# The Best Places
# To Kiss
# In Northern California

### Second Edition

"No matter how distant or exotic the destination, you will find it in this beguiling book."

*The Toronto Star*

"This travel series will help you plan your next vacation, using your heart as a guide. There's even a listing of great outdoor locations and a miscellaneous category—for places you can kiss anytime."

*First for Women*

"Never has a travel book had so much heart-stirring fun cover-to-cover."

*Santa Rosa Press Democrat*

"If you need a place for that special occasion, you are sure to find what your hearts need inside."

*Oakland Tribune*

"Our hearts went pit-a-pat when we received our kissing guide."

*The New Yorker*

"More delightful travel hints abound in The Best Places To Kiss. Be sure to include this one in your travel collection."

*San Francisco Examiner*

Other Books in *THE BEST PLACES TO KISS*... Series

*The Best Places To Kiss In The Northwest*  $10.95

*The Best Places To Kiss In Southern California*  $10.95

*The Best Places To Kiss In And Around New York City*  $10.95


Any of these books can be ordered directly from the publisher.

Please send a check or money order for the total amount of the books, plus $1.50 for shipping and handling per book ordered, to **Beginning Press**, 5418 South Brandon, Seattle, Washington 98118.

# The Best Places
# To Kiss
# In Northern California

*Second Edition*

by
Paula Begoun, Pam Hegarty,
and Tomi Jo Taylor

Beginning Press

Art Direction and Production: Lasergraphics
Cover Design: Rob Pawlak
Typography: Lasergraphics
Editor: Miriam Bulmer
Printing: Bookcrafters
Contributors: Avis Begoun

Copyright 1990, 1992 by Paula Begoun

First Edition: June 1990
Second Edition: June 1992
1 2 3 4 5 6 7 8 9 10

**Best Places To Kiss**™ is a registered trademark of Beginning Press
ISBN 1-877988-05-7

This book is distributed to the U.S. book trade by:
Publisher's Group West
4065 Hollis Street
Emeryville, California 94608
(800) 788-3123

This book is distributed to the Canadian book trade by:
Raincoast Books
112 East Third Avenue
Vancouver, British Columbia V5T 1C8
CANADA

## Special Acknowledgments

To Avis Begoun, for her extremely creative and romantic original idea for this book.

# Dedication

Kissing is a fine art. To our partners, who helped us hone our craft.

## Publisher's Note

Travel books have many different formats and criteria for the places they include. We would like the reader to know that this book is not an advertising vehicle. As is true in all the **Best Places To Kiss** books, none of the businesses included here were charged fees, nor did they pay us for their review. This book is a sincere effort to highlight those special parts of the region that are filled with romance and splendor. Some places were created by people, such as restaurants, inns, lounges, lodges, hotels, and bed and breakfasts. Some places are untouched by people and simply created by G-d for us to enjoy. Wherever you go, be gentle with each other and gentle with the earth.

The recommendations in this collection were the final decision of the publisher, but we would love to hear what you think of our suggestions. It is our desire to be a reliable source for your amorous outings, and, in this quest for blissful sojourns, your romantic feedback assists greatly in increasing our accuracy and resources for information. Please feel free to write Beginning Press if you have any additional comments, criticisms, or cherished memories of your own from a place we directed you to or of a place you discovered on your own.

We would love to hear from you!

**Beginning Press**
5418 South Brandon
Seattle, WA 98118

"As usual with most lovers in the city,
they were troubled by the lack of that
essential need of love—a meeting place."
*Thomas Wolfe*

*"When kisses are repeated and the arms hold
there is no telling where time is."*

Ted Hughes

# TABLE OF CONTENTS

The Fine Art of Kissing . . . . . . . . . . . . . . . . . . . . . . . . . . . . . . . . . . . . xi
  Why It's Still Best To Kiss In Northern California . . . . . . . . . . xi
  You Call This Research? . . . . . . . . . . . . . . . . . . . . . . . . . . . . . . . . xi
  What Isn't Romantic . . . . . . . . . . . . . . . . . . . . . . . . . . . . . . . . . . xii
  Rating Romance . . . . . . . . . . . . . . . . . . . . . . . . . . . . . . . . . . . . . xiii
  Kiss Ratings . . . . . . . . . . . . . . . . . . . . . . . . . . . . . . . . . . . . . . . . xiv
  Cost Ratings . . . . . . . . . . . . . . . . . . . . . . . . . . . . . . . . . . . . . . . xiv
  What If You Don't Want To Kiss? . . . . . . . . . . . . . . . . . . . . . . . xv
North Coast . . . . . . . . . . . . . . . . . . . . . . . . . . . . . . . . . . . . . . . . . . . . 1
Wine Country . . . . . . . . . . . . . . . . . . . . . . . . . . . . . . . . . . . . . . . . . 47
San Francisco . . . . . . . . . . . . . . . . . . . . . . . . . . . . . . . . . . . . . . . . . 93
East Bay . . . . . . . . . . . . . . . . . . . . . . . . . . . . . . . . . . . . . . . . . . . . 141
South of San Francisco . . . . . . . . . . . . . . . . . . . . . . . . . . . . . . . . 153
South Coast . . . . . . . . . . . . . . . . . . . . . . . . . . . . . . . . . . . . . . . . . 161
Gold Country . . . . . . . . . . . . . . . . . . . . . . . . . . . . . . . . . . . . . . . 209
Lake Tahoe Area . . . . . . . . . . . . . . . . . . . . . . . . . . . . . . . . . . . . . 227
Big Sur . . . . . . . . . . . . . . . . . . . . . . . . . . . . . . . . . . . . . . . . . . . . . 239
Personal Diary . . . . . . . . . . . . . . . . . . . . . . . . . . . . . . . . . . . . . . . 243
Index . . . . . . . . . . . . . . . . . . . . . . . . . . . . . . . . . . . . . . . . . . . . . . . 248

"Love expands; it not only sees more and enfolds more, it causes its object to bloom."

Hugh Prather

# THE FINE ART OF KISSING

## Why It's Still Best To Kiss In Northern California

Northern California is a splendid part of the world, filled with all the things you might require for a romantic experience. From the dazzling lights of San Francisco, it is only a short drive to the mountains, forests, rugged shorelines, and sandy beaches. Regardless of the season, misty mornings, sultry afternoons, and cool evenings are standard. The seasons themselves are all exhilarating and temperate: mild, warm winters; lush autumns; vivid springs; perfect summers. In short, there probably is not a more diverse, yet compact place in the world in which to pucker up.

From the north coast and the wine country to San Francisco, the Bay Area, and the fascinating terrain of the south coast—all will ignite your imagination and passions. If you've ever longed for a special place where you can share closeness, you can find it here. Wine tastings, bed and breakfasts, hot-air balloon rides, vibrant nightlife, alluring restaurants, country hikes, lofty woods, city streets filled with extravagant shopping, expansive parks, not to mention the ocean and the bridges and the valleys and the entertainment and ... in short, Northern California is an adult carnival. From shore to valley, the vitality and romance here are contagious, and when you're accompanied by the right someone, the only challenge will be to find the lovable niche that serves your hearts best.

## You Call This Research?

This book was undertaken primarily as a journalistic effort. It is the product of earnest interviews, travel, and careful investigation and observation. Although it would have been nice, even preferable, kissing was not the major research method used to select the locations listed in this book. If smooching had been the determining factor, several inescapable problems would have developed. First, we would still be researching, and this book would be just a good idea, some breathless moments, random notes, and nothing more. Second, depending on the mood of the moment, many kisses might have occurred in places that do not meet the requirements of this travel guide. Therefore, for both practical and physical reasons, a more objective criterion had to be established.

You may be wondering, if we did not kiss at every location during our research, how we could be certain that a particular place was good for such an activity? The answer is that we employed our reporters' instincts to evaluate the heartfelt, magnetic pull of each place visited. If, upon examining a place, we felt a longing inside for our special someone to share what we had discovered, we considered this to be as reliable as a kissing analysis. In the final evaluation, I can guarantee that once you choose where to go from among any of the places listed, you will be assured of some degree of privacy, a beautiful setting, heart-stirring ambience, and first-rate accommodations. When you get there, what you do romantically is up to you and your partner.

## What Isn't Romantic

You may be skeptical about the idea that one location is more romantic than another. You may think, "Well, it isn't the setting, it's who you're with that makes a place special." And you'd be right. But aside from the chemistry that exists between the two of you without any help from us, there are some locations that can facilitate and enhance that chemistry, just as there are some that discourage and frustrate the magic in the moment.

For example, holding hands over a hamburger and fries at McDonald's might be, for some, a blissful interlude. But the french-fry fight in full swing near your heads and the preoccupied employee who took a year and a day to get your order will put a damper on heart-throb stuff for most of us, even the most adoring. No, location isn't everything; but when a certain type of place combines with all the right atmospheric details, including the right person, the odds are better for achieving unhindered and uninterrupted romance.

With that in mind, here is a list of things that were considered to be not even remotely romantic: olive green or orange carpeting (especially if it is mildewed or dirty); anything overly plastic or overly veneered; an abundance of neon (even if it is very art deco or very neo-modern); most tourist traps; restaurants with no-smoking sections that ignore their own policy; overpriced hotels with impressive names and motel-style accommodations; discos; the latest need-to-be-seen-in nightspot; restaurants with officious, sneering waiters; and, last but not least, a roomful of people discussing the stock market or the hottest and latest business acquisition in town.

Above and beyond these unromantic location details, unromantic *behavior* can negate the affection potential of even the most majestic surroundings. These are mood killers every time: any amount of moaning over the weather; creating a scene over the quality of food or service, no matter how justified; worrying about work; getting angry about traffic; incessant back-seat driving, no matter how warranted; groaning about heartburn and other related symptoms, no matter how painful or justified.

## Rating Romance

The three major factors that determined whether or not we included a place were:

1. Surrounding splendor
2. Privacy
3. Tug-at-your-heartstrings ambience

Of the three determining factors, "surrounding splendor" and "privacy" are fairly self-explanatory; "heart-tugging ambience" can probably use some clarification. Wonderful, loving environments are not just four-poster beds covered with down quilts and lace pillows, or tables decorated with white tablecloths and nicely folded linen napkins. Instead, there must be more plush or other engaging features that encourage intimacy and allow for uninterrupted affectionate discussions. For the most part, ambience was rated according to degree of comfort and number of gracious appointments, as opposed to image and frills.

If a place had all three factors going for it, inclusion was automatic. But if one or two of those criteria were weak or nonexistent, the other feature(s) had to be superior before the location would be included. For example, if a breathtakingly beautiful panoramic vista was in a spot that was inundated with tourists and children on field trips, the place was not included. If a fabulous bed and breakfast was set in a less-than-desirable location, it would be included if, and only if, its interior was so wonderfully inviting and cozy that the outside world no longer mattered.

## Kiss Ratings

If you've flipped through this book and noticed the miniature lips that follow each entry, you're probably curious about what they mean. The rating system notwithstanding, *all* the places listed in this book are wonderfully special places to be, and all of them have heart-pleasing details and are worthwhile, enticing places to visit. The tiny lips indicate only our personal preferences and nothing more. They are a way of indicating just how delightfully romantic a place is and how pleased we were with our experience during our visit. The number of lips awarded each location indicates:

> ❤ Romantic Possibilities
> ❤❤ Very Romantic
> ❤❤❤ Irresistible
> ❤❤❤❤ Sublime

## Cost Ratings

We have included additional ratings to help you determine whether your lips can afford to kiss in a particular restaurant, hotel, or bed and breakfast (almost all of the outdoor places are free; some charge a small fee). The price for overnight accommodations is always based on double occupancy; otherwise there wouldn't be anyone to kiss. Eating establishment prices are based on a full dinner for two, excluding liquor, unless otherwise indicated. Because prices and business hours change, it is always advisable to call each place you consider visiting, so your lips will not end up disappointed.

## Restaurants

Inexpensive                 Under $25
Moderate                    $25 to $50
Expensive                   $50 to $80
Very Expensive              $80 to $110
Unbelievably Expensive      $110 and up

## Lodging Rating

Very Inexpensive            Under $75
Inexpensive                 $75 to $90
Moderate                    $90 to $125
Expensive                   $130 to $175
Very Expensive              $185 to $240
Unbelievably Expensive      $250 and up

# What If You Don't Want To Kiss?

For most couples, romance isn't easy. Some people I interviewed resisted the idea of best kissing locales. Their resistance stemmed from expectation worries. They were apprehensive that once they arrived at the place of their dreams, they'd never get the feeling they thought they were supposed to have. They imagined spending time setting up itineraries, taking extra time to get ready, making the journey to the promised land, and, once they were there, not being swept away in a flourish of romance. Their understandable fear was, What happens if nothing happens? Because in spite of the best intentions, even with this book in hand, romance is not easy.

Having experienced situations like this more than once in my life, I empathize, but I'm prepared with solutions. To prevent this anti climactic scenario from becoming a reality, and to help you survive a romantic outing, consider following the suggestions. When you make decisions about where and when to go, pay close attention to details; talk over your preferences and discuss your feelings about them. For some people there is no passion associated with fast pre-theater dinners that are all but inhaled, or with walking farther than expected in overly high, high heels, or with finding a place closed because its hours have changed. Keep in mind the impossibility of second-guessing traffic patterns in San Francisco, along the coast, or through the wine country. My strong recommendation, although I know this is difficult, is not to schedule a romantic outing too tightly or you will be more assured of a headache than an affectionate interlude.

Do not discuss money, family, or the kids. If you have a headache, take some aspirin now and not later. Regardless of how good-looking the person at the next table is, remember that distractions are never considered to be in romantic good taste. How different factors might affect your lips, not to mention your mood, is something to agree on before you head out the door, not after—or during.

Remember that part of the whole experience of an intimate time together is to allow whatever happens to be an opportunity to let affection reign. Regardless of what takes place, that is what is romantic. For example, remember the incredibly intense scene in the film *Body Heat*, where Kathleen Turner is standing in the hall and William Hurt smashes through the door (even though it appears to be unlocked) and rushes into her waiting arms, tumbling them both to the floor? Well, how romantic would it have been if Kathleen had started fretting about having to clean up the broken glass, get the door fixed, and repair her torn underwear? Or remember the scene between Kevin Costner and Susan Sarandon in *Bull Durham* where he throws his full cereal bowl against the wall, cleans the kitchen table with a sweep of his arm, then picks Susan up and throws her passionately on the table? How romantic would that have been if Kevin had started complaining about the broken china in his hair and the spilled milk running down his arms? Get the idea?

So, if the car breaks down, the waiter is rude to you, your reservations get screwed up, or both of you tire out and want to call it a day, you can still be endearing and charming. Really, it only takes an attitude change to turn any dilemma into a delight.

# NORTH COAST

## Sausalito

### Hotel/Bed and Breakfast Kissing

**CASA MADRONA HOTEL
AND RESTAURANT, Sausalito**
**801 Bridgeway**
**Hotel (415) 332-0502, (800) 288-0502**
**Restaurant (415) 331-5888**
Moderate to Very Expensive

*Heading north to Marin County on Highway 101, take the first exit (Alexander Avenue) after you cross the Golden Gate Bridge. This winding road proceeds downhill and then automatically connects to Bridgeway. The hotel is located on the left side of the road, after the second traffic light in the town.*

Meandering Casa Madrona is one surprise after another. The rooms display the creative work of no fewer than 16 local designers, and each room is more interesting than the last. As you climb to your accommodations on the tiered walkway, this multilayered hotel reveals every sort of style—from blushingly romantic to endearingly strange. Describing all of the 34 rooms at Casa Madrona would require a book by itself. You name it and you can find it here, in a variety of combinations: spacious to cozy, French country to contemporary, brilliant sunlit harbor views, skylights, fireplaces, and on and on. The two of you need only to decide what composite you want. Continental breakfast is included in the cost of the room.

If an overnight stay is not possible, the restaurant at Casa Madrona is a heart-stirring alternative. The dining area has a remarkable panoramic view of Sausalito Bay; the visual refreshment outside the windows will beautifully complement your meal inside. All of the tables have glorious views, but the tables nearest the windows have it all. Lunch is served Monday through Saturday, dinner nightly, and brunch on Sunday. The eclectic cuisine, with Mediterranean influences, is beautifully prepared. After you've dined, take a stroll hand-in-hand through the town of Sausalito. Or, if you are staying at the hotel, you can stroll back to your private, individualized haven at Casa Madrona.

◆   **Romantic Suggestion:** One way to get to Sausalito or Tiburon and not get stuck in traffic is to take the ferry. The **GOLDEN GATE FERRY**, (415) 332-6600, leaves from the San Francisco Ferry Building, located at the foot of Market Street, and makes its way across the bay every day of the week. The more romantic times are during off-peak hours on most weekdays, but even when the boat is thick with commuters, this is a genuinely San Francisco way to sightsee in the Bay Area.

## Restaurant Kissing

**ALTA MIRA RESTAURANT, Sausalito**
**125 Buckley Avenue**
**(415) 332-1350**
Expensive to Very Expensive

*Heading north to Marin County on Highway 101, take the first exit (Alexander Avenue) after you cross the Golden Gate Bridge. This winding road proceeds downhill and then automatically connects to Bridgeway. Once you enter the town of Sausalito, turn right on Bay Street. Go to Buckley Avenue, turn right, and follow the signs to the Alta Mira.*

A more impressive location for brunch or an afternoon nosh would be hard to find. Tucked away on a hillside overlooking Richardson Harbor and the San Francisco skyline, this terraced restaurant is a prime spot for a leisurely meal together. The view from up here is so vibrant that it becomes an integral part of the interior. Leave yourselves plenty of time to take in the entire panorama.

◆ **Romantic Warning:** The Alta Mira is also well known for its hotel accommodations, though why anyone would want to stay here is beyond me: the hotel has been in desperate need of renovations since the 1960s. The rooms are tacky, the floors creak, the bathrooms aren't big enough for one person, let alone two, and the mildewy smell throughout is fairly unpleasant. Our suggestion is to stay elsewhere and enjoy the view from the restaurant during breakfast, lunch, or dinner.

### SCOMA'S, Sausalito
**588 Bridgeway**
**(415) 332-9551**
Moderate

*Heading north to Marin County on Highway 101, take the first exit (Alexander Avenue) after you cross the Golden Gate Bridge. This winding road proceeds downhill and automatically connects to Bridgeway. Continue on Bridgeway to the restaurant on the right side of the road.*

Classic seafood dishes are served in this very pretty, very classic dining room that is made even more enticing by its dynamite location on the shore of Sausalito. The view from the glass-enclosed room is breathtaking regardless of the weather. After dinner, a walk along the shore to watch the moon's reflection on the water is a spectacular way to end your evening.

◆ **Romantic Alternative: HORIZON'S,** 558 Bridgeway, Sausalito, (415) 331-3232, (Moderate), has a casual atmosphere that offers the same outstanding, expansive view as Scoma's. The dark-wooded interior is fronted by a wall of windows that open onto a deck poised directly over the bay. From here you can survey the entire area from the Bay Bridge to the home-covered hills of Tiburon. A hot cup of coffee or cocktails from this vantage point can turn out to be an inspiring affair.

**THE SPINNAKER, Sausalito**
**100 Spinnaker Drive**
**(415) 332-1500**
Moderate

*Take Highway 101 north across the Golden Gate Bridge to Alexander Avenue. Follow Alexander Avenue to the east until it becomes Bridgeway. Continue following Bridgeway to Anchor Street and turn right. Anchor Street becomes Spinnaker Drive; the restaurant is at the end of the road.*

I once heard someone refer to Sausalito as one, big beautiful view of San Francisco and it's true: this little town is one of the best vantage points from which to ogle the city skyline. And among the restaurants situated to best display this spectacle is The Spinnaker, which is located on a rocky point next to the Sausalito Yacht Harbor. Windows span the entire length of one wall, from floor to ceiling, looking out onto the bay. During the day, you can watch a sailboat slip by or a ship in the distance against the picturesque background of San Francisco. At night when it is clear, the city lights are dazzling. The menu is filled with variety and includes seafood, poultry, and beef for dinner, salads, sandwiches, and light meals for lunch. The food is always satisfying, but also always secondary to the splendid setting, where couples can and should prefer to fill up on romance.

◆ **Romantic Alternative: THE CHART HOUSE,** 201 Bridgeway, Sausalito, (415) 332-0804, (Moderate to Expensive), may be a name you know. Most major cities have one. But I've never seen a Chart House with a better view than the one in Sausalito, which is right on the water. The huge picture windows frame the bay and the San Francisco skyline, the food is always good, and in my opinion the salad bar at The Chart House is the best in the Bay Area.

## *Outdoor Kissing*

### RODEO BEACH AT THE MARIN HEADLANDS
### (415) 331-1540

*Head north from San Francisco on Highway 101. Take the Alexander Avenue exit and follow the signs to Golden Gate National Recreation Area. At Bunker Road continue 3 miles to the beach.*

This expanse of white sandy beach is not a secret among locals, but you can be effectively alone during most weekdays before summer vacation releases eager kids from the classroom. A more beautiful scenic area for rambling through surf cannot be found so near to San Francisco. Colored stones of jasper and agate are scattered along the shore. Bird Island, just a short distance from shore, is often blanketed with fluttering white birds. In the distance, rolling hills and jagged cliffs make distinguished tableaux against the bright blue sky. There are plenty of hiking trails nearby that will lead you over intriguing terrain to breathtaking overviews of the area. You won't be at a loss for ways to spend time here; you only need to be prepared for sun, wind, and long, loving hours together.

◆ **Romantic Note: GOLDEN GATE NATIONAL RECRE-ATION AREA**, (415) 331-1540, contains more than 70,000 acres of protected coastline, pristine woodland, mountain terrain, rugged hillsides, and meticulously maintained city parks. To say that there is a diverse assortment of places to discover here is at best an understatement. It is hard to believe that such a massive refuge can exist so close to San Francisco. Hiking, picnicking, swimming, or any other outdoor activity you can think of is possible in this awesome stretch of land with something for the most ardent wilderness lovers and the tamest urban dwellers. It is simply there for your pleasure, provided by Mother Nature and the Golden Gate National Park Association.

# Tiburon

## Restaurant Kissing

**CAPRICE RESTAURANT, Tiburon**
**2000 Paradise Drive**
**(415) 435-3400**
Expensive

*Once you enter the town of Tiburon, follow Paradise Drive along the water to the end of Waterfront Park, about three blocks. The restaurant will be on your right.*

The Caprice will delight the most finicky of gourmands. Divinely quaint, with a reclusive hobbitlike aura, the homey wood-framed building sits snugly on a stone embankment above the gently swirling waters of Raccoon Strait looking across to Angel Island. Its small dining salon is warmed by a radiating fireplace, and large windows allow perfect ringside water viewing. In the distance, San Francisco and the Golden Gate Bridge are in clear view. Lunch and dinner are served daily and the food is wonderful. It would be difficult for you not to give in to the loving atmosphere this place generates.

◆ **Romantic Suggestion:** After brunch or an early dinner at the Caprice, continue up Paradise Drive till you reach **PARADISE BEACH PARK**. This quiet little corner of the world is a wooded landscape that overlooks the distant hills beyond the bay and the San Rafael Bridge. Depending on the time of day and season, this place could be yours alone, and there is enough strolling and picnicking turf here to make it a lover's point of interest.

◆ **Second Romantic Suggestion: SAN RAFAEL AVENUE** in Tiburon wraps around a cove with a simply glorious view of the sunset. You can walk slowly along this neighborhood street and watch the fading colors of day as they surrender to nightfall.

## GUAYMAS, Tiburon
### 5 Main Street
### (415) 435-6300
Inexpensive to Moderate

*From Highway 101, take the Tiburon Boulevard off-ramp; follow Tiburon Boulevard east about five miles to Main Street. Guaymas is on the corner.*

In every way, Guaymas reflects a south-of-the-border feel and flavor. The restaurant, named for a Mexican fishing town, emphasizes authenticity. Instead of Americanized versions of Mexican food, at Guaymas you'll find menu selections that include tamales or pork wrapped in banana leaves, fresh fish served with guero chile-tomato butter, and green poblano chiles stuffed with chicken and raisins. Some dishes may sound more exotic than your taste buds would care to sample, but they are all truly delicious. You can choose a table in the adobe dining room, which is accented with bright colors and a corner fireplace, or one outside on the waterfront deck. The patios are heated with gas warmers, making them pleasant even on cool nights. Of course, during the day the stunning view of the bay and San Francisco makes it difficult to resist outdoor dining. If there's one thing I know about the fishing villages of Mexico, it's that they take life slow and easy. At Guaymas, that's exactly the way they want you to enjoy your meal. In this casual, yet romantic, setting you'll find that very easy to do.

◆ **Romantic Note:** Guaymas is located next to the ferry landing, making it a nice excursion from San Francisco. But be sure to check the departure schedules both in the city and in Tiburon so you won't get stuck without a way back.

## SAM'S ANCHOR CAFE, Tiburon
### 27 Main Street,
### (415) 435-4527
Inexpensive

*From Highway 101, take the Tiburon Boulevard off-ramp and follow Tiburon Boulevard east about five miles to Main Street. Sam's is to the right.*

Tiburon has the bright distinction of being the sunny spot of the Bay Area. Not always, but on many days, when other parts of San Francisco and Marin County are veiled in fog, Tiburon is basking in sunshine. That's why deck dining is so popular in this small community, and no doubt why people come from miles away to have lunch at Sam's. The waterfront deck is right next to a yacht harbor; miles beyond, the city of San Francisco is its backdrop. (This makes Sam's even better on sunny days, when the view across the water is crystal clear.) Sam's serves up casual fare—burgers, omelets, and salads—in a casual setting: blue-and-white-checked vinyl cloths cover the tables and customers sit on plastic chairs. In fact, this place is so casual, the sea gulls aren't shy about sharing your french fries if you aren't paying attention to your plate. But that comfortable feeling is just what makes kissing at Sam's so special. There is no proper etiquette to adhere to, no refined rules, just the sun, the sea, the breeze, and your desire to enjoy a warm afternoon together.

◆ **Romantic Note:** Sam's also has an inside dining area for cold days and the dinner hours. In the evening, the menu features pasta, seafood, and light entrees.

◆ **Romantic Alternative:** Deck dining is also available at other restaurants along Main Street in Tiburon. **MR. Q'S**, 25 Main Street, Tiburon, (415) 435-5088, (Inexpensive to Moderate), has the advantage of a second story from which to enjoy the view, but its food, ranging from egg dishes to seafood and baby back ribs, is inconsistent. **CHRISTOPHER'S**, 9 Main Street, Tiburon, (415) 435-4600, (Moderate to Expensive), has a small deck, too, but the restaurant is not open for lunch, and the only time to take advantage of it is during early-evening meals or on the weekends for brunch. Christopher's does serve a nice American-style dinner inside and the floor-to-ceiling windows along the back wall look out onto the water and the San Francisco skyline.

# Mill Valley

## Hotel/Bed and Breakfast Kissing

**MOUNTAIN HOME INN**
**AND RESTAURANT, Mill Valley**
**810 Panoramic Highway**
**(415) 381-9000**
Moderate to Expensive

*Drive north on Highway 101 to Stinson Beach, take the Highway 1 exit, and turn left onto Highway 1. In three miles turn right on Panoramic Highway and proceed to the inn.*

Mountain Home Inn, situated on the north side of Mount Tamalpais, stands guard over the surrounding East Bay hills, the Tiburon peninsula, San Francisco, and Mount Diablo. It is a handsome, refurbished lodge, with redwood vaulted ceilings and huge windows, where excellent food and sublime views combine to create a rare treat among dining experiences. The inn also has 10 cozy guest rooms, several of which boast their own fireplace, Jacuzzi, and deck. All have views of purple mountain majesty.

## Restaurant Kissing

**EL PASEO, Mill Valley**
**17 Throckmorton**
**(415) 388-0741**
Moderate

*Take Highway 101 north to the East Blithedale off-ramp. Follow East Blithedale about two miles to Throckmorton and turn left to the restaurant.*

The Spanish name is very misleading: El Paseo is anything but the cantina your mind conjures up. Instead it's one of the loveliest, most intimate French restaurants in Northern California. The deep, rich decor and the dining room's brick walls reflect a European elegance and style. A candlelight dinner at one of the cozy tables for two is an experience in indulgence. Among the fine offerings from the menu are escargots with blue cheese butter, roast baby rack of lamb with rosemary, and a dark-and-white-chocolate mousse. The restaurant has won a number of culinary awards, and deserves them all. El Paseo also deserves a prize for romance. You'll find this delightful restaurant a wonderful environment for kisses and other expressions of love.

◆　　**Romantic Alternative:** You would never know this is an intimate dining room from the outside, because **GIRAMONTI**, 655 Redwood Highway, Mill Valley, (415) 383-3000, (Moderate), is located in a building filled with retail and office space. But inside, you will find a darling place for a cozy dinner. Giramonti overlooks Shelter Bay and some of Marin's rolling hills. The charming room is decorated in rose tones with floral wallpaper, a wood-beamed ceiling, fresh, fragrant flowers, and antiques. Wonderful Italian dishes are served by a friendly staff. The pastas are superb and priced quite reasonably. At Giramonti, the ambience and cuisine combine to create a romantic dining experience you can share and savor.

◆　　**Second Romantic Alternative: PIAZZA D'ANGELO**, 22 Miller Avenue, Mill Valley, (415) 388-2000, (Moderate), is another great place for lunch, dinner, or brunch on the weekend, if you are in the mood for Italian. It's more modern in appearance, with red tile floors, track lighting, textured walls, and windows framed with blond wood. Open kitchens to the side allow the scent of Piazza D'Angelo's delicious individual pizzas, pasta specialties, and meat dishes to tantalize and entice diners. And the food tastes as good as it smells. On warm days, the restaurant sets up tables on the patio for dining in the sunshine.

# Larkspur

## Restaurant Kissing

**LARK CREEK INN, Larkspur**                                          ◆◆◀
**234 Magnolia Avenue**
**(415) 924-7766**
Moderate

*Take Highway 101 to the Paradise Drive/Mount Tamalpais exit. Go west on Mount Tamalpais for about one mile, then turn right on Corte Madera Avenue, which becomes Magnolia Avenue. The restaurant is a half mile down on the right.*

As you wind through the remote wooded neighborhoods of Larkspur, you may be surprised to see this yellow frame home on what would otherwise be another curve in an out-of-the-way country road. Though this place feels remote, it is one of the more renowned dining spots in the North Bay. Lark Creek Inn deserves its reputation and, in spite of its popularity, the environment is still conducive to a romantic interlude. The interior is highlighted by a glass-domed ceiling shaded by lofty redwoods. When the weather warms, the restaurant's garden, situated near a babbling creek, serves as an extension to the dining room. The only thing left to mention is the food, which is sheer heaven most of the time; the rest of the time it is merely excellent.

**REMILLARD'S, Larkspur**                                             ◆◆◀
**125 E. Sir Francis Drake Boulevard**
**(415) 461-3700**
Expensive to Very Expensive

*From the north: Take Highway 101 to the Sir Francis Drake Boulevard exit. Follow Sir Francis Drake Boulevard east. From the south: Take Highway 101 to the Richmond Bridge/San Anselmo exit. Follow the signs to the Richmond Bridge until you are on East Sir Francis Drake Boulevard.*

The structure that houses Remillard's was built more than a hundred years ago. Back then it was the Green Brae Brick Kiln, and it supplied bricks for such San Francisco landmarks as Ghirardelli Square, The Cannery, and the St. Francis Hotel. Now, a century later, and after more than a million dollars in renovations, Remillard's retains its historic charm while offering all the contemporary advantages of a fine French restaurant. The dining room, constructed of solid brick walls and ceiling, is shaped like a large tunnel. As you'd expect in such a place, it's dark, but low light reflects off the walls from sconces and from candles on the tables. White linens and exotic flowers brighten the room a bit more. Though the restaurant is rather large, the tables are situated to provide a cozy and quaint feeling. The French cuisine receives high praise from food critics and from customers. The kitchen creates fantastic sauces, and those who know the menu well suggest the fresh poached salmon in a chive sauce or the fillet of beef with green peppercorns and calvados sauce. The dessert souffles are decadent, but to pass them over would be a shame. Instead, order one and linger for a while in a place where the past provides the setting for modern-day romance.

# Greenbrae

## Restaurant Kissing

JOE LOCOCO'S, Greenbrae
300 Drakes Landing Road
(415) 925-0808
Moderate to Expensive

*Take Highway 101 to Sir Francis Drake Boulevard. Follow Sir Francis Drake Boulevard west to Barry Way and turn left. Go one block and take another left on Drakes Landing Road.*

An irresistible aroma fills the air as you enter Joe LoCoco's. As you pass the open kitchen, you cannot doubt that you will be totally satisfied with your meal. And then, as you look ahead, into the dining room, you cannot doubt that you also will be pleased with the restaurant's romantic atmosphere. The restaurant is bathed in the soft glow of candlelight and pastel hues. The decor is contemporary and artistic; the peach-colored walls are adorned with paintings. Exquisite floral arrangements add another gentle touch of color. Large windows open to the water and views of Mount Tamalpais during the day. At night, the deep darkness outside contrasts beautifully with the pretty interior. The Italian dishes served here are hearty, not heavy. The kitchen turns out marvelous homemade pastas, delicious wild game, and fresh seafood dishes. Because the restaurant has such a great reputation, reservations are almost always needed at dinner. Make yours well in advance and plan a special evening out. Or, you can choose Joe LoCoco's for lunch, and enjoy an afternoon rendezvous.

# Muir Woods

## Restaurant Kissing

THE PELICAN INN
RESTAURANT AND PUB, Muir Woods
Highway 1
(415) 383-6000
Moderate

*Take Highway 101 north over the Golden Gate Bridge into Marin County. Take the Stinson Beach/Highway 1 exit and follow the signs for Muir Woods, which will lead you directly to the inn.*

Among the redwoods, between the pines and alders, dabbed with touches of honeysuckle and jasmine, is The Pelican Inn, a magical place out of the past. This 16th-century-style country cottage, hidden in the Golden Gate National Recreational Area, is a shelter for weary, hungry travelers, as well as the habitat for the "little folk" of days gone by. All this will be clearly evident as you approach the inn, especially when the weather assists in the magic. Sea mist often mingles with the mountain air to create a foggy veil that contributes to the sense that you are moving back through time to England of Olde.

You can take your schooner of ale or pot of tea to a table near the stone hearth of the brick fireplace and allow this daydream to continue for as long as you dare. Or you can simply snuggle close together, watching the embers flicker and glow in the dimly lit room as you wait for the innkeeper to bring you your afternoon or evening feast. You can partake in this unique atmosphere for lunch and dinner every day but Monday.

◆ **Romantic Warning**: The guest rooms in The Pelican Inn are called "rustic" by the owners, but from our point of view "rundown" would be a more descriptive word. If you happen to be in a pioneer frame of mind, the rooms could pass muster. Besides, there are the mystical, cinematic setting and acres of forest and nearby beaches to stimulate your imagination.

◆ **Romantic Possibility**: Nearby **MUIR BEACH STATE PARK** is a well-frequented expanse of white sandy shoreline. While too much smooching is probably out of the question, you can still claim your own spot, lie back, listen to the ocean's serene rhythms, and concentrate on each other.

## Outdoor Kissing

### HIGHWAY 1
*From the Golden Gate Bridge out of San Francisco, follow the signs for Highway 1.*

Northern California Coast Highway 1 is an exhilarating roller-coaster ride of a lifetime. The road writhes its way along terrain that would otherwise seem impassable. Following the ocean from atop towering cliffs, each turn capriciously switches back on itself, hugging the edge so closely that you may feel more like you're hang-gliding than motoring along. At other times, feeling the ocean mist on your face and hearing the roar of the surf, you can imagine you're boating instead of just driving.

Be sure to allow enough time to travel this highway at a leisurely, touring pace. There are scads of turnoffs that will demand your attention, so the slower your speed, the easier it will be to stop at any given point and enjoy. The picture-perfect profile of the surf pounding against death-defying palisades continues on forever. Each corner, each turn, has a view so like Eden that a warning seems in order: driving and kissing don't mix! Before you indulge, be sure you are parked and not negotiating the narrow turns on Highway 1.

◆ **Romantic Warning**: If you are in a hurry to get to points north at a faster clip, do yourselves and the rest of the traffic on Highway 1 a favor and take Highway 101.

## MUIR WOODS AND MOUNT TAMALPAIS
**Panoramic Highway**
**(415) 388-2070**

*Take Highway 101 north to Marin County. Turn off at the Stinson Beach/ Highway 1 exit, and follow the signs for Muir Woods and Mount Tamalpais.*

If you long to be secluded and near nature, you need only cross the Golden Gate Bridge into Marin County and drive along Highway 1 to the crest of Mount Tamalpais. This is without question one of the most absorbing drives the area has to bestow. The S-curved road coils along the edge of this windswept highland, and each turn exposes another vantage point from which to scan the scenery: land cascading down to Marin; the pattern of overlapping hills. As you continue your excursion, you can choose to remain in the car or venture out into the hills with a *fete champetre* (picnic) in hand. Here, in the midst of earth's simple gifts, a loaf of bread, a jug of wine, and thou are all you need.

◆ **Romantic Suggestion**: The **STEEP RAVINE TRAIL**, whose trailhead is at the Pantoll Station on the Panoramic Highway, is a magnificent deep-forest journey to views of the ocean and bay. This one is my sister's romantic favorite, and she ought to know: the idea for this book was hers.

MARIN HEADLANDS
**Northwest of the Golden Gate Bridge**
**(415) 331-1540**

*From the north: Heading south on Highway 101, take the last Sausalito exit. Follow signs to the park. From the south: Heading north on Highway 101, take the Alexander Avenue exit. Follow signs to the park*

What is it about the Golden Gate Bridge that evokes passion in all who see it? Find out for yourselves by visiting the Marin Headlands. A precipitous road hugs the cliff above this graceful sculpture of a bridge. Several viewpoints are perfect for windblown kisses before the Golden Gate with the San Francisco skyline as a backdrop. The scene is truly magical when fog rolls, cradling the arching span and city skyscrapers in cottony billows of mist. Intrepid romantics can continue on the winding road to the edge of the Pacific, hike inland to secluded, grassy picnic spots, or comb rocky beaches for sea-swept caresses.

◆ **Romantic Alternative:** Marin is blessed with several outdoor sanctuaries. If you're in Tiburon, stop by the **RICHARDSON BAY AUDUBON CENTER**, 376 Greenwood Beach Road, Tiburon, (415) 388-2524. The charmingly restored Victorian house is picture perfect in this setting on the gentle bay waters. A short loop trail leads you up to the crest of a hill for kissing before a lofty panorama of Angel Island, San Francisco, Sausalito, and the coastal mountains.

# Olema

## *Hotel/Bed and Breakfast Kissing*

POINT REYES SEASHORE LODGE, Olema
**10021 Coastal Highway 1**
**(415) 663-9000**
Inexpensive to Expensive

*On Highway 1 at the Sir Francis Drake Boulevard intersection.*

This grand new lodge with a turn-of-the-century motif is a bit imposing from the outside, being so close to the street it looks like it might bend over and swallow it. Don't let this deter you. Inside, the ambience is at once polished and provincial, commodious and cozy. All rooms have mesmerizing views of the inn's pleasantly landscaped backyard and the forested hills of Point Reyes beyond. The upper-story rooms are particularly appealing, with their high peaked ceilings and picture windows. In several, you can light a flame in a ceramic tile fireplace, and then in each other as you kiss on the bay window seat in front of this dreamy panorama. From the ground-floor rooms, step through the private entrance to the garden and nestle into a sun-warmed Nantucket wooden chair for the afternoon. In the evening, play a spirited game on the antique billiards table or try your hand at a puzzle in the game room downstairs. Continental breakfasts are served in a sunny room that opens to the backyard and is warmed by an immense stone hearth festooned with dried flowers.

## ROUNDSTONE FARM, Olema

**9940 Sir Francis Drake Boulevard**
**(415) 663-1020**
Moderate

*Call for directions to the bed and breakfast.*

Serenity welcomes you with a whispered caress in this quiet inn. Step into the spacious living room with its wood stove and soaring, skylighted ceiling and you are at once drawn to the bucolic view framed by a wall of picture windows. An emerald meadow slopes below, set with a sapphire pond and punctuated with the innkeeper's extraordinary Connemara and Arabian horses, all brushed on a canvas of rolling hills and forested horizons. Several of the peaceful, uncluttered rooms, with their simple lacquer furnishings and soft florals, share this pastoral scene. All have fireplaces to perpetuate the setting's gentle spirit long after night cloaks the land in darkness.

◆    **Romantic Alternative:** For traditional bed-and-breakfast charm, try **TEN INVERNESS WAY**, 10 Inverness Way, Inverness, (415)

669-1648, (Moderate to Expensive). Rooms are cozy, homespun, and overlook the inn's cheerful English gardens. Generous country repasts are served in the sun-soaked breakfast room. A player piano delights guests by the stone hearth in the parlor. Best of all, a hot tub sheltered in its own petite cabin can be reserved for private, candlelight soaks for two.

◆   **Second Romantic Alternative: THE HOLLY TREE INN**, 3 Silverhills Road, Inverness Park, (415) 663-1554, (Moderate to Expensive) is another homespun bed and breakfast that complements this country setting. Warm hospitality, old-fashioned guest rooms, evening appetizers, and full breakfasts invite unpretentious caresses. For the utmost in seclusion, ask about the Sea Star Cottage. Several miles from the inn, this petite house is reached by a long wooden walkway built over the tidal waters next to the yacht club. Watch the ducks swim beneath you at high tide while you soak in the hot tub on the deck. The cottage and parts of the inn are a bit weatherworn and would improve with a dab of sprucing up.

# Inverness and Point Reyes

## Hotel/Bed and Breakfast Kissing

**BLACKTHORNE INN, Inverness Park**
**266 Vallejo Avenue**
**(415) 663-8621**
Moderate to Expensive

*Heading north on Highway 1, look for the sign for a left turn to Inverness (near Point Reyes Station). Turn left onto Vallejo Avenue (the Knave of Hearts Bakery is on the corner). When you think an inn can't possibly be this far down this narrow country lane, look for the small sign with "266" on the right.*

Nesting high in the trees, this popular, four-story, wooden castle with twin turrets, high-peaked gables, and multipaned windows is crowned with an octagonal tower and surrounded by an expansive moat of a redwood deck, complete with a fireman's pole to the drive below. Inside, classical music casts a cultivated spell in the spacious, cathedral-ceilinged living room with its immense stone hearth. Spiral staircases lead up and down to the guest rooms. The Overlook has a Juliet-style balcony overlooking the living room, a private outdoor terrace, and stained glass windows. The Eagle's Nest occupies the octagonal tower, with windows on all sides looking out to the treetops and a steep ladder to its sun deck. The bath for this room, however, is across a 40-foot-high outdoor walkway leading to the uppermost deck. There is a jetted hot tub available for the use of the guests, where, in true California spirit, clothing is optional after dark. For the most part this is a unique bed and breakfast, but it can feel cramped and crowded when occupancy is full, which it usually is most of the year.

◆ **Romantic Warning**: The town of Inverness, which borders the Point Reyes National Seashore, is the entry point into this area. Even though this wee small village is somewhat quaint, it is too well traveled to be a truly romantic option all by itself. However, a stay at one of the special bed and breakfasts in the area can be utterly romantic. For more information regarding accommodations, both romantic and not so romantic, write to: INNS OF POINT REYES, P.O. Box 145, Inverness, CA 94937.

**DANCING COYOTE BEACH
GUEST COTTAGES,** Inverness
**12794 Sir Francis Drake Boulevard
(415) 669-7200**
Inexpensive to Moderate

*Call for directions to the cottages.*

Four cottages here are all nestled in the shade of sturdy pine and cypress trees on Tomales Bay. Each cottage has access to private beachfront a few feet from its front door. Fireplaces, skylights, floor-to-ceiling windows, galley kitchens, and pastel shades of green and peach adorn each bungalow. This getaway is made to order when you're in need of time to jointly embrace tranquillity.

**MACLEAN HOUSE, Inverness**
**P.O. Box 651**
**(415) 669-7392**
Inexpensive

*From the town of Inverness, on Highway 1, turn left on the Inverness*
*Highway. Go two short blocks and take a sharp right on Hawthornden Way.*
*MacLean House is on your left as you go up the hill, but Hawthornden is a*
*divided road, so you must make a U-turn at the top and come back down to*
*the parking area.*

This charming bed and breakfast is two blocks from the main street
of Inverness and only minutes from the ocean. As you drive up the road
you will see the house set upon a hill, a brick-and-stone dwelling set
amidst gardens and trees. This Scottish-style guest house has only two
rooms; both are homespun and uncomplicated. Before or after a hard
day of combing the seashore hand-in-hand, you can lounge on the
trellised deck where breakfast and afternoon tea are served along with
shortbread and sherry. As you recline on the terrace, you'll see Tomales
Bay in the distance, framing the horizon in picturesque harmony with
the landscape.

◆ **Romantic Suggestion:** Along the western edge of Tomales Bay,
in Tomales Bay State Park, is **HEART'S DESIRE BEACH**. It's worth
a visit. Even if you believe that names have no meaning, it still may be
interesting to test the truth of this one for yourselves.

**THE NEON ROSE, Point Reyes**
**76½ Overlook Road**
**(415) 663-9143**
Moderate

*Call for directions.*

The Neon Rose is an amazing, unique retreat on a hill overlooking
Tomales Bay. You walk through a delightful, small, very private garden
and into your own modern white stucco-and-wood little cottage. The
view from up here is a broad vista of Point Reyes and the bay. The cottage

has a fully equipped kitchen, a chic bedroom opening onto a cozy living area with a Jacuzzi tub, wood stove, and complete stereo system. An abundant supply of breakfast foods are provided for you to prepare at your convenience. If only home were like this! The Neon Rose bed and breakfast is the ultimate in privacy. You could stay here for days and feel blissfully content.

## *Restaurant Kissing*

**MANKA'S RESTAURANT, Inverness**
**Argyle Avenue and Callendar Way**
**(415) 669-1034**
Expensive

*Heading north on Highway 1, look for the sign for a left turn to Inverness (near Point Reyes Station). In Inverness, turn left onto Argyle Drive at Manka's sign.*

Tiny Inverness is known for its surprising restaurants, and Manka's is the most unexpected of all. Up a steep side street, deep and dark in the nighttime forest, this turn-of-the century hunting lodge is a magnet for locals and visitors alike. A fire blazes in the first of three intimate dining rooms, while tapers flicker on linen-cloaked tables. Serene melodies from the grand piano waft through the room along with the mouth-watering aromas of seasonal specials. Appetizers might include clam and mussel soup with fennel and cilantro puree or grilled polenta with local wild mushrooms. Some entrees, like the guinea hen and the skirt steak, are grilled in the fireplace. Manka's serves dinner Thursday through Monday only.

# Outdoor Kissing

## POINT REYES NATIONAL SEASHORE
## (415) 663-1092

*Just off Highway 1, about 35 miles north of San Francisco.*

I'm usually of the opinion that facts are not the least bit romantic. They're great if you feel like absorbing data, but they won't create a groundwork for snuggling. For example, knowing that Point Reyes National Seashore has geologically noteworthy formations and protected wildlife may not do much for you. What might entice you is knowing that you are likely to fall in love with acre after exquisite acre of wild land, colored by winter grass, patterned with chiseled rock, cascading waterfalls, calm sandy beaches, precarious primitive coastline, and turbulent eddies of water crashing against haystack rocks and spewing streams of water into the fresh air above. Now that has meaning! You can almost feel the ground move under your quickening feet as you see ahead the crest of a ridge while you traverse one of the many trails that interlace this prime hiking kingdom. Some trails end near the edge of the land, where the ocean reveals itself nestled between interwoven hills. Regain your composure. Now is the moment to create lasting memories.

There are too many spectacular treks in this area to list in this book. Realistically, not everyone who wants to find romance owns hiking boots or, for that matter, sturdy thighs and a disposition that can survive the walk. For a beautifully written examination of the hikes available, I strongly recommend the book *Point Reyes Secret Places and Magic Moments*, by Phil Arnot. His descriptions and instructions are accurate and fairly easy to follow.

◆   **Romantic Suggestion:** Three of my favorite places in Point Reyes National Seashore are **ALAMERE FALLS, TOMALES POINT,** and **WILDCAT BEACH.** Each is dramatically different from the others, and the natural glory that exists here is worth discovering for yourselves. Check at the ranger station for hiking information about these areas, or use the book by Phil Arnot mentioned above.

◆   **Second Romantic Suggestion: FIVE BROOKS STABLES,**
(415) 663-8287, is a fabulous horse ranch with hourly rentals at Point
Reyes National Seashore.

## WHALE WATCHING, Point Reyes
*From numerous viewpoints along the Coast Trail in the Point Reyes National
Seashore, and especially from Point Reyes Lighthouse, (415) 669-1534, at
the end of Sir Francis Drake Boulevard due west of Inverness.*

If you have always secretly longed to witness firsthand the passage of
whales on their yearly migration to warmer waters, then the Northern
California coast is a great place to live out your fantasy. December to
April is the best time to witness this odyssey, particularly when the
weather conditions are clear and sunny. Be sure to go early in the
morning, about the time when the sun is radiantly warming the cool
morning air. As you stand at the edge of a cliff towering over the depths
below, you will have a tremendous view of this tortuous coastline. Find
a comfortable position, snuggle close together, and be patient. This
performance is intermittent at best and requires careful study and
diligence. Be prepared for an amazing encounter.

Picture the open, endless ocean, lined with staggered cliffs haloed
with green and gold chaparral for as far as the eye can see. Allow your
eyes to slowly scan the calm, azure waters. Then suddenly, in the
distance, breaking the still of a silent, sun-drenched spring morning, a
spout of bursting water explodes from the surface. A giant, arched black
profile appears boldly against the blue sea, followed by an abrupt tail slap
and then stillness once more. It's hard to explain the romance of that
moment, but romantic it is. Perhaps it's the excitement of observing
such an immense creature gliding effortlessly through the water with
playful agility and ease. Or perhaps it's the chance to celebrate a part of
nature's mysterious aquatic underworld together.

# Bodega Bay

## Hotel/Bed and Breakfast Kissing

**BAY HILL MANSION, Bodega Bay**
**3919 Bay Hill Road**
**(707) 875-3577 or (800) 526-5927**
Inexpensive to Expensive

*Call for directions.*

   Set on a hillside above the village, this gleaming white mansion with a Queen Anne motif is Bodega Bay's most romantic retreat. In the evening, wine and appetizers draw guests into the spacious parlor with its immense wood stove and bay window overlooking the sunset. One cabinet is filled with jewellike jelly jars filled with the inn's own chutneys and jams. A fresh femininity of soft, light hues and dainty florals flows throughout the inn. Several of the guest rooms have multi-angled walls, with windows overlooking the village and sea; you'll feel as though you're kissing inside a diamond. In the Whale Watch, the octagonal walls soar to a high turret, lifting your imagination, and your love, upward.

   ◆ **Romantic Warning:** Weddings and private parties are a specialty here. Be sure to call ahead to ensure you won't feel like an uninvited guest.

# Valley Ford

## *Hotel/Bed and Breakfast Kissing*

**THE INN AT VALLEY FORD, Valley Ford**
**14395 Highway 1**
**(707) 876-3182**
Inexpensive

*On Highway 1, just south of Bodega Bay, on the west side of the road.*

Bed and breakfasts are known for their cordial, cozy warmth; that is the earmark of this genre of lodging. Given the right touches, there is nothing quite as affection producing as staying someplace that diligently attends to matters of the heart. This means the aroma of fresh-baked scones and croissants, a well-tended fireplace, cushy antique decor, snuggly quilts piled with oversized pillows, sizable rooms, and a conspicuous amount of responsive loving care. The Inn at Valley Ford has seen to all that and more. The one drawback to this place is its communal bathroom facilities. There is something disconcerting about running into someone you don't know en route to the powder room or, worse, finding it occupied when you're in need. The reason we make an exception to our policy in this case is because one of the shared bathrooms here is a suite unto itself. In fact, you may decide to stay in there and forget about returning to your own room. The feature that will surely spark your interest is the large, tiled, walk-down shower, which is large enough to qualify as a small playfield. With space to spare, it can accommodate two people who want to emerge clean, giggling, and inseparable.

# Cazadero

## Hotel/Bed and Breakfast Kissing

**TIMBERHILL COUNTRY INN
AND TENNIS RANCH, Cazadero**
35755 Hauser Bridge Road
(707) 847-3258
Unbelievably Expensive

*Drive north on Highway 1. Five miles north of Jenner, turn right onto Meyers
Grade Road (first right after Seaview Plantation Road) and climb to the ridge.
Follow this country road for 13.7 miles from Highway 1. Six miles down, the
Meyers Grade Road turns into Seaview and then Seaview turns into Hauser
Bridge Road, which ends at the ranch.*

Why would a tennis ranch be considered a perfect place to unite in
a soul-connecting embrace? After all, if you don't like cuddling a racquet
or chasing balls in the hot afternoon sun, you're probably thinking of
ignoring this selection altogether. But be open-minded. Even if you
can't tell a tennis racquet from a baseball bat, you can still enjoy this
retreat, because all around you are 80 wooded acres of nature's finest
greenery, far removed from the pressures of the real world. The ranch is
home to 10 handsome cedar-log cabins, all with the appropriate romantic accoutrements: fireplace, view, sun deck, and extreme privacy. From
your own patio you can watch the sunset paint the country hills with a
kaleidoscope of color. Even the dining room has a serene elegance that
enhances the enticing meals, all prepared by a skilled chef. The acres of
woodland that ramble on endlessly next to the ranch will tempt you to
take long hikes. Or stay on the grounds and swim, or relax in the Jacuzzi
till the day journeys into night and dinnertime nears. If you want to get
far enough away from civilization to create some country magic, then
Timberhill Ranch may be your answer.

◆    **Romantic Note:** The daily room rate here includes all meals.

# Jenner

## Hotel/Bed and Breakfast Kissing

**FORT ROSS LODGE, Jenner**
**20705 Highway 1**
**(707) 847-3333**

Inexpensive to Expensive

*On the west side of Highway 1, just north of Jenner.*

The setting for this place is impeccable. The main building rests on a rocky pinnacle that pirouettes above the rugged azure sea and is encircled by rolling meadows dotted with wildflowers and dried golden brush. Nearby are dense woodlands of redwood and fir trees that house a newer, upscale section of the lodge. Each of the rooms bordering the ocean has sliding glass doors that open onto a private deck overlooking the unobstructed beauty of the Pacific. A glass-enclosed hot tub with the same view is available for guests, and many rooms come with their own sizable soaking tub for more private, interpersonal use. And the price is more than reasonable for such a stellar location. In spite of all this, I'm not certain Fort Ross Lodge is really romantic. The rooms are really tacky: lumpy, sagging beds; ugly brown carpeting; secondhand furnishings; and a VCR in each room (for kissing purposes a VCR is not considered to be a heart-tugging feature). But then again, there's that view and your own private deck. I guess you'll have to decide for yourselves, because I can't seem to make up my mind.

## Restaurant Kissing

**RIVER'S END RESTAURANT, Jenner**
**Highway 1**
**(707) 865-2484**
Moderate to Expensive

*On the west side of Highway 1, just north of the town of Jenner.*

The view of swirling white water and turbulent eddies that explode over and around the rock outcroppings of the Pacific Ocean can change at night into a placid, almost surreal, composition. As sunset nears, a single path of sunlight glosses the surface, illuminating only the water and the horizon, with the hills veiled in darkness. Evening announces its finale with a crescendo of colors that fade slowly to black. From the deck and dining room of River's End Restaurant, this daily, sparkling performance is yours to behold. If you've timed it right, nightfall and the last taste of your succulent, well-prepared dinner will occur simultaneously. Whether taking care of your appetite or spending a starry-eyed evening together is what you had in mind, both desires will be fully satiated.

◆   **Romantic Note:** The days and hours that the restaurant are open vary, depending on the season, but it is usually closed December and January.

◆   **Romantic Warning:** River's End is also a lodge with guest rooms that have the same view as the restaurant, only closer to the water. Why the warning? Because the decor can only be described as tacky and old, which hardly makes the rooms romantic. The price and scenery are certainly desirable, so if proximity to the ocean and bargain accommodations are paramount concerns, this place is a gem.

◆   **Romantic Alternative: JENNER BY THE SEA**, Coast Highway 1 at Jenner, (707) 865-1192, (Moderate), in any other setting might be considered a little too rustic or too casual, and too near the highway for a romantic dinner. Here on the Sonoma coast, however, almost any restaurant with a large fireplace and hearth, windows that survey the meandering Russian River emptying into the Pacific, and a kitchen staff that prepares very fresh seafood dishes is indeed a special spot.

# Gualala

## Hotel/Bed and Breakfast Kissing

**THE OLD MILANO HOTEL, Gualala**
38300 Highway 1
(707) 884-3256
Moderate to Expensive

*The hotel is one mile north of the town of Gualala, on Highway 1. Watch for a small, easily missed sign for the hotel on the west side of the road.*

This modest turn-of-the-century bed and breakfast has an irresistible quality. It is unsurpassed for its invitation to modern gracious living and in its enthusiasm for country finery. Every corner—the dining area, suites, furnishings, and gardens—reflects a heartfelt tenderness. As you turn from the road down the sandy driveway to the main house, you will readily appreciate the enveloping seclusion. The main building and the adjoining cottages are settled on a three-acre estate with the ocean only a stone's throw from the front door. At night, safe in the confines of your own bed, the sound of the surf will lull you to sleep. In the morning, after a late, lazy breakfast of freshly baked breads and an assortment of other delicacies, you can stroll along the shore and look back at the slice of heaven the two of you found together.

◆ **Romantic Note:** Be sure to ask about the caboose accommodations if you want a totally different, romantically bawdy adventure.

**ST. ORRES INN AND RESTAURANT, Gualala**  
P.O. Box 523
(707) 884-3303
Inexpensive to Expensive

*As you head north out of Gualala on Highway 1, the spires of St. Orres will appear on the left. If you reach Anchor Bay, you have gone too far.*

Finding words that succinctly express the richness and architectural intrigue of this bed and breakfast is a challenge. Your hearts and thoughts will succumb to the dream world you enter here at St. Orres. Rising above a cloistered sandy cove, this structure appears suddenly out of nowhere, a fascinating hand-carved, wood-and-glass Russian-style chalet. The stained glass windows of this inn's two intricately crafted towers twinkle in the daylight. This same prismatic light bathes the interior in a velvety amber hue. On the main floor, the distinctive dining room uses the light to its full potential: it illuminates a petite indoor arboretum. The food there lives up to its surroundings. The guest rooms here are varied, from simple to splendid; there are even cottages scattered about the grounds, each with its own spirit and tone. Some have a perfect unobstructed ocean view, others have sun decks, fireplaces, and sunken tubs. Wherever you finally settle at St. Orres, your own dream world is guaranteed to come quickly alive.

◆     **Romantic Suggestion**: Several beaches are accessible from Highway 1. Keep watch for the signs, as they pop up inconsistently. **SHELL BEACH**, just south of Gualala, is one of those windswept beaches you reach via a tree-sheltered trail. Beachcombing along here is a wonderful way to spend an afternoon.

## WHALE WATCH INN, Gualala
35100 Highway 1
(707) 884-3667
Expensive to Very Expensive

*On Highway 1 just north of Gualala, on the west side of the road.*

Most modern hotels or resorts remind me of suburban condominium developments: functional, but not very romantic. On the other hand, newness can sometimes be inventive, fresh, and artistic. When you take innovative architecture and combine it with a thrilling setting, you end up with the Whale Watch Inn, which oversees the rugged, treacherous shoreline and sandy beach inlet of Anchor Bay. The music of the rushing water resounds through the five compact buildings that make up this complex. The wood exterior is stained a weathered seaside gray that harmonizes with the landscape. The inn boasts only 18 suites, each with its own flair. Skylights, sun decks, whirlpools, and fireplaces enhance the plush furnishings and pastel fabrics. There is an overpowering air of loving feeling here that will influence your stay and inevitably encourage you to return.

◆　**Romantic Footnote**: Each room at the Whale Watch contains a small diary. The entries are all from previous guests. As you read over the thoughts and experiences from the past, take time to discuss the entry you would like to leave for the next visitors.

◆　**Romantic Alternative**: Across the street and up from the Whale Watch Inn is the **NORTH COAST COUNTRY INN**, 34591 South Highway 1, Gualala, (707) 884-4537, (Moderate), residing on a forested hillside with a view of the Pacific in the distance. The four rooms here have an assortment of french doors, private decks, large bay windows (two with ocean views), fireplaces, skylights, kitchenettes, and comfortable (although dated) American furnishings. There is also a steamy outdoor hot tub for soaking tired spirits back to life. Breakfast is delivered to your room for the most intimate dining possible. Having said all that, I must also inform you that this attractive redwood home is located right next to Highway 1, which is hardly what you would call secluded and intimate. But at these prices and with this quality, it can be a fine place to stay on the coast.

## Outdoor Kissing

**ROTH RANCH, Gualala**
**37100 Old Stage Road**
**(707) 884-3124**

*Head north on Highway 1 for one mile past the town of Gualala. Turn left on Pacific Woods Road. This road dead-ends at Old Stage Road, where you turn left. The ranch is two miles down the road.*

The Sonoma coast's shoreline is the perfect setting for a gallop through surf and sand, especially if you know how to ride a horse. The waves splash against the horses' hooves as you ride effortlessly alongside someone you love. Sigh! Of course, the clincher would be to stop along the way for a hearty lunch and a playful frolic in the foam. Given that scenario, it is hard to pass up a trail ride at Roth Ranch. They offer healthy, energetic horses for a journey that begins in dense forest and ends with romantic memories. In between, you can admire the long, empty beaches, eat lunch, and soak up some sun just by saddling up and trotting along the trail.

◆    **Romantic Note:** Horse rentals are by the hour, or you can request three-hour excursions that include lunch or dinner on the beach.

# Elk

## *Hotel/Bed and Breakfast Kissing*

**ELK COVE INN, Elk**
**6300 South Highway 1**
**(707) 877-3321**
Moderate

*The inn is located 15 miles south of Mendocino, on the west side of the road next to Highway 1.*

This is one of those places I almost passed up. The unassuming facade of the main house looked plain and uninviting, and on top of that, I was tired and felt more like the *Accidental Tourist* than a romantic travel writer. Thank goodness, I have learned from past experience never to write off a place based solely on its outward appearance. Often I have found that what waits inside is more precious than anything I could have dreamed possible. Elk Cove Inn is such a place.

The guest rooms here are idyllic, spacious getaways that contain the kind of details lovers can appreciate. Some have bay windows, fireplaces, high beamed ceilings, skylights, stained glass windows, and private decks. One cabin even has a hand-painted tile shower, with its own floor-to-ceiling view of the ocean. The views are stunning, with a sunset that will leave you speechless (which makes kissing that much easier). As if that weren't enough, Elk Cove Inn is renowned for its daily gourmet breakfast, which leaves you satisfied until dinner. Did I forget to mention the driftwood-scattered beach below the inn? This is one place that you really should check out for yourselves.

## HARBOR HOUSE, Elk

**5600 South Highway 1**
**(707) 877-3203**
Moderate

*Just outside of Elk, on the west side of Highway 1.*

The word "rustic" usually makes me nervous. It's hard to know exactly what is meant by the term. Rustic can conjure up images of knotty wood paneling, alcove sitting areas next to bay windows, crackling fireplaces, and feather-down quilts three inches thick. It can also suggest paneling that is falling off the walls, drafty fireplaces that provide no warmth, and torn quilts that have seen better days. This inn by the sea is best described as a rustic sanctuary—of the first type and not anything like the second type. It is a place where the hours drift by and your mood is enhanced by the tranquillity around you.

The inn is constructed of redwood and resides on a bluff with awesome views of the water and the private beach below. The sweeping bay window in the dining room looks out onto haystack boulders and sea-worn rock arches that dot the ocean's surface. In this imposing setting, exceptional gourmet breakfasts (for guests only) and dinners are served with flair. The food is as pure as the location, with preference given to homegrown vegetables and herbs. You will find everything about Harbor House amorous and relaxing.

The moderate price for staying here includes breakfast and dinner for two. There are 10 rooms at Harbor House and almost all are decidedly romantic. The Seaview and Oceansong cottages have private decks, fireplaces, and ocean views. The Cypress and Harbor rooms are spacious and have fireplaces and incredible ocean views.

# Albion

## Hotel/Bed and Breakfast Kissing

**ALBION RIVER INN, Albion**
**3790 North Highway 1**
**(707) 937-1919, (800) 479-7944**
Inexpensive to Expensive

*On the west side of Highway 1, near the town of Albion, six miles south of Mendocino.*

Albion River Inn is a very popular location along the north coast, but that in no way hampers its romance potential. If, after a long day of touring, you want a secluded, beautiful place to watch the golden sunset turn the sky to fiery red as the ocean thunders against the shore below, this is the place to be. The inn sits on a precipice directly on the coast towering above Albion Cove and the Pacific. All of the 20 rooms have superlative views. Or you may prefer one of the suites (numbers 1–5, 10–13 and 16), where you can soak in a spa-size bathtub while a sizzling fire fills the room with an amber glow.

If you want to take a walk during your stay, a private headland pathway takes you to great vistas of the expansive water and sky. Included in the cost of the room is a generous breakfast of home-baked breads, homemade granola, eggs to order, fresh fruit, and juices, served in the inn's restaurant. The food is truly delicious and the view mesmerizing.

◆   **Romantic Note:** It is recommended that you call one or two months ahead of time to book weekends, holidays, or any time during the summer.

# Restaurant Kissing

**THE LEDFORD HOUSE, Albion**
**3000 North Highway 1**
**(707) 937-0282**
Moderate to Expensive

*Off Highway 1, just south of Little River, on the east side of the road.*

Sited on a bluff with a spectacular view of the ocean, The Ledford House is one of the most elegant places for dinner along the coast. Candlelight casts flickering shadows on whitewashed walls, creating a warm, gentle feeling throughout. When the area is shrouded in fog (which occurs more often than some would like to admit), The Ledford House becomes still more cozy and inviting. There is little doubt that this place offers a touching environment for dining and kissing.

◆     **Romantic Note:** Be sure to call for reservations. This restaurant, like many others in this part of the world, is closed during the winter.

◆     **Romantic Option: LITTLE RIVER RESTAURANT,** 7750 North Highway 1, Little River, (707) 937-4945, (Inexpensive to Moderate), is probably one of the most unlikely locations for a restaurant, whether or not you are in the mood for romance. This obscure, tiny, thoroughly pleasing place to dine is attached to the back of the town's gas station and post office. A remarkably adept kitchen staff serves fresh fish, creatively prepared, at two seatings to a cozy group of seven tables. (Now this is what I call intimate!) Dinner is served Friday through Monday only; the reasonably priced entrees include soup and salad.

# Little River

## Hotel/Bed and Breakfast Kissing

GLENDEVEN, Little River
8221 North Highway 1
(707) 937-0083
Inexpensive to Expensive

*On Highway 1, just south of Mendocino, look for the Glendeven sign on the east side of the road. Turn right into the driveway.*

This is country living at its best. The charming New Englandesque farmhouse is poised on verdant meadowland brushed by fresh ocean air. Glendeven has 12 unique guest suites, and each is more engaging and provocative than the last. My first reaction was to utter a sigh of "Wow!" The entire bed and breakfast is replete with affectionate details and cozy furnishings. Fireplaces, balconies, redwood paneling, french doors leading to a sunny deck, large tiled bathrooms, and spacious, airy rooms are distributed throughout. Of special interest for those looking for heart-stirring accommodations are the Bayloft, Briar Rose, and Pinewood suites. The Bayloft, in particular, is an incredible place to spend a weekend on the coast. If this room doesn't help set the mood, nothing will.

HERITAGE HOUSE, Little River
5200 North Highway 1
(707) 937-5885, (800) 235-5885
Expensive to Unbelievably Expensive

*About two miles south of Mendocino, on the ocean side of Highway 1.*

Kiss before one of the most spectacular panoramas on California's northern coast at this spellbinding hostelry. The estate embraces no fewer than 72 guest rooms in a series of small buildings terraced above the Pacific. Almost all of the uniquely decorated rooms have private entrances and share a dazzling view of a pristine cove where waves crash majestically against rugged cliffs. Kissing on the private deck of a "Sunset" room is pure inspiration. In the evening, throw open the windows to welcome the Pacific's music and share warm kisses by the fire or sink into the double tub beneath the starry skylight. Unbelievably, the view from the Carousel Suite is even more sensational. A two-sided fireplace warms both the living room and bedroom. Dim the track lights and indulge in the double whirlpool or splash in the dual-headed shower, then cuddle with towels heated by the towel warmer.

◆ **Romantic Note:** Room rates include breakfast and dinner for two served in the elegant dining room perched above the Pacific. The menu changes daily, but could include saffron mussel bisque, or crab and smoked almond salad to start; grilled salmon with artichokes, leeks, and pistachios, or African pheasant with spicy vegetable pot-stickers as an entree; and luscious desserts. The restaurant is open to envious non-guests if room is available after guests are accommodated.

◆ **Second Romantic Note:** The movie *Same Time, Next Year* was filmed here, but if you're thinking of kissing in the room where Alan Alda and Ellen Burstyn romanced, reserve months in advance. In fact, reserve as far in advance as possible for any room here. Heritage House is closed in December and January.

**RACHEL'S INN, Little River**
**8200 North Highway 1**
**(707) 937-0088**
Moderate to Expensive

*The inn is two miles south of Mendocino, on the ocean side of Highway 1.*

From the front door of this charming inn, I followed a footpath through a meadow in the adjacent state park. The trail wove its way through more meadows, past small groves of gnarled trees; the sound of the Pacific grew ever nearer. Suddenly, it climaxed at a stunning seascape of rugged cliffs, mighty surf, and an azure ocean that stretched as far as the imagination. Below, waves sent miniature waterfalls rippling over sculptured rocks and seals played gleefully in the breakers. Only the Rachel Inn's simple but romantic accommodations could call me away.

The Garden Room, in the 1860s main house, is the most secluded, with its private entrance and love seat by the fire. All four rooms in the contemporary barn feature fireplaces. The Mezzanine Suite is especially feminine and crisp, with its white wicker and pink cushions. The suite's private deck overlooks the back lawn, where deer frequently graze at sunset: a magic end to your day on the coast.

◆    **Romantic Alternative**: Just across the street from Rachel's, **STEVENSWOOD**, 8211 North Highway 1, Little River, (707) 937-2810, (Inexpensive to Very Expensive), offers contemporary, crisp rooms with fireplaces, mini-bars, remote-control televisions, and phones. Generous evening appetizers and wines and gourmet breakfasts are served in the cheerful, firelit common room. Stevenswood is set back from the road on nicely landscaped grounds; my only objection is that the rooms seemed to be designed for traveling executives, a style that is not always perfect for kissing.

# Mendocino

If there is one place that is representative of coastal life in Northern California, it is Mendocino. The only words that appropriately fit this uncommon seaside town are "quaint" and "serene." Well, at least during the winter that's true. Other times of the year, "crowded" best characterizes this Cape Cod-style village. Its quiet streets are lined with whitewashed storefronts that house small specialty shops ripe for browsing. There are also enviable bed and breakfasts that are frequently fully booked on weekends—months in advance. Of course, the main attraction is the view of the tranquil bay and rocky shoreline that surround Mendocino. In essence, this town offers the yin and yang of getaway spots. The very elements that make it so wonderful are also why everyone and their cousins know about it. Still, there is the off-season, when the crowds and sun are less prevalent and fog shrouds the area in a veil of misty white. And that's what down comforters, fireplaces, and snuggling close are there for.

# Hotel/Bed and Breakfast Kissing

**AGATE COVE INN, Mendocino,**
**11201 North Lansing Street**
**(707) 937-0551, (800) 527-3111**
Inexpensive to Expensive

*Call the inn for directions.*

One element of a romantic place to stay is a view that overlooks a hypnotic seascape with the surf close enough to serenade you all night long. The Emerald and Obsidian rooms at Agate Cove make that fantasy come true. These oceanfront accommodations are cozy and comfortable. And the generous full breakfast served in the inn's extremely pleasant, window-outfitted dining room has a ringside view of the potent, rugged shoreline. There are 10 country-style cottages here at Agate Cove Inn, but the best are the ones with the view. The rooms that face the courtyard offer very little privacy.

**BREWERY GULCH INN, Mendocino**
**9350 North Highway 1**
**(707) 937-4752**
Very Inexpensive to Moderate

*Just south of Mendocino, on the inland side of Highway 1.*

A deer pranced by as I made my way up the long drive to this enchanting inn. From the moment I stepped through the weathered garden gate, I felt as though I'd entered a storybook land of tangled vines, daffodils, crowing roosters, and a friendly golden retriever. This is a genuine country inn, an embrace of serenity, generous hospitality, and old-fashioned romance. Share an old title from the shelf in the spacious Garden Room, while firelight glows on expectant cheeks. Snuggle beneath the hand-sewn quilt in the Orchard Suite or jot down an ode to love at its writing desk. Imagine the stories the antiques in the Victorian Room could tell as you cuddle by the hearth. In the morning, a hearty breakfast may beguile you into adding your own chapter to this charming story.

**THE HEADLANDS INN, Mendocino**
**Howard Street and Albion Street**
**(707) 937-4431**
Moderate to Expensive

*From San Francisco, go north on Highway 101 to Cloverdale, head west on Highway 128 to Highway 1, and proceed north to Mendocino. Turn left to the business district and go two blocks to Howard Street. Turn right, and in a block and a half you will find the inn on your left.*

There are five distinctive, although small, rooms at the Headlands Inn. The interior is an interesting blend of rustic and charming, and the views of the churning white water of the Pacific are outstanding. Each room has its own fireplace and gorgeous views of the water; there is also a cottage that is the ultimate in privacy. In the morning, be prepared for an exceptional breakfast brought directly to your room. Do not be surprised to find Mexican egg souffles, peach or blackberry crepes with Amaretto sauce, and fresh pastries and fruits on your personalized tray.

**MENDOCINO VILLAGE INN, Mendocino**
**44860 Main Street**
**(707) 937-0246, (800) 882-7029**
Inexpensive to Moderate

*Call for directions.*

This inn has an assortment of simple to charming guest rooms with everything from private entrances to fireplaces, bay windows, and canopied beds. Of the 12 rooms, the best are the French Country, Diamond Lil, Quilt Cabin, Captain's Quarters, and Teddy Roosevelt: they all have the best details the inn has to offer. Perhaps the highlight here is the gourmet breakfast with homemade cornbread, muffins, cheddar scones, banana pancakes, and quiche. You are likely to find a combination of these and more waiting for you in the morning.

## REED MANOR, Mendocino

**10871 Palette Drive**
**(707) 937-5446**
Expensive to Unbelievably Expensive

*Going north on Highway 1, take the Little Lake Street exit. Turn right on Lansing, then right on Palette. The inn is on the right.*

For opulently voluptuous kissing in this earthy village, check into this stately new manor. All of the palatially sized guest rooms feature gas fireplaces, ample whirlpools, sumptuous decor, mini-fridges, coffee makers, teapots, televisions tucked away in cabinets, and VCRs hidden in bedside drawers. Telescopes on private decks invite viewing the quaint town below and the ocean beyond; a complimentary split of wine provides the perfect toast to it all. Pull back the flouncy curtains and sink into the bubbling tub while watching the gas flames in the cheerful Morning Glory's hearth. In the Napoleon, a double-sided fireplace glows in both the bathroom, with its whirlpool and dual-headed shower, and the silvery French Provincial bedroom. Josephine's Garden opens to a delightful redwood patio laced with colorful blooms. A Continental breakfast of nut breads, fruit, and locally made apple juice is wrapped and delivered to your room in the evening, so you can enjoy it at your leisure in the morning.

## SEA ROCK INN, Mendocino

**11101 North Lansing Street**
**(707) 937-5517**
Inexpensive to Moderate

*Call for directions.*

The Sea Rock Inn is next door to the Agate Cove Inn and has the same sweeping view of the sea and rocky headlands. The rooms here range in style from basic and unassuming to private cottages hidden by cypress trees to rooms with spectacular water views and heat provided by Franklin stoves and wood-burning fireplaces.

**STANFORD INN BY THE SEA,** Mendocino
**44850 Comptche-Ukiah Road**
**(707) 937-5615, (800) 331-8884**
Expensive to Unbelievably Expensive

*Just south of Mendocino, turn inland from Highway 1 onto Comptche-Ukiah Road.*

This expansive lodge is the perfect marriage of quintessential luxury and a woodsy naturalness true to its ruggedly beautiful setting. Step onto your private deck as the sun setting on the far horizon sprinkles its golden glow across the Pacific, over the inn's herd of graceful llamas grazing in the meadow, past terraced gardens with their cornucopia of flowers and vegetables, to your expectant lips. If the evening chills, cuddle by the firelight in your wood-paneled room, pop open the complimentary bottle of burgundy, and slide a mood-setting CD into your stereo. Each room has a fireplace, private balcony, stereo, television, VCR, and a sleigh or four-poster bed. In the morning, take a dip in the alluring new greenhouse-enclosed pool or luxuriate in the spa and sauna. Then indulge in an elaborate champagne breakfast of cereals, yogurt, pastries, fruits, and more, served in the cozy firelit parlor. Don't forget to toast the north coast.

◆   **Romantic Note:** See the coast in style on one of the inn's state-of-the-art mountain bikes, available at no cost to guests. Or rent a canoe for a romantic paddle along the Big River, inland to secluded kissing spots where only the forests remain virgin.

**WHITEGATE INN,** Mendocino
**499 Howard Street**
**(707) 937-4892**
Moderate

The Whitegate Inn is a traditionally Victorian, extremely elegant bed and breakfast. The six guest rooms all have ocean or village views, some have fireplaces, and the beds are draped with thick, white down comforters. Observing the bay from the huge parlor window is a delightful way to while away a morning, after partaking in the gracious continental breakfast served in the dining room.

# Restaurant Kissing

**CHOCOLATE MOOSSE CAFE, Mendocino**
**390 Kasten Street, at Albion**
**(707) 937-4323**
Inexpensive

Plan on light romance at lunch or dinner in this cozy, casual cafe, especially on a chilly, foggy day when firelight warms the room. This is the kind of place where specials written on the blackboard can range from salmon smoked over applewood to a saucy lasagne or an garlic chicken. Decadent desserts, such as the irresistible blackout cake, and gourmet coffees make even a dreary day enjoyable when shared by two.

◆     **Romantic Alternative:** If the sun is shining, choose a table on the patio of **THE MENDOCINO CAFE**, Lansing at Ukiah, Mendocino, (707) 937-0836, (Inexpensive). Creative salads, soups, sandwiches, and light entrees are served along with a view of the village and headlands beyond.

**THE GRAY WHALE BAR AND CAFE, Mendocino**
**45020 Albion Street**
**(707) 937-5763**
Moderate

*As you turn west off Highway 1 onto Main Street, look for Lansing Street and turn right. The next block is Albion, where you turn left to the bar.*

The epitome of North Coast dining and lounging is to be found here at The Gray Whale. The ambience is a careful combination of country Victorian refinement and laid-back California spirit. Whoever handled this renovation knew what they were doing. It takes a great deal of skill to meld the warmth of the past with the finesse of the present and yet create the illusion that nothing has changed in 100 years. The substantial cobblestone fireplace fills the dining rooms with a burnished light that flickers warmly against redwood paneling. The tables are placed far enough apart to provide for discreet conversation. A window-framed sun porch at the front of the lounge houses the cafe, which overlooks the bay and street scene. Complementing this atmosphere is a menu of fresh fish, meats, and produce that are exceptionally well prepared and savory.

◆    **Romantic Note:** The Gray Whale Bar and Cafe is located on the ground floor of the **MACCALLUM HOUSE INN**, (707) 937-0289, (Inexpensive to Expensive), under separate management from the restaurant. This inn is, to say the least, one of the most unusual bed and breakfasts I've ever seen. The meandering array of rooms and suites range in style from overly rustic to unusually romantic. For the purposes of kissing, the best units are The Barn and The Barn Apartment. The Barn has a massive stone fireplace, cozy sitting area, and a large picture window overlooking the bay. The Barn Apartment is similar, with the addition of a very sensual, very large bathroom. For the most part, however, this is not what we would call the best kissing place in Mendocino.

## MENDOCINO HOTEL DINING ROOM, Mendocino      ◆◆◀
**45080 Main Street, between Lansing and Kasten**
**(707) 937-0511, (800) 548-0513**
Expensive

Victorians wouldn't have dreamed of kissing whilst they dined at this refined restaurant 100 years ago, but you may be inspired to a quick, secret caress. Arrive early to ease yourselves back in time by the fire in the elegant lobby, with its tapestried settees and Persian carpets. Candles flicker on the tables in the dining room, casting a nostalgic glow on the rich, red wall coverings and faceted glass partitions. Appetizers to share include aphrodisiacal oysters and Brie baked in puff pastry, followed by such continental favorites as petrale sole and prime rib served with Yorkshire pudding. For lunch or an early dinner, the hotel's Garden Room is a gloriously lush greenhouse setting, especially inviting when the sun streams in to bless your love.

# Outdoor Kissing

### MENDOCINO COAST BOTANICAL GARDENS
### (707) 964-4352
$5 adult admission fee

*West side of Highway 1, just south of Fort Bragg.*

Just like new love, these natural gardens unfold before you with ever-expanding layers of beauty, each one surprising and evocative. Don't be fooled by the entrance, little more than a rustic garden shop by a roadside cafe. Once beyond the gate, you can stroll hand-in-hand past formal plantings of colorful annuals, following walkways festooned with rhododendrons, over hillsides laced with hydrangeas and meadows mellow with heather. Wander to the very farthest reaches of the garden and you will happen upon a stunning seascape with welcoming benches perched high above the crashing surf. Hug each other closely while fishing boats bob in the cool Pacific and foghorns call mournfully. In the winter you may even see a whale pass by, its spout punctuating the allure of the sea.

### MENDOCINO HEADLANDS AND
### BIG RIVER BEACH STATE PARK
*The coastal headlands and park surround Mendocino on all sides.*

Perhaps more than any other attraction in Mendocino, the headlands and Big River Beach State Park are the primary draws of this region. The protected, flawless curve of land is an easily accessible place to see, hear, and feel nature in all its magnitude and glory. On a calm, sun-filled day, the glistening ocean reveals hidden grottos, sea arches, and tide pools, as foamy white surf encircles the rock-etched boundary of Mendocino. If you happen to be here December through March, you may see a school of whales making its way down the coast. On days when the thick ocean fog enfolds the area in a white-gray cloak, this is still a prime place to explore and daydream. Dress warmly and allow the cool mist to tingle against your cheeks as you taste the lightly salted air that wets your lips.

Here you are—with the wind sailing through your hair, the fog concealing your movements, and someone special next to you.

◆    **Romantic Option: RUSSIAN GULCH STATE PARK**, (707) 937-5804, just north of Mendocino, off Highway 1, is a small campground with redwood-lined trails, rocky coves, lovely inlets, a quiet bay, and campsites at the water's edge. There aren't many tent spaces available here, so it is advisable to make reservations well in advance.

◆    **Second Romantic Option: MACKERRICHER STATE PARK**, (707) 937-5804, three miles north of Fort Bragg off Highway 1, is a wondrous assortment of nature's most attractive features: waterfalls at the end of forested trails, grass-covered headlands overlooking the Pacific, white sandy beaches, rolling dunes, and haystack rocks where harbor seals spend the day sunning themselves. The most outstanding feature of this state park is its distance from Mendocino; the extra few miles make it less popular, and thus it has a definite kissing advantage.

# WINE COUNTRY

## Sonoma Valley and Napa Valley

*From San Francisco, take Highway 101 north to Highway 37 east. Highway 37 connects with Route 12 (the Sonoma Highway), which leads north through the Sonoma Valley, and with Route 29, which accesses the Napa Valley.*

The hills in this holiday countryside are given over to vineyards and the succulent grapes they produce. Once you visit this region you will understand the vivacious, impetuous temperament that is the hallmark of the wine country, its robust regard for living life to its fullest. The boroughs and hamlets of the area are well stocked with an enormous selection of bed and breakfasts, restaurants, spas, wine tasting rooms, hot-air balloon companies, and the most remarkable picnic turf around. The roughest part of your travels here will be making a choice about where to concentrate your time. In line with the discriminating criteria of this book, we do earnestly describe the Napa and Sonoma valleys as brimming with the creme de la creme of romance.

**Romantic Consideration:** The number of wineries scattered throughout these picturesque hills and valleys is staggering. Even if you were merely to sip your way in and out of the tasting rooms for a week, you would make only a nominal, intoxicating dent in the possibilities that exist here. Because this book is about sentiment and not about choosing a vintage wine, we've chosen a handful of the lesser-known, out-of-the-mainstream wineries we found to be the most appealing for embracing and tasting, both the wine and each other.

# Sonoma

*From San Francisco, take Highway 101 north to Highway 37 east. Highway 37 connects with Route 12, which goes north to the town of Sonoma.*

In spite of its popularity and tourist appeal, Sonoma is still an interesting place for a rendezvous. The village is wrapped around a village square shaded by sprawling oak trees and sculpted shrubbery. Weaving around this central area are flowering walkways, a gently flowing fountain, a duck pond, and park benches. Around the square's perimeter, branching out in all directions, is an array of shops, restaurants, and wineries that have retained much of their original charm. Commercialism is softened to a purr instead of a roar.

Consider starting your day at a local espresso shop or bakery to gather all of the necessities for a breakfast picnic on the square's cool green lawn. The rest of your day can be spent gallivanting through the wineries and tasting rooms that line the surrounding lush hillsides and valleys. When evening arrives and you come back to where you began the day, you'll find enough gourmet dining options in Sonoma to keep both of you happy.

◆ **Romantic Warning**: Summer crowds in Sonoma can be overpowering all week long and unbearable on the weekends. Off-season is the best time to find a degree of solitude as well as comfortable weather conditions.

◆ **Romantic Option**: **TAYLOR'S OF SONOMA FLORIST SHOP**, 933 Main Street, Sonoma, (707) 938-1000, is a business that embodies the irresistible appeal of the past. The stone house stands alone on a side street just off the town square; its wrought-iron fence, wooden stairway, and stone threshold leading inside seem Lilliputian in dimension and style; and bouquets of flowers in a multitude of colors and fragrances occupy every inch of available space.

## Hotel/Bed and Breakfast Kissing

**SONOMA HOTEL RESTAURANT, Sonoma**
**110 West Spain Street**
**(707) 996-2996**
Inexpensive

*On the northwest corner of the plaza, at the intersection of West Spain Street and West First Street.*

Consider the life-style of the well-heeled West around the turn of the century. Whatever images you conjure up, you'll find thriving at the Sonoma Hotel Restaurant. You enter the lobby through two antique wooden doors. Once inside, you notice a chaise lounge next to a massive stone fireplace topped by a mantel lined with hurricane lamps. A ceiling fan spinning overhead circulates aromas from deep within the kitchen. The dining area has three separate seating areas from which to choose. The area closest to the front receives softly filtered daylight through sheer curtains hanging from ceiling-tall windows. The rear section has a library theme with subdued lighting. Oak tables and paneling lend a rustic simplicity to the restaurant. Here your desire for good food, privacy, and a taste of the past can be indulged.

◆ **Romantic Warning:** The hotel part of this landmark building is nice but a little too rustic. There are impressive, massive antique furnishings in some of the rooms, but they tend to overpower the space, which feels cramped and small. Five of the rooms have their own baths and are really quite charming, but the floors creak a little and the bathrooms are tiny.

◆ **Romantic Suggestion: THE VICTORIAN GARDEN INN**, 316 East Napa Street, Sonoma (707) 996-5339, (Inexpensive to Moderate), resides in the bucolic neighborhood of Sonoma. The home's ordinary exterior is enveloped by a trellised walkway and garden. Behind the house is a swimming pool takes up the entire backyard. The inn offers four distinctive, comfortable overnight options, including a separate, very cozy cottage. Several have private entrances, wicker furnishings, fireplaces, sitting areas, and country-style antiques. Breakfast is a continental array of local ground fruit, granola, fresh juice, and pastries.

**TROJAN HORSE INN, Sonoma**
**19455 Sonoma Highway**
**(707) 996-2430**
Moderate to Expensive

*About one mile west of Sonoma Plaza. Where Highway 12 (the Sonoma Highway) jogs north, look for the inn immediately on the left.*

A pleasant surprise lies hidden inside the Trojan Horse Inn. Although I was tired and the weather dreary upon my arrival, stepping over the threshold of this 1887 Victorian inn rejuvenated me. The spacious, cheerful parlor appears to be abloom with bright spring flowers radiant in the sunshine. Country plaid sofas, floral accent chairs, and copious bouquets of silk flowers are at once homey and charming. In the evening, the hospitable innkeepers and their lucky guests partake of local wines, cheese, and conversation before the glowing hearth. Decor in the guest rooms ranges from the virginal Bridal Veil, with its billowing white lace canopy and curtains and corner wood stove, to the erotic Victorian Room, with its rich, Bordeaux satin bedcoverings. If your taste runs toward the less extravagant, try the placid Walden Pond or no-nonsense Jack London. All rooms are furnished with noteworthy antiques. In the morning, a full breakfast—perhaps melon with yogurt-ginger sauce, blueberry pancakes, and locally made sausage—ensures a hearty start to a day of wine tasting.

## Restaurant Kissing

**PASTA NOSTRA, Sonoma**
**139 East Napa Street**
**(707) 938-4166**
Moderate

*Less than half a block from Sonoma Plaza.*

Take a cliche, add a dash of California freshness, and *voila!* You have this delightfully creative Italian bistro. High peaked ceilings and a series of open rooms hint at the original framework of this former Victorian home. The restaurant is both airy and cozy, highlighted with little white lights and oil lamps flickering on the tables. The menu has both classic and inventive dishes, such as succulently sweet veal marsala, homemade caramelized carrot pasta, and cream-cheese ravioli. My favorites were the specials: a Maui onion stuffed with sausage, then topped with cheese and baked, and the spinach fettuccine with sauteed tarragon chicken.

## *Outdoor Kissing*

### BUENA VISTA WINERY, Sonoma
### 18000 Old Winery Road
### (707) 938-1266

*From Sonoma Plaza, head east on East Napa Street. Turn left after the railroad tracks onto Old Winery Road. The winery is about one mile from the plaza.*

I had gathered my picnic goodies in Sonoma Plaza: award-winning sourdough from the Sonoma Bakery, homemade deli meats and mustard from the Sonoma Sausage Company, and scrumptious pesto jack from the Sonoma Cheese Company. All I needed was a smooth chardonnay and a peaceful picnic spot. I found both at Buena Vista. Tangled ivy over rugged stone walls lends an ancient feel to this winery, California's oldest. A bevy of picnic tables are set by the woodsy creek and on a hillside terrace, all shaded by sweet-scented eucalyptus trees. The cool tasting room offers a small selection of fine gifts to commemorate your time together; a mezzanine gallery showcases local art.

### HACIENDA WINERY, Sonoma
### 1000 Vineyard Lane, P.O. Box 416
### (707) 938-3220

*At the Sonoma town square, turn right onto East Napa Street and go one mile. At Seventh Street East, turn left and follow the signs on Castle Road.*

If you've ever wondered which winery has the most romantic setting in the Napa/Sonoma Valley, Hacienda Winery may provide your answer. Its sensual setting is a tour de force of gardening skill and ageless beauty. The walk from the dusty, unpaved parking area up to the stone cellar and tasting room is a stroll through venerable moss-covered trees and pinery. As the path narrows and turns, the city environs disappear behind you and ahead you face a vine-covered world. The grounds of the estate are etched with fragrant flowers, and strategically placed picnic tables provide exalted seating for gazing upon acre after acre of sinuous terrain. As far as the eye can see, rows of burgeoning grapevines are bordered with jade forest. A wildly flirtatious outing is here for the asking; your part is to do the asking and subsequent romancing.

◆ **Romantic Option:** In keeping with the spirit of a day spent stimulating your palate at the wineries, you'll want a dinner that is European and traditional. **MAGLIULO'S**, 691 Broadway, Sonoma, (707) 996-1031, (Inexpensive to Moderate), obliges with just that. Its rustic, Victorian setting of wrought iron and wood is accented by pastel colors. Here you can relish incredible Italian cuisine and sensational desserts. Dinner and lunch are served seven days a week, plus an enchanting Sunday brunch.

# Glen Ellen

## *Hotel/Bed and Breakfast Kissing*

**GAIGE HOUSE, Glen Ellen**
**13540 Arnold Drive**
**(707) 935-0237**
Moderate to Expensive

*Driving north on Highway 12, turn left onto Arnold Drive (look for the sign to Glen Ellen). Gaige House is a half mile west, on the right side.*

A symphony of bird songs greeted me as I entered through the garden gate of this small-town inn, an impressive Italianate Victorian that seems to have taken root in this rural setting. Inside, an eclectic collection of antiques punctuated with the occasional art deco sculpture fills the double parlors. You'll never run out of conversation pieces as you enjoy your afternoon wine and cheese by the fire. The guest rooms are spacious and uncluttered, the furnishings comfortable and tasteful, the bathrooms modern. Kissing by your own fire will warm you in two of the rooms. The grandest room has its own private wraparound deck, a king-size carved cherry-wood bed with canopy, and an immense bathroom with a whirlpool large enough for four (but much more enjoyable with just two!). After a day of wine tasting, enjoy a rejuvenating dip in the inn's pool before dinner.

### GLENELLY INN, Glen Ellen
### 5131 Warm Springs Road
### (707) 996-6720
Inexpensive to Moderate

*Driving north on Highway 12, turn left onto Arnold Drive (look for the sign to Glen Ellen). Take a right onto Warm Springs Road; the inn is located on the right in one-third mile.*

This 1916 railroad inn is a legacy of Glen Ellen's heyday, when San Franciscans thought this woodsy town an invigorating getaway. The inn's setting is still enchanting, nestled at the base of a steep hill, shaded by the gnarled branches of century-old oak and olive trees. Now it is enhanced with a whirlpool and a brick courtyard in the lower garden, and a double hammock in the more naturally landscaped upper terrace. Although the architectural design is from an era when standard rooms were smaller, the fresh, bright decor, Norwegian down quilts, and claw-foot tubs make them cozy. You can sip your wine by your own wood stove in the suites or enjoy it by the fire in the common room. All the rooms have private entrances: no need to tiptoe in after a late-night swing in the hammock.

## Outdoor Kissing

**JACK LONDON STATE HISTORIC PARK, Glen Ellen**
**2400 London Ranch Road**
**(707) 938-5216**
$5 per car, day-use fee

*From Glen Ellen center, head west uphill on London Ranch Road.*

Pack a picnic lunch and stop at **GLEN ELLEN WINERY**, 1833 London Ranch Road, (707) 935–3000, on your way up to Jack London State Historic Park. Besides being a fascinating historical site, it offers one of the most pastoral picnic sites in the country, with lovely wooded paths for old-fashioned country constitutionals after lunch. Picnic tables are set amongst the trees, but I prefer to bring a blanket and spread it out on the rolling lawn over-looking the small cottage where London penned his romantic adventures. A forested trail leads to the granite ruins of Wolf House, the castle that London was building for himself and his beloved wife, Charmian. Wolf House burned down before they could move in, and London died shortly after. Nearby is another grand stone structure, The House of Happy Walls, which Charmian built as a memorial to the love of her life. It holds memorabilia from their life and exotic travels together.

# Kenwood

## Restaurant Kissing

**KENWOOD RESTAURANT, Kenwood**
**9900 Highway 12**
**(707) 833-6326**
Moderate to Expensive

*On the west side of Highway 12, about 10 miles north of Sonoma, two miles north of Glen Ellen.*

Plan a sun-soaked luncheon or arrive before sunset for dinner at this lovely restaurant. The view of the pastoral fields and vineyards surrounding it is intoxicating. Inside, the setting is serene, with a high peaked ceiling of rubbed wood paneling and exposed beams; white-washed walls brushed softly with contemporary, almost impressionistic paintings; bentwood rattan chairs; and white linen cloths set with silver and fine china. The continental menu, featuring escargot, duck, salmon, and sweetbreads (or a club sandwich, if you prefer), is enhanced by an extensive selection of Valley of the Moon wines.

# Santa Rosa

## Hotel/Bed and Breakfast Kissing

**THE GABLES, Santa Rosa**
**4257 Petaluma Hill Road**
**(707) 585-7777**
Moderate to Expensive

*From Highway 101, take Rohnert Park Expressway east. In two and a half miles, where it dead-ends at Petaluma Hill Road, take a left. The inn is about four miles up on the left.*

Sweets are the way to my heart, so when homemade cappuccino bars and herb tea were laid out by the Italian marble fireplace in the parlor, I knew I was in for a special evening. We could have spent hours relaxing in the twin blue velvet settees, listening to classical music and admiring the antiques, such as the lovely Venezuelan harp, and the voluptuous bouquets of dried flowers. Instead, our curiosity aroused, we set out to see if our room was as gracious. We swept up the grand mahogany curving staircase to find guest rooms refined yet unpretentious, spacious yet embracing. In several, the unusual architecture of this high Victorian Gothic Revival home, with its 15 gables crowning keyhole-shaped windows, became part of the decor. The Sunrise's eye-catching ceiling forms an eight-sided semicircle; the Meadow has five angles. Several rooms are blessed with fireplaces to warm up your kissing. In the morning, the country gourmet breakfast of fruit, home-baked breads with homemade jam, main entree with sausage, and strudel dessert is served by the marble fireplace in the formal dining room.

**VINTNERS INN, Santa Rosa**
**4350 Barnes Road**
**(707) 575-7350, (800) 421-2584**
Moderate to Very Expensive

*From Highway 101, take the River Road exit west (four miles north of downtown Santa Rosa). Take the first left onto Barnes Road.*

As I drove towards Vintners Inn, through tidy rows of grapevines, I felt as though I had crossed through a magic portal and found myself in southern France. This complex of sand-colored buildings with red tile roofs has more the feel of a vintner's private estate than a hotel. A fountain splashes in the central plaza; from the rooms, french doors open to patios or iron grillwork balconies overlooking 50 acres of surrounding vineyards. Upper-story rooms have high peaked ceilings. All the rooms are spacious, clean, and uncluttered, with antique pine and contemporary furnishings. Their oversized, oval tubs invite long soaks. You can savor a mellow chardonnay by the fireplace in many of the rooms. In the evening, sink into one of the overstuffed sofas by the fire in the library. A continental buffet breakfast is served in the main building; enjoy home-baked breads and fruit in the bright sun room overlooking the lawns or savor a Belgian waffle together by the wood-burning hearth with a skylighted cathedral ceiling above.

## *Restaurant Kissing*

**HOTEL LA ROSE DINING ROOM, Santa Rosa**
**308 Wilson Street**
**(707) 579-3200**
Moderate

*From Highway 101 North, take the Downtown Santa Rosa exit. Turn left onto Fifth Street, then take the second right onto Wilson. The hotel is on the corner of Wilson and Fifth streets.*

The locally quarried granite exterior of this 1907 depot hotel casts a somber face, but inside, the parlor and dining room are delightfully inviting. An ebony grand piano, played by a computer, greets diners with clear, bell-like melodies. The mauve, green, and sand color scheme is restful; the tables are elegantly laid out with white linen, fine china, and silver. You can relax with an aperitif on the love seat before the wood-burning fire, then sit down to savor almond-encrusted baked Brie, breast of chicken stuffed with leeks and served with pistachio-orange sauce, or eggplant and almond crepes.

◆    **Romantic Note:** Rooms in this old establishment don't compare with the restaurant for kissing ambience, but are a real bargain at less than $50 midweek.

## JOHN ASH & CO. RESTAURANT, Santa Rosa
**4330 Barnes Road**
**(707) 527-7687**
Expensive

*From Highway 101, take the River Road exit west (four miles north of downtown Santa Rosa). Take the first left, onto Barnes Road. The restaurant is adjacent to Vintner's Inn.*

The view of the vineyards encircling this elegant restaurant is as beguiling as the fruit of their vines. Floor-to-ceiling cathedral windows frame a panorama to match any painter's masterpiece. In the evening, an inviting fire casts a warm glow inside this showcase for Sonoma Valley foods and wines. The menu changes seasonally, but is as contemporary and fresh as the decor. It may include a locally grown duck appetizer, Sonoma rabbit braised in red wine, or roasted local lamb in a walnut, thyme, and wild honey sauce. Wine for every taste is offered, from private reserves to a chardonnay made from grapes from the surrounding vineyards to cognacs blended by John Ash himself.

# Geyserville

## Hotel/Bed and Breakfast Kissing

**HOPE-MERRILL HOUSE,** Geyserville
**21253 Geyserville Avenue**
**(707) 857-3356**
Inexpensive to Moderate

*From Highway 101 North, take the Geyserville exit and continue north on Geyserville Avenue one mile to the inn.*

Staying at this faithfully restored turn-of-the-century Victorian in lackluster Geyserville is like finding a valuable gem in your grandmother's musty attic. The Eastlake Stick-style home showcases Victorian intricacies alongside modern amenities. Stunning, silk-screened Bradbury wall coverings and ceilings add the proper flourish to the white linen cutwork comforter and white wicker accent pieces in the Vineyard View Room and to the floral sofa and flouncy draperies around the bay window in the Bradbury Room. Contemporary indulgences in some rooms include gas fireplaces and whirlpool tubs.

◆   **Romantic Note:** For $30, the inn will prepare a gourmet picnic lunch for two to enjoy in wine country, including an appetizer, entree, salad, dessert, fruit, and a bottle of the innkeeper's wine, all packed in a keepsake basket. Reserve ahead.

## Restaurant Kissing

**CHATEAU SOUVERAIN,** Geyserville
**Independence Lane**
**(707) 433-3141**
Expensive

*From Highway 101, exit at Independence Lane. The winery is on the west side of the freeway.*

You'll kiss like sovereigns at this chateau, a majesty in stone crowning a vineyard-laden knoll. Swirl up the regal stone steps to the main dining room, where picture windows on three sides frame a view that is as intoxicating as the nearly 100 fine wines offered here. The sound of lead-crystal wineglasses clinking toasts rings above the classical melodies that waltz through the elegant restaurant. A massive fireplace, magnificent bent brass chandeliers highlighting a cathedral ceiling, and soft, neutral tones enhance the ambience. In the warmer months, tables are set on the grand terrace overlooking the vineyards. The cuisine is equally luxuriant, with such appetizers as ahi tartare or white truffle risotto with smoked salmon and entrees including Sonoma lamb with mushrooms, caramelized pearl onions, and cabernet sauce, or macadamia nut-encrusted sea bass. One of the royal desserts is Tira Misu, "Lift me up," but by then you'll already feel you've found heaven.

◆   **Romantic Note:** Wine tasting is offered in **THE CAFE**, Chateau Souverain's more casual and less pricey alternative to the restaurant. The decor is refreshingly modern, with geometric murals gracing the walls and live jazzy music on Friday and Saturday evenings.

◆   **Second Romantic Note:** Chateau Souverain is closed Monday and Tuesday. Reservations are highly recommended for lunch, dinner, and Sunday brunch.

## HOFFMAN HOUSE, Geyserville
**21712 Geyserville Avenue**
**(707) 857-3264**
Expensive

*From Highway 101 North, take the Geyserville exit. Continue north on Geyserville Avenue about a mile and a half.*

Another of Geyserville's surprising gems, this charming restaurant serves creative gourmet dishes in a delightfully casual setting with just a touch of elegance. In the warmer months, tables are set on this Victorian's wraparound porch, with sweet-scented wisteria flowing over its trellis. In winter, a gas fire warms the cozy parlor of a lounge and the dining room with its cane-back chairs and pastel floral cloths topped with white linen. The food is as sparkling as a champagne-laced kiss, with such appetizers as home-smoked salmon or cream of wild mushroom soup with a blend of shiitake, oyster, and chanterelle mushrooms. Seasonal dinner entrees may include pork chops stuffed with pears, apples, raisins, and walnuts and topped with bourbon and apple syrup.

# Healdsburg

## *Hotel/Bed and Breakfast Kissing*

**BELLE DU JOUR INN, Healdsburg**
**16276 Healdsburg Avenue**
**(707) 431-9777**
Moderate to Expensive

*Take Highway 101 65 miles north of San Francisco to the Dry Creek Road exit and turn right to Healdsburg. At Healdsburg Avenue turn left and go one mile to the inn.*

The Belle du Jour Inn is situated on six acres of rolling hills lined with vineyards and profuse greenery. As you enter the driveway you will see white cottages nestled amidst tall oak trees that oversee the majestic landscape. All of the cottages have private entrances and are totally modern and exceedingly comfortable. Each of the four guest rooms has an assortment of amenities that are hard to choose among. One cottage has a fireplace, whirlpool tub, and french doors that open to a trellised deck; another has high vaulted ceilings, a wood-burning stove, and a whirlpool tub. Breakfast in the morning is a bountiful display of fresh fruits, crab quiche, gorgonzola polenta, apple turnovers, and fresh muffins. You can enjoy this feast on the garden deck or in the privacy of your own room. The Belle du Jour is a place where you can wind down and experience the calm of the countryside.

## CAMELLIA INN, Healdsburg
## 211 North Street
## (707) 433-8182
Inexpensive to Moderate

*From Highway 101 North, take the second Healdsburg exit (Central Healdsburg). Follow Healdsburg Avenue past the plaza to North Street and turn right. The inn is two and a half blocks up on the left.*

With a spectrum of rooms that will appeal to almost any bed-and-breakfast fancier, this inn is as multipetaled and feminine as a camellia blossom. The double parlors of the 1869 Victorian, where cheese and beverages are served each evening, welcome you with a gentlewomanly softness. Delicate pink walls trimmed with intricate, leaf-motif plasterwork cast a dawn glow over the hardwood floors, Oriental carpet, floral sofa, and tapestried chair. The bouquet of nine uniquely decorated guest rooms includes one with a massive, half-tester bed from a Scottish castle; one with a Mexican brass sink, gas stove, and double whirlpool; and one with a cutwork lace canopy and white wicker accent furniture. In summer, you'll feel fresh as a flower after a dip in the backyard pool.

## THE GRAPE LEAF INN, Healdsburg
## 539 Johnson Street
## (707) 433-8140
Inexpensive to Moderate

*Call for directions to the inn.*

This kissing place in Healdsburg was a total surprise. In an otherwise ordinary suburban group of houses, my attention was diverted by this conspicuously purple bed and breakfast housed in a refurbished Queen Anne-style home. You have to see it for yourselves. The inn, a winsome and welcome combination of eccentricity and solace, has seven suites with seven personalized styles. From the outside it's hard to imagine that there is room for one room, much less seven, but not only is there more than enough space, the accommodations are ample, the decor jubilant, and the design fascinating. There are skylights, multicolored windows, separate sitting areas, five whirlpool baths for two, and hardwood floors covered by Oriental rugs. Breakfast in the morning is a substantial array of egg dishes, fresh baked breads, fresh fruit, and juice. An overnight stay here will be a surprising concoction of fun and good old-fashioned romance.

## HAYDON HOUSE, Healdsburg
321 Haydon Street
(707) 433-5228
Inexpensive to Expensive

*From Highway 101 North, take the second Healdsburg exit (Central Healdsburg). Follow Healdsburg Avenue to Matheson at the plaza. Turn right on Matheson, then right on Fitch, then left on Haydon. The inn is the third house on the left.*

The high-gabled, storybook Victorian behind the main house called to me on this quiet residential street. I half expected Hansel and Gretel to come skipping down its front walk. Instead, I discovered rooms so romantic that you will create your own happy endings here. Cathedral ceilings crown both upstairs rooms, with skylights above double whirlpools. The Pine Room is awash in white, with a stunning Battenburg lace canopy and a crocheted spread; the gentle scent of the dried flower wreath above the headboard whispers of sweet dreams. Ralph Lauren accents in paisleys and plaids lend a more masculine feel to the Victorian Room. In the main house, the Attic Suite is the most unusual, with its bed and claw-foot tub tucked into the sloping eaves.

## MADRONA MANOR, Healdsburg
1001 Westside Road
(707) 433-4231
Moderate to Very Expensive

This landmark restaurant and bed and breakfast is considered to be one of the finest in the area, and the setting, without doubt, is definitely romantic. Make a reservation and see what dining in country luxury is all about. The stately mansion is surrounded by beautifully landscaped and maintained gardens and woods. The backyard holds a swimming pool and carriage house. Inside, the dining room is the scene for sumptuous evening meals and unusually romantic breakfasts (for guests only). There are some who would say that this is the best place for miles around to eat, sleep, and kiss.

There 18 rooms at Madrona Manor. All have fireplaces and old-world charm; some have balconies and sitting rooms. The Garden Suite is by far the most private of all.

**HEALDSBURG INN**
**ON THE PLAZA, Healdsburg**　　　　　　
**116 Matheson Street**
**(707) 433-6991, (800) 491-2324**
Inexpensive to Moderate

*In the town of Healdsburg, just one block east of Healdsburg Avenue, on the park green.*

I was a bit skeptical when I entered the lobby area of the Healdsburg Inn. The narrow ground floor, where the gift shop is located, is attractive but not appealing. But once I had walked up the grand staircase that led to the bed-and-breakfast area on the second floor, I was enthralled with what I saw. The rooms encircle an enormous mezzanine; each suite has a private bath, some have fireplaces, and all were decorated affectionately in American antiques, with thick down comforters, firm canopied beds, and cozy sitting areas trimmed in pastel colors and textured country fabrics. The rooftop garden and solarium are a charming setting for hearty, savory breakfasts and afternoon tea served with cake and cookies that are creamy and richly decadent.

## *Restaurant Kissing*

**JACOB HORNER, Healdsburg**　　　　　　
**106 Matheson Street, on the plaza**
**(707) 433-3939**
Moderate

*In the town of Healdsburg, just one block east of Healdsburg Avenue, on the park green.*

Toast to a love that only improves with age at this congenial restaurant on the plaza. The award-winning wine list offers many fine selections by the glass, so you can sip a superb chardonnay while your partner quaffs a classic cabernet and both sigh with contentment. Tiny white lights add sparkle to the earthy oak wainscoting topped with forest green wall coverings; leafy green plants hang above etched glass partitions. A generous salad comes with your dinner of pork with pineapple chutney or Petaluma duck with nectarine sauce, the perfect accompaniment to wine country's cornucopia of romance.

# Outdoor Kissing

### RUSSIAN RIVER WINE ROAD
### Highway 128 to Chalk Hill Road

*From Healdsburg follow Healdsburg Avenue north till it becomes Alexander Valley Road. Follow this road to Highway 128 and turn south. Highway 128 branches off to the east; to the west is Chalk Hill Road.*

The handful of wineries along this backwoods road are set apart from the rest of the Napa Valley by their isolation and beauty. Coiling through the hillsides and ravines, your path crisscrosses the tributaries and creeks of the Russian River. Along the way, the vineyards, redwoods, and forests take turns revealing their distinctive virtues and profiles. Whenever you see a sign along here that says "WINERY," it means you're invited to stop and rest for a bit under the shade of a tree or in the coolness of a cellar tasting room.

### RUSSIAN RIVER AREA WINERIES
### (707) 869-9212, (800) 253-8800 for tourist information

More than 50 wineries grace the Russian River area, which stretches from the Pacific Coast inland to Healdsburg, then north through Geyserville. Many are family-run operations that are far off the beaten path and a joy to discover together. The following wineries offer quiet, romantic picnic spots for the price of the wine you'll savor with the repast you've packed in your basket. *Salud!*

**ROBERT STEMMLER VINEYARDS**, 3805 Lambert Bridge Road, Healdsburg, (707) 433-6334, has cafe tables on a shaded, redwood deck overlooking sun-soaked vineyards, plus several picnic tables beneath the trees with plenty of shade but not much view. Open daily from 10 A.M. to 4:30 P.M.

**BELLEROSE VINEYARD**, 435 West Dry Creek Road, Healdsburg, (707) 433-1637, is reached along a winding farm road, then up a long, gravel drive. Two picnic tables set next to an old red barn overlook rolling vineyards with mountains on the horizon. Roaming chickens and weatherworn antique farm equipment emphasize the rural setting. Open Tuesday through Thursday from 1 P.M. to 4:30 P.M., and Friday through Sunday from 11 A.M. to 4:30 P.M., in summer; Friday through Monday from 11 A.M. to 4:30 P.M. in the winter.

**HOP KILN WINERY**, 6050 Westside Road, Healdsburg, (707) 433-6491, offers one of the most romantic picnic spots in the area. Sun-soaked picnic tables border a pond hemmed with vineyards and home to a family of mallards. More tables are in the cozy, shaded garden. Wine tasting takes place in the impressive stone historic landmark that was once a hop kiln and now doubles as a small gallery for local art. Open daily from 10 A.M. to 5 P.M..

**ROCHIOLI VINEYARDS AND WINERY**, 6192 Westside Drive, Healdsburg, (707) 433-1385, equals Hop Kiln in its intoxicating picnic setting. Spend a lazy afternoon lingering at a table on a shaded patio with an ambrosial view of rolling vineyards backdropped by mountains.

**KORBEL CHAMPAGNE CELLARS**, 13250 River Road, Guerneville, (707) 887-2294, is a superb stop for romance if you're heading to the coast. The tasting room is one of the grandest in the land—a spacious, elegant chamber complete with crystal chandelier in a castlelike stone building. Before tasting, take a bubbly tour of the winery or the stunning gardens April through October. Colorful flowers and towering shade trees enhance the picnic area, but noises from the busy street aren't as conducive to vintage kissing.

# Napa

## Hotel/Bed and Breakfast Kissing

**OAK KNOLL INN, Napa**
**2200 East Oak Knoll Avenue**
**(707) 255-2200**
Expensive

*Take Highway 29 heading north. Just outside the town of Napa, turn right onto Oak Knoll Avenue and continue about a half mile to the inn.*

The rooms here are the most impressive I've seen anywhere, plus the location is as far removed from the madding crowd as you could ever hope for. The inn's stone entrance and wrought-iron gate only suggest the splendor that lies inside. Once you enter the courtyard area, where the two wings of suites surround the aqua blue swimming pool, you will realize that you have stumbled upon a tranquil retreat. Besides the handful of other guests, there is nothing else for miles around but the fertile vineyards and lush meadows and woodlands of the Napa Valley. The interior of each suite has a remarkable 17-foot-tall wood-beamed ceiling, floor-to-ceiling draped window, fireplace set into an inlaid stone wall, gorgeous bathroom with marble floors, and french doors that open onto the inner courtyard. If I were you, I wouldn't hesitate on this one, it is that special.

## Restaurant Kissing

**PETRI'S, Napa**
**Monticello Road and Vichy Avenue**
**(707) 253-1455**
Moderate to Expensive

*On the east side of Napa, Trancas Road ends and turns into Highway 121, called Monticello Road. As you head toward Lake Berryessa, look for Vichy Avenue on your right. The restaurant is at this intersection.*

Before you cast yourselves adrift on the backroads to find the sovereign wineries of this region, you may want to visit this amiable establishment filled with congenial charm and hearty pasta. The elfin cottage is so well camouflaged by flowering gardens hugging close the vine-covered stone exterior that you could miss it completely. Two glass doors open into the main dining areas, where wood-beamed ceilings, tile floors, wood tables, and rough-hewn stone walls all make a charming backdrop for your meal. Sauce-laden pastas accompany continental dinners that are sure to please the most discriminating elfin gourmets.

◆ **Romantic Suggestion**: Personally, I find the town of Napa too industrial and citified to be a romantic destination, especially when there are so many other quaint, delightful villages to recommend. But there is a bed and breakfast in Napa that is just too outstanding and too exceedingly romantic for me not to include it. **THE OLD WORLD INN**, 1301 Jefferson Street, Napa, (707) 257-0112, (Inexpensive to Expensive), is beautiful and inviting. Each of the eight rooms is unique, with features that include private decks, canopied beds, large bay windows, private Jacuzzi, skylights, and comfortable furnishings. There is also a huge outdoor hot tub in the backyard. The buffet breakfast and evening wine and hors d'oeuvres fest are both generous and superb.

## Outdoor Kissing

**NAPA VALLEY WINE TRAIN, Napa**
**1275 McKinstrey Street**
**(707)253-2111 or (800) 522-4142**
$14.50 to $29 round-trip train fare
$22 to $25 prix fixe lunch; $45 prix fixe dinner

*From Highway 29 north, take Highway 121 (Silverado Trail) toward Lake Berryessa. Bear left at a fork onto Soscol Avenue. Turn right on First Street, then turn left on McKinstry Street. The train depot is on your left.*

The depot was buzzing with an undercurrent of excitement as we waited for the wine train to pull in. Already we had been transported back to an era of elegance, when rail travel still had the air of romance.

The train's arrival was announced and passengers flowed gleefully from the station's tapestry sofas, souvenir shops, and small art gallery to board a line of beautifully restored 1915 Pullman cars. Ours was the last on this string of pearls. Once inside, we settled into plush, tufted golden velvet chairs that faced the picture windows but swiveled for an all-around view. Glowing wood paneling, stenciled ceilings, and etched glass partitions highlighted the elegant setting. After our chicken/mushroom terrine appetizer, we stepped through the back door to the sunny observation platform to toast each other and kiss as the vineyards rolled slowly by. Lunch in the dining car was served with the aplomb of yesteryear, from the pastry-encrusted soup to the fillet marinated in red wine to the decadent multilayered torte. Although the slow-moving trip lasted three hours, everyone sighed with reluctance as we pulled back into the Napa depot.

◆ **Romantic Suggestion**: One car is devoted to wine tasting. For $5, you can try four wines from the extensive selection.

◆ **Romantic Note:** The view of the vineyards is the best facet of the wine train experience and can't be seen after dark. If you want to ride a dinner train, which departs at 6:30 P.M. and returns at 10 P.M., go in the warmer months when the days are longer.

◆ **Romantic Warning:** Not everyone adores the wine train. Some locals have protested against it, citing noise, increased traffic congestion and pollution. You may even see two or three "NO WINE TRAIN" signs, which to me is sour grapes.

## THE SILVERADO TRAIL

*This stretch of highway follows the east side of the Napa Valley starting from the south, in the town of Napa, and going north to the town of Calistoga.*

Only two major roads traverse the Napa Valley: Highway 29 and the Silverado Trail. At some points these roads are separated by only one or two miles, but in spirit and atmosphere they are eons apart. Highway 29 is just that, a highway, encumbered with cars, billboards, tourists, gas stations, and other "civilized" necessities. In contrast, the Silverado Trail is a meandering drive through nature at its purest: contiguous, undulating hillsides endowed with a profusion of vineyards, forests, and olive groves. As you map out your course through the wine country of Napa Valley, it would be a grievous mistake not to allow enough time to cruise along this absorbing roadway. The wineries that branch off in a network of backroads are less commercial and more personal than those that line the main road. Plus, when you do require provisions or restaurants, the towns of Napa, Yountville, Oakville, Rutherford, St. Helena, and Calistoga are practically across the street.

# Yountville

## *Hotel/Bed and Breakfast Kissing*

**CROSSROADS INN, Yountville**
**6380 Silverado Trail**
**(707) 944-0646**
Expensive to Very Expensive

*Inn is perched on a hillside above the Silverado Trail. Heading north, look for a sign on the right just before the Yountville Crossroad.*

If your day of kissing in wine country has you walking on air, ascend hand-in-hand to the lofty Crossroads Inn, perched high above the rolling, vineyard-laden hills. The view from its spacious, firelit living room and redwood deck is as enchantingly mellow as Napa's best cabernet. Pour each other a glass of sunset, then pour yourselves into one of the guest rooms' double whirlpools that share this same magnificent view. In the Puddleduck, the whirlpool nests in the outermost corner, with windows on either side looking over the valley to the west and a wild ravine to the north. Hiking trails climb up the forested hills above to views that stretch as far as San Francisco on a clear day. A feeling of airiness flows throughout this inn, especially when the late-afternoon sun fills the rooms with a glowing embrace. Step through the sliding glass doors of your room to the deck to kiss as if you're walking on air.

## OLEANDER HOUSE, Yountville
### 7433 St. Helena Highway
### (707) 944-8315
Moderate to Expensive

*Call for directions.*

As dawn slips its rosy cloak over the Napa Valley, guests at the Oleander House often tiptoe to the backyard for a wake-up soak in the hot tub while enjoying their first cup of coffee. Sometimes a strange *whoosh* pierces the morning and a brightly colored, hot-air balloon floats overhead. Although this inn is on one of Napa's busiest routes, you'll find a peaceful blend of old-fashioned bed and breakfast and modern architecture and amenities inside. You can kiss by the fireplace in all of the upstairs guest rooms. High peaked ceilings, private balconies, and uncluttered, softly-hued decor lend a sense of simplicity and spaciousness. In the morning, after the hot tub and coffee, guests join in the dining room for healthy, hearty breakfast specialties like cinnamon apple flan and locally made chicken sausage.

◆ **Romantic Note:** One of Napa Valley's most popular restaurants, **MUSTARD'S GRILL**, 7399 St. Helena Highway, Yountville, (707) 944-2424, (Moderate), is next door to the Oleander House. Always crowded, it has a boisterous atmosphere that is not conducive to intimate dining, but it has an extensive wine list and will appeal to those looking for a fun, relaxed luncheon spot.

## VINTAGE INN, Yountville
### 6541 Washington Street
### (707) 944-1112, (800) 351-1133
Moderate to Very Expensive

*From Highway 29, take the Yountville exit (California Drive). Turn left on Washington Street. The inn will be on the left just past Vintage 1870.*

Soft classical music breezes through the serene lobby with plum-colored chairs and brick hearth. Above, set in the high peaked, blond wood-paneled and -beamed ceiling, slowly churning fans seem to beckon you to discover this small estate. Brick and blue clapboard buildings are set amongst fountains, reflecting pools, and flowers. Guest rooms are equally peaceful, enhanced by wood-burning fireplaces, neutral tones, jetted baths, and a complimentary bottle of wine to set the mood. Although the Villas encompass two rooms, I found the commodious Deluxe and Superior rooms more convivial to kissing, especially those with marble fireplaces and contemporary padded and upholstered headboards. In the afternoon, a dip in the inn's outdoor heated pool will rejuvenate you for a night of romance.

## Restaurant Kissing

**DOMAINE CHANDON, Yountville**
**1 California Drive**
**(707) 944-2892, (800) 736-8906**
Expensive to Very Expensive

*Take Highway 29 north from Napa and take the Yountville exit to California Drive.*

Domaine Chandon is considered by many to be the most beautiful dining setting in the entire Bay Area, and I have to agree that the inlaid stone walls and arched wood-beamed ceiling and doorways are all luxurious. The only obstacles to an intimate dining atmosphere is the room's large size, popularity, and poor acoustics, which make for a somewhat noisy evening. It is still a stunning place to dine, though; the food is very good and often superb, and the champagne is superior. Schedule yourselves here before prime eating hours and you're likely to find the experience rapturous. Call for information regarding seasonal hours.

**FRENCH LAUNDRY, Yountville**
**6640 Washington Street**
**(707) 944-2380**
Expensive

*Just off Highway 29 heading north, turn right on Washington Street to the restaurant.*

This appealing restaurant is housed in a brick, two-story, affectionately renovated country building where superlative meals are prepared and served. Reputed to be one of the finest in the Napa Valley, it is also one of the most charming and one of the most difficult to get a reservation at, requiring perhaps weeks in advance for weekends. This isn't a well-marked location; you need to look closely or you will mistake the building for a lovely country home. Dinner is served Wednesday through Sunday only. A remarkable prix fixe meal changes nightly. The food and the atmosphere are like a dream come true.

## MAISON ROUGE, Yountville
**6534 Washington Street**
**(707) 944-2521**
Expensive

*From Highway 29, take the Yountville exit (California Boulevard). Turn left on Washington Street. The restaurant is on the right just before Vintage 1870.*

You know when you see "Soup of the Sentiment" rather than "Soup of the Day" on the menu that the chef/owner spices his cooking with passion. You can share the passion by sharing the fine cuisine at this intimate, unpretentious restaurant. The decor is French-Californian, with an eye-catching collection of china plates highlighting champagne pink walls. Nosegays of colorful flowers blossom in mineral bottles on each table. Creative dishes may include a smoked salmon appetizer with warm crabmeat-and-caviar mousse and a spicy sour cream sauce, or an entree of chicken breast stuffed with a veal-truffle mousse and served with a fresh tomato-tarragon sauce. In the warmer months, romance beckons in the back courtyard, with its tangled weave of wild grapevine.

◆   **Romantic Note:** On Sunday through Friday evenings in winter, Maison Rouge's prix-fixe, three-course dinner, at less than $20, is one of the Napa Valley's best romantic bargains.

# Oakville

## Outdoor Kissing

**VICHON WINERY, Oakville**
1595 Oakville Grade
(707) 944-2811
*From Highway 29, in the town of Oakville, turn west on Oakville Grade Road and follow the sign to the winery.*

The view from up here is a gorgeous sylvan expanse of neatly arrayed vineyards blanketing sloping hills that surge down into the valley below. In the distance, forested peaks go on for as far as the eye can see. A picnic area on a knoll overlooks this bewitching landscape. As long as you're in this setting, you might as well indulge in a very California kind of afternoon and pack a picnic basket that includes a vintage bottle of wine, fresh cheeses, and sweet, ripe fruit. The winery is open seven days a week from 10 A.M. to 4:30 P.M.

◆ **Romantic Note:** Speaking of gourmet California-style picnic lunches, the absolute best place for 100 miles around is the **OAKVILLE GROCERY**, on Highway 29 in Yountville. Its intriguing collection of pates, cheeses, olives, cured meats, and salads are all luscious to look at, delectable to eat, and outrageously expensive to buy. This is gourmet heaven, except for the price tags.

# Rutherford

## Hotel/Bed and Breakfast Kissing

**AUBERGE DU SOLEIL RESTAURANT AND LOUNGE, Rutherford**
180 Rutherford Hill Road
(707) 963-1211, (800) 348-5406
Expensive to Very Expensive

*From Highway 29, just past the town of Rutherford, turn right on Zinfandel Lane. This lane intersects with the Silverado Trail, where you turn right again. Look for Rutherford Hill Road and turn left up the hill.*

High above the Napa Valley, perched atop a ridge, Auberge du Soleil has a commanding perspective of the entire countryside. Ensconced in hills with flourishing olive groves, the restaurant and lodge are so well integrated with the landscape that they seem to be organically linked. Walls of cream-colored stucco, light pine-paneled ceilings, wooden tables, and a Spanish-style hearth all add to this effect. The dining room and lounge are designed to supply premium viewing pleasure from every nook and corner of the restaurant. The tables in the lounge are positioned near a fireplace large enough to generate ample warmth. A late-evening visit will allow you to drink in the watercolor hues of day yielding to night. Whether you indulge in a dining adventure here or simply toast each other in the bar, the potential for romance is more than likely—it's guaranteed. Breakfast, lunch, and dinner are served seven days a week, and each has its own affectionate appeal.

◆ **Romantic Note:** Auberge du Soleil also has some of the most well-known and certainly first-class accommodations in the area. In fact, its 48 exceptional rooms here are all unbelievably expensive but also unbelievably spacious and beautiful. Some of the rooms have Jacuzzi tubs, but all have fireplaces and terraces that overlook the Napa Valley. These are stunning retreats, which on the outside look a tad like a suburban development, but not inside. Inside everything is simply perfect.

◆ **Romantic Suggestion:** Rising above Auberge du Soleil is **RUTHERFORD HILL WINERY**, 200 Rutherford Hill Road, Rutherford, (707) 963-1871, or (707) 963-7194 on weekends, just off the Silverado Trail and up Rutherford Hill Road. It is a heart-tugging spot to bring a picnic with your own tempting specialties for a leisurely lunch and wine-tasting event. Spread your blanket under the shade of a sprawling tree overlooking the splendid view of the valley. Then, as the cool of evening approaches, you can saunter down to Auberge du Soleil and toast the beginning of an amorous night.

## RANCHO CAYMUS INN, Rutherford
### 1140 Rutherford Road
### (707) 963-1777, (800) 845-1777
Moderate to Very Expensive

*Take Highway 29 north to Route 128 and turn right; 200 yards down and on your left is the inn.*

Rancho Caymus Inn is a definite change of pace from most of the bed and breakfasts and other inns in the wine country—or anywhere in Northern California. Each room is outfitted in a Southwestern Spanish motif. The tile bathroom floors, knotty hardwood floors, stucco fireplaces, and Native American-designed blankets and throw rugs all create a handsome individual appearance. The spacious rooms are a bit on the dark side, but the spirit is warm.

The 26 rooms, some quite large, come in five variations, including some with their own fireplace, wet bar, Jacuzzi, balcony, and full kitchen. This may not be the most romantic overnight stay in the area, but the location, architecture, and courtyards make it a good base camp for relaxing and touring the idyllic surrounding environs.

A complimentary continental breakfast is served in the Rancho Caymus Inn's **GARDEN GRILL RESTAURANT**. The Spanish atmosphere and decor are congenial and inviting. The tiled floors, wooden tables, colorful tapestries, and gracious service are all a pleasure. A full breakfast is available for an extra charge. Be sure that one of you tries the Caymus Eggs—scrambled eggs topped with creamy rich guacamole, cheese, and chiles, presented with a glass of bubbling champagne. The restaurant is open to the public for both breakfast and lunch (dinner is not served).

# St. Helena

## Hotel/Bed and Breakfast Kissing

**CHESTELSON HOUSE, St. Helena**
**1417 Kearney Street**
**(707) 963-2238**
Inexpensive to Moderate

*From Highway 29 North, turn left onto Adams at the first light in St. Helena.*
*Take the second right onto Kearney; the inn is the second house on the left.*

Located on a residential street two blocks from the center of this small wine- country town, the inn is reminiscent of the old-fashioned bed and breakfasts, when Victorians were sweetly decorated and hospitality was down-to-earth friendly. Firelight warms the parlor and adjacent dining area, where the gourmet breakfasts of the innkeeper-turned-caterer delight guests. Step through your private entrance to the inn's most romantic retreat, a cozy suite with the bright, airy feel of a cabana. Ceiling-high bay windows frame the bed's headboard, with sparkling white shutters to swing closed for private kissing.

**LA FLEUR, St. Helena**
**1475 Inglewood Avenue**
**(707) 963-0233**
Moderate to Expensive

*From Highway 29, turn west onto Inglewood Avenue. The inn is just past the*
*Villa Helena Winery on the left.*

Vintage intimacy and romance are La Fleur's raison d'etre. From the moment we entered this enchanting 1882 Victorian, we knew we were in for a memorable encounter, even for wine country. Our royal retreat for the evening was the Prince Edward Room, with its majestic, billowing crowned valance over the bed and a stunning, floor-to-ceiling black marble hearth. Rococo gilt mirrors and wall sconces highlighted lavender walls and a claw-foot tub waited in the bathroom. In the Antoinette Room even Marie would toast its French femininity, with hand-painted shutters, bounteous ruffles and floral fabrics, red tile fireplace, and private veranda overlooking the vineyards. The Library Room is decidedly Victorian, with the original tile fireplace, cool green walls, shelves lined with books, and swag drapes crowning the bay window looking out to the rose garden. In the morning, linger in the sunny breakfast room over a glorious buffet of fresh baked goods, egg dishes, fruit, and more. *Bon appetit!*

◆  **Romantic Note:** Part of your intimate stay here is a private tour and tasting at the petite Villa Helena Winery next door.

## MEADOWOOD, St. Helena
900 Meadowood Lane
(707) 963-3646 or (800) 458-8080
Very Expensive to Unbelievably Expensive

*From Highway 29 in St. Helena, turn right on Pope Street. Go two miles to the Silverado Trail (just past a narrow stone bridge), and cross it diagonally to the left onto Howell Mountain Road. Look for the Meadowood sign on the left.*

I couldn't help but imagine Jay Gatsby and Daisy on the croquet lawn at Meadowood, dressed all in white, he with his bucks and she with her wide-brimmed hat, sharing a knowing smile and that first blossoming kiss. Although tucked away in the forested foothills of wine country, Meadowood could well be a grand old resort on some New England shore, with its tiers of gables, gray clapboard, and sparkling white trim and balustrades. Relaxation and rejuvenation are the essence of Meadowood; it has its own manicured croquet lawns, a golf course, tennis courts, swimming pools, health club, and massage studio. The secluded guest rooms are scattered discreetly amongst the resort's 256 wooded acres. Private entrances, stone hearths, private balconies in the treetops, skylighted cathedral ceilings, and subtle, softly hued decor create a sense of serenity. Even the bathroom's tile floors are heated, so as not to startle your toes.

The restaurant (Expensive to Very Expensive) at Meadowood perpetuates the theme of rejuvenating serenity. A blazing fire warms the cozy lounge for appetizing kissing. The dining room is at once spacious and intimate, with high peaked ceiling, plush private booths, and elegant table settings. The extensive selection of wines, including 250 from the Napa Valley alone, will please any palate, as will the homemade foie gras on artichoke salad appetizer or the paella Catalan with lamb sausage and chicken blended with the traditional seafoods. A chocolate souffle with sour cherries and amaretto sauce is the perfect romantic dessert, especially when shared by two.

### VILLA ST. HELENA, St. Helena
**2727 Sulphur Springs Avenue**
**(707) 963-2514**
Expensive to Very Expensive

*Head north on Highway 29 (the St. Helena Highway). Past the town of Rutherford and just before St. Helena, turn west onto Sulphur Springs Avenue. Follow this road up and around to a wooden corral fence that may or may not be open, and continue up the drive to the villa.*

Most bed and breakfasts are older homes that have been transformed to offer visitors the pleasures of homey living with a sprinkling of extras that make you feel spoiled and totally pampered. There are as many different ways of achieving that as there are bed and breakfasts. What makes Villa St. Helena so special is that both these ingredients are abundantly present. There are only three guest rooms, located in opposite wings of this architecturally renowned Spanish mansion, located down the glass-enclosed promenades. The rooms are simple, well kept and comfortable, but the setting is outstanding. The 20-acre estate is situated on a hillcrest overlooking Napa Valley. Within, the grand interior becomes your exclusive residence, and the immaculate grounds and courtyard are your playground. There are three common rooms in the center of the house, and each of them has a sizable fire-place and is exceedingly romantic and comfortable. Although, this huge home can be a bit drafty during the winter, that only makes cuddling by the fireplace more desirable.

As you awaken from a lazy nap in your private suite, you may want to slip into your swimsuit, pour a glass of the complimentary wine provided in your suite, and lounge by the pool for an afternoon of carefree fun. At twilight you can explore the restaurants of St. Helena, returning to the opulence of your weekend villa while the evening is still young. If you happen to be in the mood to spend an evening or a weekend in the lap of luxury, this is it.

## WINE COUNTRY INN, St. Helena
**1152 Lodi Lane**
**(707) 963-7077**
Moderate to Very Expensive

*From Highway 29, turn right onto Lodi Lane, north of downtown St. Helena. The inn is on your left.*

Sometimes wine is best served with a splash. The outdoor pool at this unassuming inn is a tranquil place to enjoy it, set on a knoll above tree-hemmed vineyards. Many of the rooms in the three buildings share this placid view, including the parlor, where a continental breakfast is served each morning by the warmth of the wood stove in the winter and that of the rising sun on the deck in the summer. Each guest room is individually decorated with an old-time country flair. The mini-suite in the Brandy Barn is particularly romantic, with white wicker furniture in the sitting room and a private deck where you can raise a well-aged cabernet to your ageless love.

◆   **Romantic Warning**: You can't please all the people all the time. I found the decor and color schemes in some of the rooms unattractive. Also, the small, modern baths gave a motel feel to this otherwise appealing inn.

ZINFANDEL INN, St. Helena
800 Zinfandel Lane
(707) 963-3512
Expensive

*From Highway 29 just south of St. Helena, turn east on Zinfandel Lane to the inn.*

The four guest rooms in this stately bed and breakfast, although not posh, are extremely comfortable, immaculate, and absolutely perfect for an amorous escape. The stone and wood exterior of the home has the proportions of a mansion. Three of the suites are immense, with an assortment of dazzling attributes: one has a large stone fireplace, wood-beamed ceiling, and sweeping bay windows that look out to the garden; another has a tiled Jacuzzi, private deck, and stained glass. The Zinfandel Inn will provide a heavenly touch to your wine-country escape.

## *Restaurant Kissing*

SHOWLEY'S AT MIRAMONTE, St. Helena
1327 Railroad Avenue
(707) 963-1200
Moderate to Expensive

*In the town of St. Helena, just off Highway 29 going north, turn right on Hunt Street. Just before the railroad tracks turn left at Railroad Avenue. Look for a white building on the west side of the street.*

There are a handful of award-winning restaurants in the Yountville-Rutherford-St. Helena section of the wine country. The international and regional crowds that flock to this part of the world keep a handful of chefs busy to almost distressed proportions. It is a feat to continually execute smashing meals that keep pace with the finicky palates of these visiting connoisseurs. Showley's, though not as in-vogue as some of the other restaurants in the area, does a superior job of keeping up with the demand. Inside this large, unembellished white stucco building is a simple, subdued interior where you will find cordial service and a unique international menu that is as interesting as it is well presented. The Santa Fe lasagne, with chiles and chevre layered in flour tortillas with cilantro pesto, was great, and the shrimp etoufee was perfect.

**TERRA RESTAURANT, St. Helena**
**1345 Railroad Avenue**
**(707) 963-8931**
Expensive

*In the town of St. Helena, just off Highway 29 going north, turn right at Hunt Street. Just before the railroad tracks, turn left onto Railroad Avenue. Look for the stone front of the restaurant on the west side of the street.*

To my way of thinking, antiques and icons of the past do not automatically induce thoughts or actions that lead to kissing (or even hugging, for that matter). But blend the artifacts of days gone by with appropriate contemporary flourishes, and *voila!* You have all the romantic atmosphere you could ever need. Terra Restaurant has that welcome mix of yesterday and today. The 100-year-old stone building has a noble yet heartwarming quality. As you enter, prepare yourselves for a walk into provincial pleasure. It is like setting foot in a miniature French castle. The wood beams that loom overhead, the burnt red tile floor, and the stone walls are complemented by contemporary paintings and fixtures. Here is a setting fit for award-winning dining. The menu comprises an ingenious assortment of fresh fish and game, accompanied by intriguing sauces and side dishes. The grilled quail with pecorino cheese and pumpkin ravoli, the grilled salmon with Thai red curry sauce, the grilled squab with chanterelle mushroom and roasted garlic sauce are all exquisite.

◆   **Romantic Note:** Terra is another hard-to-get-into place (serving dinner only), particularly on weekends. Take kissing precautions and call ahead.

**TRA VIGNE, St. Helena**
**1050 Charter Oak Avenue**
**(707) 963-4444**
Moderate

*Just off Highway 29 at the south end of St. Helena, on the east side of the road.*

Imagine a place so popular that they give confirmation numbers along with your reservation. The host informed us that giving out a number the way many hotels do "saves a lot of heartache when people insist they made a reservation, but we don't have them written down. People will do anything to eat here!" Why the intense competition for a table? The reason will be apparent from the moment you glimpse the handsome burnt orange brick exterior of Tra Vigne. You enter wrought-iron gates into a tree-shaded brick courtyard dotted with tables for outdoor seating. Inside, the seductive interior with 25-foot ceilings, stunning oak bar, and towering wrought-iron french windows is very impressive. The tables are individually spotlighted from above, which means the room is soft and subdued, but you won't have to squint to look into each other's eyes. Every detail here is attended to with sophistication and panache, including the food.

Lobster tortellini and clams in a tomato-saffron broth; cracker-thin pizza with caramelized onions, thyme, and gorgonzola cheese; and seared raw venison with chestnuts, dried cherries, and pecorino cheese are all tantalizing and beautifully presented. And the desserts are absolutely erotic. About that confirmation number they give you—get one of your own and don't lose it!

◆ **Romantic Option: TRILOGY RESTAURANT,** 1234 Main Street, St. Helena, (707) 963-5507, (Expensive), is a food lover's paradise. Inside this simple storefront location 10 tables draped in white and peach are all that's available for diners who wish to sample the delicate French cuisine served for both lunch and dinner. Sauteed duck with port and figs or grilled yellowfin tuna with lemon, caper, and dill butter are some of the traditional entrees you'll find here, always done to perfection.

## Outdoor Kissing

### BALE GRIST MILL STATE
### HISTORIC PARK, St. Helena
### (707) 942-4575
$5 day use fee

*The park is on the west side of Highway 29, a few miles north of downtown St. Helena.*

Just as love invites us to see things in a new way, veering off the beaten path can reveal hidden facets of the wine country. This cool, forested park is a short drive and a world away from sun-soaked vineyards. Stroll along restful paths that flow past a gurgling stream hemmed with wildflowers in early spring. One easy trail leads to a restored wooden grist mill and its 36-foot water wheel, which you can tour together on weekends to experience life in simpler, earthy times. Or follow the path through meadow and forest to a kissing spot that nature has saved just for you.

◆   **Romantic Note:** Tree-shaded campsites are available just up the road at **BOTHE-NAPA STATE PARK**, 3801 St. Helena Highway, Calistoga, (707) 942-4575.

### BURGESS CELLARS, St. Helena
### 1108 Deer Park Road
### (707) 963-4766

*Take the Silverado Trail going north. Turn right onto Deer Park Road. As you wind up the mountain toward the town of Angwin, look on the left side of the road for the entrance to Burgess Cellars.*

There are many reasons why you should visit one winery rather than another. If you are a consummate oenophile, you may be lured by the exceptional quality of the grapes at a particular estate or the rare vintage at an established vineyard. But it is also a treat when you become acquainted with the offerings of a small up-and-coming winery and can take pride in your secret discovery. All this and more are sublime reasons to seek out Burgess Cellars in the hills of Napa Valley. In addition to its winemaking craft, Burgess is famous for some of the most striking views of the Napa countryside. Your feelings and taste buds will soar to new heights here.

◆ **Romantic Suggestion:** The drive up to Burgess Cellars along **DEER PARK ROAD** is stupendous. As you weave up this twisting road, enjoy marvelous vistas of the ravines and dells below.

# Angwin

## Hotel/Bed and Breakfast Kissing

**FOREST MANOR, Angwin**
**415 Cold Springs Road**
**(707) 965-3538, (800) 788-0364**
Moderate to Expensive

*Take the Silverado Trail just past the town of St. Helena. Turn right onto Deer Park Road at the red blinking light. The road winds up through the hills for five and a half miles to Angwin. At Cold Springs Road, turn left. When the road forks, go right. (If you take the left fork you will dead-end at Los Posados State Forest.) Forest Manor is at the end of Cold Springs Road.*

Forest Manor is the ideal destination for a weekend sojourn. Here you can renew your relationship with each other and with the good life. This English Tudor estate is located on the outskirts of Napa Valley, backed by boundless woodlands, more than 20 acres, and a neighboring 100-year-old winery. This special domicile has exotic furnishings from the Orient and an open staircase that ascends four flights to two of the three guest rooms. Your suite (there are only three available) will have its own breakfast nook, a roaring fireplace, comfortable furnishings, and the relaxing quiet of nature all around. A generous Continental breakfast is graciously provided. In the dewy morning or under the stars at night you can submerge yourselves in the outdoor whirlpool. During the heat of midday, dive into the 53-foot-long swimming pool for more invigorating recreation. At the end of your stay, consider packing a treasure chest with mementos of your visit—perhaps a bottle of wine, a menu from a favorite restaurant, or love notes wrapped up for hiding in the forest. Then, on your return visit, you can retrace your steps, dig up your cache, and create anew the treasures of the past.

# Calistoga

### Hotel/Bed and Breakfast Kissing

**FOOTHILL HOUSE, Calistoga**
**3037 Foothill Boulevard**
**(707) 942-6933, (800) 942-6933**
Moderate to Expensive

*Head north on Highway 29 to the town of Calistoga. Stay on Highway 29, which becomes Highway 128 after you cross Lincoln Avenue. On the west side of the road, just past the town of Calistoga, one block north of Petrified Forest Road, Foothill House will be on your left.*

When I first saw this country farmhouse, I drove right by it. My initial impression was not the best. The nondescript frame house with its highway frontage disappointed me. I thought, "This can't be romantic!" But lessons learned in the past made me turn around and go back. Once again I found that I must never judge a book by its cover. The outside of Foothill House gives no indication of the rapture and ease that wait inside.

The sizable rooms overflow with everything your sentimental hearts could desire: a four-poster bed, a patchwork quilt, a private sun deck, a fireplace stacked with logs waiting for a hearthside sip of sherry, and Jacuzzi tubs. There is also a newly built separate cottage with a Jacuzzi bathtub and fireplace. If that weren't enough, after a full day of sweeping your way through the wineries and health spas of this county, you'll return to find the bed neatly turned down, fluffy fresh towels, wine, and the piece de resistance—a ceramic canister of hot, chewy, chocolate chip cookies. (Yes, cookies and wine sound a bit odd, but taste these phenomenal little gems before you form an opinion.)

In the morning, depending on your mood, partake of an impeccable breakfast in your room or in the glass-enclosed patio. As you linger over the last morsel of a pear tart souffle, homemade muffins, and fresh apple pie, you will be revitalized for an encore performance of the day before.

◆ **Romantic Alternative**: Located in a neighborhood setting two blocks from the town center, the **SCOTT COURTYARD**, 1443 Second Street, Calistoga, (707) 942-0948, (Moderate), is an attractive bed and breakfast. The white trellised courtyard forms the boundaries of this hideaway, where a gated pool and hot tub area are also available. The peach-colored home and detached cottage look fresh and appealing, and inside the rooms are very casual and spacious with cane furniture and bright fabrics. Full breakfast is served family-style in the dining room.

## LA CHAUMIERE, Calistoga
### 1301 Cedar Street
### (707) 942-5139
Moderate

La Chaumiere is a charming stucco home turned stylish bed and breakfast, located just four blocks from the town center. Draped in bountiful foliage, it feels more like a country hideaway than you would expect from this neighborhood location. The showcase here is a spacious two-tiered deck built around a massive redwood tree that shades an enormous hot tub, and I mean enormous. This setup has to be seen to be believed, but you can see it only if you stay here; a six-foot-high fence keeps everything very private and secluded.

There are two nicely decorated rooms in this petite residence and the living room is wonderfully cozy, but the space is really too small to share with another couple that you don't know. My suggestion is to stay here when you are traveling the wine country with another romantic couple and have the entire house to yourselves. The owners don't live on the property so you will be quite alone. Other amenities include a well-stocked wine and liqueur cabinet for your personal use; a full breakfast and hors d'oeuvres in the evening are beautifully presented.

**SILVER ROSE INN, Calistoga**
**351 Rosedale Road**
**(707) 942-9581**
Moderate to Expensive

*From the Silverado Trail, just outside of Calistoga, turn north onto Rosedale Road.*

Silver Rose Inn is a fabulous bed and breakfast located a discreet distance from Calistoga—far enough away from the spa scene, which can get a bit crowded, that you'll feel elated about staying here. This large, newly constructed estate is spread over an oak-studded knoll that has been lovingly landscaped to blend with the nearby foothills and leas. The hallmark of this place is an impressive rock garden with a flowing waterfall that spills into a huge stone-etched swimming pool adjoining the capacious Jacuzzi. And, of course, framing the entire backyard are hundreds of striking rosebushes that give the inn its proud appellation. The rooms are not quite as outstanding as the common areas, but they are indeed nice and inviting. The innkeepers at the Silver Rose Inn are continually making changes that add to their guests' comfort. What you can be assured of is that all the rooms are quite comfortable and attractively furnished, and have views of the nearby vineyards.

## *Outdoor Kissing*

**CHATEAU MONTELENA, Calistoga**
**1429 Tubbs Lane**
**(707) 942-5105**
$5 tasting fee

*From Highway 29, turn right onto Tubbs Lane (follow signs for Old Faithful Geyser). The winery is past the geyser on your left.*

Imagine kissing on your own private island, in the midst of a placid lake hemmed by vineyards with a castle of a winery on the hill above you. This is Chateau Montelena, one of the wine country's ultimate picnic spots. Jade Lake, with its serene waters, family of ducks, and red lacquered, geometric bridges arching to two tiny islands, beckons visitors from the cool tasting room. As I strolled along the shore, a young couple embraced in the shade of the awning above their picnic table. They had been engaged here, I was told by the wine pourer, and now were celebrating their second anniversary. The scene, like a happy ending to an old-fashioned romantic movie, brought tears to my eyes. You can be the stars of your own love story.

◆   **Romantic Note:** A picnic on your private island costs only foresight. Weekends are nearly impossible to secure, but call ahead to reserve a spot for a special weekday. Picnicking is allowed only on the two islands, which are reserved for the entire day.

## HESS VINEYARDS, Napa
**4411 Redwood Road**
**(707) 255-1144**
$2.50 tasting fee

*From Highway 29 North, turn left at the stoplight onto Redwood Road and follow signs to Hess Vineyards. The winery is about five miles from Highway 29.*

A fine wine should be savored, and so should this exceptional winery and art gallery. Far removed down a quiet side road from the rush of Highway 29, Hess woos you into slowing your pace, strolling in the courtyard garden, tasting a mellow vintage, and enjoying their small but superb collection of contemporary art. The airy, uplifting gallery envelopes three floors of provocative pieces, interspersed with windows peeking into the sequestered winemaking operation, which, in this framework, appears to be a work of art in its own right. Sadly, there are no picnic tables here, but you will find plenty of food for thought for a lively luncheon elsewhere.

## V. SATTUI, St. Helena
**1111 White Lane**
**(707) 963-7774**

*About two miles south of St. Helena's center, along Highway 29.*

On a sunny weekend afternoon, it seems everyone in the Napa Valley comes to picnic beneath the shade trees at this ancient-looking stone winery. This is one of Napa's most congenial spots, with a bevy of tables and a manicured lawn all set aside for picnickers. Step into the inner recesses and you will discover a smorgasbord of delectables—some 200 cheeses, plus meats, breads, and desserts. The wine tasting room can be crowded, but press on. V. Sattui wines are sold only on the premises and their johannisberg riesling is especially luscious.

## SCHRAMSBERG VINEYARDS, Calistoga
**1400 Schramsberg Rd.**
**(707) 942-4558**

*On the west side of Highway 29, just south of Calistoga, look for a small sign that signals the turnoff for the winery.*

To say the least, there are many wonderful vineyards in the Napa Valley. One of the more distinctive and beautiful is Schramsberg. This 100-year-old estate, located in the highlands of Napa Valley, is a beacon of historical interest. The stone buildings of the winery are located far enough away from the traffic of the main road to provide quiet refuge. Because only private tours are allowed, your introduction to the world of champagne will be sparklingly intimate. After you roam through the labyrinth of underground cellars that were tunneled into the rocky ground years ago, be certain to leave enough time to stop at the wine shop. By this point you will have learned almost all the secrets of *methode champenoise*, so purchase your own bit of effervescent history to share.

## ONCE IN A LIFETIME BALLOON COMPANY
## OF CALISTOGA
**The Train Depot, 1458 Lincoln Street**
**(707) 942-6541, (800) 722-6665**
Very Expensive

*As you enter the town of Calistoga from Highway 29, turn right on Lincoln Avenue, the main street. Just past Washington Street you will notice the yellow depot building and old train cars, where your pilot will meet you.*

If you think that a balloon ride sounds like a capricious and frivolous enterprise, you're right. That's exactly what it is—a tingling, exciting, stimulating way to spend an early morning. Your excursion commences at sunrise, when the air is still and cool (yes, that means somewhere between 5 A.M. and 9 A.M.). As you step into the balloon's gondola, your eyes will gape at the towering, billowing fabric overhead, and your heart will begin to flutter with wild expectation. Once aloft, the wind guides your craft above the countryside, and the world seem more peaceful than you ever thought possible. You will be startled by the sunrise from this vantage point; daylight awakens the hills with new vigor and warmth. After your flight, a gourmet champagne brunch awaits you at a nearby hotel. "Carried away" will suddenly take on a new meaning that the two of you will keep in your hearts forever.

◆ **Romantic Note:** A caress while floating over the world on a cloudless summer morning can be a thoroughly heavenly experience. There are many hot-air balloon companies in this part of the world. Once in a Lifetime also owns **NAPA'S GREAT BALLOON ES-CAPE** and **ONCE IN A LIFETIME BALLOON COMPANY OF SONOMA COUNTY.** Check with your innkeeper or the telephone directory to find the balloon business nearest you.

## Miscellaneous Kissing

**INTERNATIONAL SPA, Calistoga**
**P.O. Box 856**
(707) 942-6122
Prices vary depending on service

**LINCOLN AVENUE SPA, Calistoga**
**1339 Lincoln Avenue**
(707) 942-5296
Prices vary depending on service

There is no place else in the United States quite like Calistoga, California. The entire town is dedicated to the rejuvenation of the body and spirit through an ingenious variety of treatments. The services at most spas range from a peaceful massage to an invigorating rubdown that will knead away any anxieties you may have brought with you from the city. The staff at International Spa and Lincoln Spa also are skilled at foot reflexology and acupressure massage. Though both places took the time to explain the benefits of these two techniques, I can only tell you that it felt great and I didn't want them to stop.

My day at both spas went something like this: first I received an exceedingly tranquilizing massage, where every muscle in my body succumbed to relaxation. As time oozed by, I was taken to another room where I was introduced to the organic mud baths. This is something you can do side by side with a loved one. If I fully describe the mud bath, you may decide not to try it; I know I didn't want to when I read about it. But take my word for it, sitting for more than an hour in something I used to get in trouble for sitting in as a kid, was the most amazing physical sensation I have experienced. It's not even vaguely romantic, but afterwards you'll feel that all you want to do is melt into your loved one's arms.

You can experiment with other services at these spas, including facials, herbal blanket wraps (also a side-by-side service), enzyme baths, mineral baths, and on and on. The longer I was there, the more I came to understand the fascination of this place. I also realized how two people sharing such an experience could feel closer to each other than ever before. I think for the first time in my life every muscle in my body was in a blissful state. I'd go back and do this again—next time for an entire week.

◆    **Romantic Note:** There are a half dozen or so spas in the Calistoga area. Some are associated with hotels, but most of the accommodations at these places are mediocre and small. You can enjoy the services of most of the spas without having to stay there. For tender cuddling after a day at the spa, find your way back to one of the idyllic bed and breakfasts this area has to offer.

# SAN FRANCISCO

## *Hotel/Bed and Breakfast Kissing*

### ARCHBISHOP MANSION

**1000 Fulton Street, at Fulton and Steiner**
**(415) 563-7872, (800) 543-5820**
Expensive to Unbelievably Expensive

The ratings in this book indicate the amorous potential of a place based on a four-kiss system, but I would change my system just to grant at least 10 kisses to the opulent, self-indulgent style of living bestowed here. The outside world melts into oblivion once you enter this august mansion turned bed and breakfast. As you cross the threshold, you can see what makes the Archbishop so magnificent. The massive foyer, a floral-patterned, hand-painted ceiling in the parlor, the stained glass dome crowning the formidable three-story staircase, and Noel Coward's grand piano in the elaborate hallway are a few of the more notable appointments.

Each of the 15 lavish guest rooms is superbly designed for intimacy. In one, a white claw-foot bathtub sits next to a fireplace. In another, the room's centerpiece is a four-poster bed from a French castle, fronting another of the 18 carved-mantel fireplaces. All of the rooms are decorated with choice antiques, have intimate detailing, embroidered linens, and graceful sitting areas; a few even have city views. Three of the rooms have Jacuzzis. A gracious staff serves wine in the parlor and a generous continental breakfast comes to your door in the morning. The surroundings and the service at Archbishop Mansion allow guests to revel in the noble, gilt-edged style of the rich and famous.

By the way, the Archbishop Mansion survived the 1906 earthquake. That alone should rate a high kissing score.

◆   **Romantic Suggestion:** Take time to enjoy quiet, tree-dotted **ALAMO SQUARE** across the street. This park crests high above the city and offers a most remarkable view of San Francisco. On a sunny day, it's a lovely spot for a picnic.

## THE BED AND BREAKFAST INN          ◆◆
### 4 Charlton Court, between Laguna and Buchanan
### (415) 921-9784
Inexpensive to Expensive

This bed and breakfast was the first of its type in San Francisco, and its age adds to the hobbit like pampering snugness that greets you upon entering. In the truest sense of the word, this inn is a hideaway, even though it is located in an area where that would seem to be an almost impossible accomplishment. The multitude of cosmopolitan shopping and dining establishments on Union Street are only steps away from the front door, yet it is a simple task for you to leave behind the pace of that urban world for this cheerful escape into contentment. The building was once a carriage house for the neighborhood. There are 10 eclectic rooms here, five with private baths, all surprisingly comfortable and quaint, including a select few that open onto their own hidden rooftop garden. Once you're both tucked under your overstuffed down comforter, you may take a fancy to your new surroundings and want to remain there for breakfast. If not, the garden or the Colonial-style library may be your choice for discussing what the rest of the day will bring.

◆   **Romantic Warning:** The less-expensive rooms share baths.

◆   **Romantic Suggestion:** Browsing hand-in-hand along **UNION STREET** is a one-of-a-kind elite shopping extravaganza. From the western edge of the Presidio to Telegraph Hill on the east, there is an endless procession of everything a curious consumer could want.

## CAMPTON PLACE HOTEL—See Campton Place
## (Restaurant Kissing)

## EDWARD II BED & BREAKFAST
**3155 Scott Street, on Scott at Lombard**
**(415) 922-3000, (800) 473-2846**
Inexpensive to Moderate

This is one of my favorite bargain kissing places. The creative accommodations are bright, cheerful, and beautifully renovated. Some of the 31 rooms feature canopy beds, whirlpool baths, and soft down comforters. Four of the rooms have Jacuzzis, 16 have private baths, and 11 share baths. The most romantic by far are the rooms with Jacuzzis and the two-room suites. The English country decor and wicker furniture in the common rooms create a summery feeling wherever you look. Breakfast in the morning is served at the inn's continental bakery next door. The lattes and fresh baked goods are some of the best in town. Even if the rooms weren't so affable, the bakery/coffee shop would be enough of a reason to find yourself stealing a kiss or two from the one you love here in the Marina District of San Francisco.

## FOUR SEASONS CLIFT HOTEL
**495 Geary Street, at Taylor**
**(415) 775-4700**
Expensive to Unbelievably Expensive

As I savored my chardonnay in the Four Seasons' exquisite Redwood Room, the velvet patina of the walls and the grand burl redwood columns seemed aglow with the vows of eternal passion whispered here through the decades. Every detail shone with polished finesse, from the rhapsody of the grand piano to the silver nut bowl to the embroidered linen cocktail napkins. The French Room Restaurant is equally posh, with the traditional European flair of Oriental carpets, plush chairs, elegant table settings and classical pillars rising to lofty ceilings set off by crystal chandeliers. Not surprisingly, the guest rooms also are romantically handsome, with deluxe furnishings, lavish swagged valances, marble baths, or, in the case of the Deluxe Suite, a spaciousness that may well be unmatched in the city. Even if you're not a guest here, an amorous rendezvous in the Redwood Room or the French Room is a must for any romantic.

## HERMITAGE HOUSE
**2224 Sacramento Street, between Laguna and Buchanan**
**(415) 921-5515**
Moderate to Unbelievably Expensive

This bed and breakfast, when compared to others of its kind in the area, is more traditional and definitely more subdued but nonetheless romantic. If you want a distinctive place for a special night away together, one with attentive service and luxurious surroundings, those requirements can be satisfied at Hermitage House. The four-story redwood mansion is a wonderful combination of formal sophistication and relaxed country charm. The classic breakfast nook, the generous morning buffet, the grand fireplace in the library, the yellow brocade Queen Anne-period furnishings, the outdoor sun deck, the garden patio, and the inviting, generous-size rooms all make for ardent accommodations. A visit here, even for only one night, will help you learn what being cozy is all about.

## THE HOTEL JULIANA
**590 Bush Street, at Stockton**
**(415) 392-2540, (800) 382-8800**
Moderate to Expensive

In the heart of downtown San Francisco, the Hotel Juliana is a pretty little inn that's sure to tug at your heartstrings and pull you into a romantic mood. Upon entering the mauve and teal lobby, you'll be met by a warming fire, a complimentary glass of wine, and the soothing sound of classical music. The rooms and suites feature soft pastel colors and floral fabrics, artistically arrayed as though the designer was attempting to create the impression of a watercolor. (The designer came very close to achieving that effect.) The rooms are comforting and appealing, the kind of place where you'll enjoy lounging and lingering. Though the European flair of the Juliana suggests simplicity, the hotel offers all the amenities and extras that can make a stay so special, especially if you are sharing your stay with a special someone.

◆   **Romantic Option:** Half a block away, the **HOTEL VINTAGE COURT**, 650 Bush Street, (415) 392-1666, (800) 654-1100, (Moderate), has one of the coziest hotel lobbies in San Francisco. A crackling fire calls to guests to sit for a while in a setting that inspires "kick-your-shoes-off" relaxation. Pretty floral bouquets and comfortable furnishings complement the tranquil atmosphere. Each of the guest rooms at the hotel is named for a California winery, but they all basically look the same. The rooms are nice and some feature bay windows, but the furniture could be updated. If you plan to spend a lot of time out and about in the city, or downstairs by the roaring fire, you can probably overlook the fact that the rooms are not perfect, especially since the rates are so reasonable.

◆   **Romantic Warning:** Bush Street, home to both the Hotel Juliana and the Hotel Vintage Court, is a busy one-way thoroughfare. Rooms close to the ground floor on the street side tend to get a lot of traffic noise, while those off the street or on upper levels seem quiet. If you don't want to deal with the sounds of the city, ask for a room that won't echo with screeching brakes and honking horns early in the morning.

## INN AT THE OPERA—See Act IV Lounge
## (Restaurant Kissing)

## THE MAJESTIC HOTEL and CAFE MAJESTIC      ◆◆◆◆
## 1500 Sutter Street, on Sutter at Gough
## (415) 441-1100, (800) 869-8966
Moderate to Expensive

If you ever want a royal spoiling, The Majestic is the place to come. Several million dollars went into transforming this mansion into a designer masterpiece. A mirrored marble entrance leads you to the imposing lobby area, where you will be greeted by a surprising mix of formality and friendliness. While the staff makes sure your room is perfectly prepared, you can appreciate the antique tapestries, etched glass, and French Empire furnishings. You may even want to sip a cocktail at the authentic 19th-century mahogany bar. But don't linger too long; there is more waiting for you upstairs. The focal point of each of the 59 rooms is a large, hand-painted, four-poster canopied bed dressed in plump feather pillows, fine linens, and plush down comforters. Radiating warmth from the rooms with fireplaces offers even more enticement to lounge like a king and queen, or prince and princess, or duke and duchess, or whatever you wish! All the suites have a king-size canopy bed, fireplace, and marble bathroom; and the deluxe rooms have canopy beds and fireplaces.

◆   **Romantic Extra: CAFE MAJESTIC**, (415) 776-6400, (Expensive), considered one of the better restaurants in San Francisco, is often is voted "most romantic restaurant" in various local polls. Open for breakfast, lunch, and dinner seven days a week (except lunch on Monday), the stately dining rooms with their lofty ceilings and mirrors are done up in shades of gray and peach. Even if you can't stay at The Majestic, try to make room in your plans for its fine food and elegant atmosphere.

## THE MANDARIN ORIENTAL HOTEL—See Silks (Restaurant Kissing)

## THE MANSION HOTEL
**2220 Sacramento Street, between Laguna and Buchanan**
**(415) 929-9444, (800) 826-9398**
Inexpensive to Unbelievably Expensive

The Mansion Hotel is a source of visual entertainment. The setting is a strange combination of flamboyant flourishes and fun. As you walk up the stairway to the entrance, a well-lit, fertile jungle lines your path. Prominent in the center of this tropical garden is a stone statue standing watch over this traditional San Francisco neighborhood. Past the Gothic doorway, the main floor is outfitted with a billiard room, a stage area where a magician entertains on weekends, and, finally, tucked around the corner, a thoroughly idyllic, crystal-chandeliered dining area. There are only a handful of tables arranged here in a glassed alcove next to a floral garden dotted with Bufano sculptures. Both continental breakfast and dinner are served in this unique setting. You will find it impossible not to give in to the obvious enchantment that accompanies your meal.

All of the rooms are graced by a crystal decanter of sherry next to a queen-size bed, and a marble fireplace or a private terrace. The Mansion Hotel is a comfortable, playful palace that the two of you can indulge yourselves in together.

## MILLEFIORI INN—See Telegraph Hill (Outdoor Kissing)

## PETITE AUBERGE                                   ◆◆◆
**863 Bush Street, between Mason and Taylor**
**(415) 928-6000**
Moderate to Expensive

The Petite Auberge is an attractive blend of the winsome pleasures of a bed and breakfast and the courtly service and practicality of a downtown hotel. Whether you choose a room with or without a fireplace, you are still assured of a cheerful place to stay. The 26 rooms here all have private baths and French country decor. Replace city life with the gracious charm of a French country inn at Petite Auberge.

Beyond the amiable accommodations, the continental dining service is first-class. The kitchen prepares both thoughtful breakfast buffets and late-afternoon samplings of hors d'oeuvres followed by a glass of wine. You can enjoy them at one of the dining tables situated adjacent to a small garden or on a love seat next to a roaring fireplace. Either choice will tempt you to linger a moment or two longer to contemplate your upcoming schedule of events.

## THE PRESCOTT HOTEL
**545 Post Street, between Taylor and Mason**
**(415) 563-0303, (800) 283-7322**
Expensive to Very Expensive

The Prescott is too large to be considered a charming European-style hotel, but that doesn't keep the management from trying to make things feel that way. The roaring fire is the focal point of what the hotel refers to as its "living room." Located to the left of the lobby, this warm area is filled with cozy furniture and early California arts and crafts. It's an ideal spot for relaxing and enjoying the hotel's hospitality. Complimentary coffee and tea are served during the day, and wine and cheese are offered in the evening.

All the rooms in the hotel are equally attractive and plush. Rich colors like hunter green and majestic purple cover the furniture and drape the windows. Cherry-wood tables and chairs, bowfront armoires, and brass accents throughout complete the decor. The suites that have sitting rooms are elegant in style and comfortable. Every modern hotel convenience is also provided. Each room includes a color television with remote control, a stocked bar and refrigerator, terrycloth robes, a hair dryer, and, in the suites, VCRs and whirlpool tubs. Those who stay on the Club Level (rooms and suites on this floor are slightly more expensive and slightly more luxurious) also receive a complimentary breakfast, a cocktail reception in the evening, and use of the exercise facilities.

◆ **Romantic Indulgence**: The Mendocino Penthouse at the top of the Prescott may be the most extraordinary suite in the city. It's a luxurious escape with two wood-burning fireplaces, rich Edwardian furnishings in the parlor and bedroom, beautiful artwork, a grand piano in the formal dining room, and a rooftop deck with a Jacuzzi and garden. Staying here is the height of romantic pampering. It's unbelievably beautiful, unbelievably expensive, and absolutely worth it if you can make room in your romantic budget!

## THE QUEEN ANNE HOTEL
**1590 Sutter Street, on Sutter at Octavia**
**(415) 441-2828**
Moderate to Expensive

As I stepped into The Queen Anne, I felt as if I had stepped into a different era where a kiss could make you blush and long for more. The century-old ambience begins in the antique-adorned foyer, where guests share tea or sherry by a blazing fire. The cedar staircase is an impressive architectural centerpiece that rises four flights. Morning sunlight streams through the banister from stained glass windows and skylights. All of the 49 rooms are decorated with handsome English antiques. Your suite may have a curved bay window, a marble-topped dresser, a bathtub with claw feet, or a wood-burning fireplace. Regardless of the mixture, each has its own grandeur to be cherished behind closed doors. After a restful night, fresh juice, croissants, coffee, and a newspaper are served in the parlor. In the afternoon, tea and sherry are served in the library.

**Romantic Suggestion**: The Queen Anne is located in one of San Francisco's most colorful Victorian neighborhoods. Don't miss this opportunity to stroll arm-in-arm down the tree-lined streets and take in some of the architectural sights only this city can offer. Be sure to visit **LAFAYETTE PARK**, up three blocks from The Queen Anne Hotel at Octavia and California. It is a beautiful place, with remarkable views and well-tended gardens. I was recently informed that this neighborhood is so touching that romance author Danielle Steel just bought one of the mansions across the street from this park. I don't know if this will help your kissing, but it is an interesting amorous footnote.

## THE REGIS HOTEL
**490 Geary Street, at Taylor**
**(415) 928-7900, (800) 827-3447**
Moderate to Expensive

The Regis Hotel can accurately be described as quaint, luxurious, and romantic. Located in the heart of San Francisco's theater district, it is also convenient. But it is what's inside that earns the Regis its reputation for romance. The rooms are decorated with choice fabrics, comfortable antiques, lace curtains, textured wallpaper, and black marble bathrooms. Some of the suites offer canopied beds and fireplaces. All of this old-fashioned charm is combined with the modern amenities that make a hotel stay so comfortable. The Regis is a short walk from much of what San Francisco is famous for: Union Square, the cable cars, galleries, good shopping, great dining, and, of course, the theaters. But for the romantically inclined, the enticing atmosphere and the charming decor of the hotel's rooms make the Regis a primary destination.

◆  **Romantic Option:** The very chic, fashionable restaurant, **REGINA'S**, (415) 885-1661, (Moderate to Expensive), is located adjacent to the hotel. The setting is thoroughly elegant and slick. Lighting is soft and a piano soloist entertains most evenings. The dining room is decorated with sketches of performers who have played local theaters and a stunning collection of opera masks. Regina's serves flavorful French-Creole cuisine and Southern-style specialties like mint juleps and praline cheesecake. Complimentary continental breakfast for guests only is also served in this atmosphere when the mood is a bit more mellow.

## SHERMAN HOUSE
**2160 Green Street, at Webster**
**(415) 563-3600, (800) 424-5777**
Very Expensive to Unbelievably Expensive

Kissing here may make your heart pitter-patter; so will the bill unless you're on the *Forbes* 100 list. If we had an Absurdly Expensive category, we'd use it for some of the rooms. Still, this exquisitely restored 1876 French Italianate-style mansion is San Francisco's most aristocratically intimate hotel and restaurant. Copious bouquets of fresh flowers, elegant furnishings, and impeccable service are de rigueur. Guest rooms are lavishly decorated. One is akin to a king's chamber, with a full canopy bed of heavy, velvet-lined, tapestry draperies; a plush window seat with a plethora of pillows and billows of drapes above; and an immense bath with a deep, black soaking tub. Another, in the Carriage

House, is strikingly different, with a chic cabana look of latticed walls, slate floors, teak-trimmed jetted tub, and freestanding fireplace.

◆ **Romantic Note**: Even if you're not a guest, the dining room is the ultimate in intimacy for breakfast, lunch, or dinner. The solarium, with sunlight streaming through its diamond-pane windows, embraces you with contented luxury during the day. Firelight warms the formal dining area, where such seasonal specials as lobster minestrone, squab salad, coq au vin of quail, and baked sea bass delight diners. Just to remind you that you're not pinching pennies here, a 20 percent service charge is added to your bill.

## SPENCER HOUSE
**1080 Haight Street, at Baker**
**(415) 626-9205**
Moderate to Expensive

I was greeted like a long-lost friend when I visited the Spencer House. That's because many of the guests are. This inn relies totally on word of mouth and repeat business. It isn't even listed in the phone book. Although Spencer House has all the trappings of a noble Victorian— spacious, firelit parlors; wood-paneled dining room; a grand staircase up to the guest rooms—the ambience is more like that of a family home. Favorite knickknacks are clustered on the coffee table. The antiques are inviting, but not so precious you're afraid to touch them. Bradbury silk-screened wall and ceiling coverings, crisp linens trimmed with antique lace, Battenburg linen comforters, gas and electric chandeliers (some with the original 1906 light bulbs), and friendly hospitality blend for an evening of pampered but relaxed romance.

## HOTEL TRITON
**342 Grant Avenue at Bush**
**(415) 394-0500**
Moderate to Expensive

If, after Alice went through the looking glass, she had needed a hotel, she might have stayed at one like the Hotel Triton. This one-of-a-kind hotel offers all-out sensory stimulation. The interior is a combination of surrealistic and unconventional details: the chairs have S-shaped backs, the divider screens are painted bright yellow with floating pastel figures, the walls are either white-and-taupe checked or sponge painted pink and iridescent gold, the crisp white bedspreads are strewn with oversized navy blue throw pillows, and the furniture has an art deco flare. In spite of the imaginative concept, each of the 140 rooms is exceedingly comfortable, adding a bit of eccentric fun to a standard hotel stay. You can even rent roller blades from the front desk. Don't ask me why—you just can.

## VICTORIAN INN ON THE PARK
**301 Lyon Street, at Fell Street**
**(415) 931-1830**
Inexpensive to Very Expensive

We entered another era as we crossed the threshold of this splendidly restored Victorian—an era of romance, chivalry, and gracious living. The grand foyer of rubbed mahogany paneling and oak parquet floors glowed with the light of the handsome brick fireplace, as if it had snatched the golden glimmering sunset as the door shut slowly behind us. As the sky grew darker, we sipped wine by the classic, ceiling-high hearth of the parlor's white tile fireplace. We could barely pull ourselves away from the graceful Queen Anne setting, with its fainting couch, fringed and embroidered lamp shades, and gracefully bowed walls. Upstairs, even more romance awaited. Full canopy beds, fireplaces, stunning Bradbury wall coverings, marble baths, and period furnishings blend to create a setting that would make any Victorian-minded guest forgo the proprieties of yesteryear.

◆ **Romantic Warning:** The basement rooms of this inn are somewhat dark for my taste and you can hear the sounds from the busy street in the upper-story rooms, but I feel the ambience of this inn charms these intrusions away.

◆ **Romantic Suggestion:** This inn is within strolling distance of **GOLDEN GATE PARK**. A sunny afternoon would be well spent enjoying a special kissing place surrounded by flowers and trees.

## WASHINGTON SQUARE INN
**1660 Stockton Street, on Washington Square**
**(415) 981-4220, (800) 388-0220**
Inexpensive to Expensive

Kissing at the Washington Square Inn is like sinking into a slice of Tira Misu ("Lift me up") cake, a favorite at nearby bakeries in this Italian neighborhood: one taste makes you sigh with pleasure. The inn overlooks verdant Washington Square and the magnificent Gothic cathedral of Saints Peter and Paul. Although this is the heart of North Beach, one of San Francisco's most vibrant areas, we felt as though we were visiting a gracious country home. A fire warms the parlor, where wine is served each evening. In the guest rooms, French and English antique wardrobes and desks blend tastefully with plush floral draperies, canopies, fresh flowers, and contemporary paintings by a local artist. In some rooms, you can pledge your *amore* on the window seat as the sun sets over San Francisco's little Italy.

## WHITE SWAN INN
**845 Bush Street, between Mason and Taylor**
**(415) 775-1755**
Expensive to Very Expensive

The White Swan Inn brings the English countryside to life in the heart of downtown San Francisco. Each of the 26 rooms is masterfully done, with its own fireplace, stately antiques, floral bouquets, and bay windows. As wonderful as the rooms are, you will also enjoy sharing high tea (served every afternoon) in the handsome fireside living room or lingering over a full breakfast in the inn's intimate dining room.

◆ **Romantic Alternative:** The lasting impression of your stay at **THE INN AT UNION SQUARE**, 440 Post Street, (415) 397-3510, (Moderate to Expensive), will be one of cozy comfort and dedicated service. All of the rooms are outfitted with sitting areas, Georgian furnishings, and lively fabrics. Each of the six floors has a small tranquil lounge with a crackling fireplace where morning breakfast, afternoon tea, or hors d'oeuvres can be enjoyed (or taken back to the privacy of your room). The grand suite on the top floor has its own sauna, whirlpool bath, fireplace, and bar.

## Restaurant Kissing

### ACQUERELLO                                    ◆◆◀
**1722 Sacramento Street, between Van Ness and Polk**
**(415) 567-5432**
Expensive

*Acquerello* is the Italian word for "watercolor," and this restaurant is as pretty as a painting. Everything about the decor—an exquisite pastel floral arrangement at the front of the dining room, the painted wood-beam ceiling and other architectural details, the white linens and pale pink china, the cream-colored walls illuminated by sconces and graced with watercolors—is artistically arranged to create the soft effect of a watercolor. While the setting alone is enough to entice a happy couple into an evening of tender togetherness, Acquerello offers an innovative menu of Italian dishes flavored with the freshest ingredients of each season. (If it's available on the night you dine—dinner is served Tuesday through Saturday only—don't miss the pumpkin gnochetti with black truffles and sage.) The extensive wine list is an opportunity for discovery. The courteous staff is always willing to help you select a marvelous meal. This restaurant is an experience waiting to be enjoyed!

◆    **Romantic Option: IL FORNAIO**, 1265 Battery Street, (415) 986-0100, (Moderate), is one link in a chain of restaurants, and something about that almost precludes romantic encounters. Almost. If rules can have exceptions, and I believe they can, Il Fornaio is certainly one of them. The restaurant in San Francisco is very contemporary inside, with black, white, terra-cotta, and marble accents; high ceilings; an open kitchen; and artwork on the walls. More romantic is dining outside, where gas lamps warm the enclosed patio, pretty flowering plants add a burst of color, and a fountain flows just outside the glass walls. A second Il Fornaio in the city is located at 101 Spear Street,

(415) 777-0330. In Marin County, a third Il Fornaio is at 233 Town Center, Corte Madera, (415) 927-4400. All of the restaurants are similar in design and ambience.

## THE ACT IV LOUNGE ◆◆◆◆
## and THE INN AT THE OPERA
**333 Fulton Street, between Gough and Franklin**
**(415) 863-8400, (800) 325-2708**
Moderate to Very Expensive

When I first walked into The Inn at the Opera, it was at the end of a long day. The way I felt, the Taj Mahal would not have impressed me. But the moment I headed down the entry hall to the inn's restaurant, my mood made a 360-degree turn for the better. I was still exhausted, but I had found another kissing place. Ah, sweet success!

The Inn at the Opera offers a softly stated environment in which you will be spoiled more elegantly than at almost any other place you're apt to stay within the Bay Area. Inviting, overstuffed pillows and comforters, chocolates at bedside, and terry-cloth robes all await you in rooms subtly designed for provocative moments. And outside your front door is San Francisco's theatrical, artistic, and political essence gathered in the cathedrallike buildings of the Civic Center.

The highlight of your stay will be to discover **THE ACT IV LOUNGE**, a bastion of refinement and gourmet cuisine. The handsome interior is accented by a marble fireplace, mahogany pillars, and muted lighting that gently illuminates the walls and furnishings. Seated at one of the handful of tables nestled about the room, you and your companion will be perfectly situated to enjoy the delights of the ensuing meal—from appetizers to after-dinner drinks—to your hearts' content. The menu changes frequently, but we were thrilled with the duck and pheasant in caramelized onions served in a puff pastry shell, and the angel-hair pasta with prawns, scallops, and caviar. You will be kissing in between every course. While Act IV is open for breakfast, lunch, and dinner daily, dinner is by far the most romantic interlude.

## AMELIO'S
**1630 Powell Street, between Green and Union**
**(415) 397-4339**
Very Expensive

From the street, Amelio's might not beckon to you. But step inside the lobby and then through the velvet curtains to the intimate dining room, and Amelio's will immediately win you over. The deep-colored walls are softened by oil paintings and the delicate light of gilded chandeliers. Tapestry-covered booths, designed so couples can sit next to each other, line the walls, with a few additional tables in the center of the room. An exotic floral arrangement provides the focal point of the restaurant. More fresh flowers and candles are placed at each elaborately set table. The French cuisine is divine—perfectly prepared and beautifully presented. You have a choice of ordering from an a la carte menu or selecting the fixed-price dinner. Amelio's is not the kind of restaurant you decide to dine at late in the day; usually, reservations are required in advance. Dinner is served Tuesday through Saturday.

## BISTRO AMBROSIA
**2080 Chestnut Street, between Steiner and Pierce**
**(415) 923-1777**
Moderate

Something about the name Bistro Ambrosia evokes the image of a dreamy kind of place. So I wasn't the least bit surprised when I saw how charming this little neighborhood restaurant is. The long, narrow dining room glows with soft candlelight and the illumination of low hanging lamps. Gigantic oil paintings on coral walls and green potted palms add a cheerful touch, and a handsome wine bar is situated along the back wall. Attentive waiters serve an eclectic array of dishes such as Pacific salmon grilled with red onions, fennel sauce, and spinach risotto, or homemade ricotta-prosciutto ravioli in a roasted tomato sauce. The wine list is small but complete, and offers a number of selections by the glass.

Bistro Ambrosia serves dinner Tuesday through Sunday. On the weekends, the restaurant offers a delightful brunch, and if it's warm and sunny outside, you can enjoy cinnamon-banana pancakes or poached eggs with hollandaise sauce on the patio.

◆   **Romantic Alternative**: A few doors down the street, **LA PER-GOLA**, 2060 Chestnut Street, (415) 563-4500, (Moderate), is a lovely Italian restaurant that serves delicious food in a romantic atmosphere. Round, linen-draped tables for two, dim track lighting, dramatic art-work on the walls, exotic floral arrangements, and a big picture window that looks out onto Chestnut Street complete this sophisticated, yet casual, dining room.

## BIX
**56 Gold Street, between Pacific and Jackson**
**(415) 433-6300**
Moderate

An intimate evening doesn't always have to be discreet, cultivated, and cosmopolitan. Especially if you find yourselves as enamored of this vivacious, energetic restaurant as we were. Bix is certainly not the place to go if you want to whisper sweet nothings to each other, but if you're looking for an incredible dinner and great entertainment, you'll love it. While you're partaking of well-prepared dishes accented with a few unusual ingredients, you might hear a torch singer or a saxophone player. Jazz is the theme here, and it shows in the mood and decor. The restaurant has two floors connected by a large staircase; booths line the walls, and tables occupy the rest of the downstairs dining area.

## THE BLUE FOX

**659 Merchant Street, between Montgomery and Kearney**
**(415) 981-1177**
Expensive

I wasn't sure what we were in for when we turned onto Merchant Street, which is actually an alley. A small sign at the door of The Blue Fox, and the valet on the curb, indicated we were in the right place, but from the appearance of things, I was afraid we had made the wrong choice.

The doors opened and The Blue Fox turned out to be exactly what we had hoped for. The restaurant is decorated in soft, peachy tones. Draped fabric and mirrors line the walls, holding together a formal dining room that is filled with dazzling light from the chandeliers. The tables, beautifully set with crystal and silver and tea roses, are spaced well, some of them even separated by large, white pillars. The cuisine is classic Italian, with an occasional surprise ingredient. The dishes routinely receive rave reviews from San Francisco's tough food critics, the wine list is wonderful, and the service excellent. We were delighted with our dinner and with the restaurant's romantic mood. In fact, we were so taken with the experience that when it came time to leave it was a surprise when the doors opened again onto that alley. The Blue Fox transported us, at least for a little while, to a very distinctive place. Dinner is Monday through Saturday.

**CAFE MAJESTIC—See The Majestic Hotel (Restaurant Kissing)**

**CAFE MOZART**                              ❖❖❖
**708 Bush Street, between Powell and Mason**
**(415) 391-8480**
Moderate to Expensive

Thick red velvet and embroidered lace hang in the windows. Outside, people walk by and cars pass back and forth, but inside you won't take any notice of them. Cafe Mozart is probably one of the most intimate restaurants in San Francisco. There are just ten tables here, each draped in white linen and set with fine china, silver, crystal, and a single red rose. Antiques, artwork, and music by the restaurant's namesake enrich the interior. The French cuisine is flavorful and beautifully presented. (The warm chocolate cake with roasted banana sauce is a lip-warming production.) This is a very romantic place for a special occasion, even if the occasion is simply that the two of you are together. Open for dinner only, Tuesday through Saturday, from 6 P.M. to 10 P.M.

## CAFE POTPOURRI
**905 California Street, between Mason and Powell**
**(415) 989-3500**
Inexpensive

I am always in search of wonderful restaurants that specialize in breakfast and cafe au lait (or latte, depending on which country's cuisine and atmosphere you prefer). This stimulating morning ritual is not to be taken lightly. What better way to start the day than with ardent clinging and a steaming cup of espresso? (Only a bona fide San Francisco couple would understand what I'm referring to.) Now, whether or not you buy any of this coffee romance, the Cafe Potpourri is still an elegant place for your morning repast. Exquisite French pastries, interesting egg dishes, and, of course, precisely made cafe au lait are always available. The kissing is up to you.

## CAMPTON PLACE DINING ROOM
**340 Stockton Street, on Stockton at Sutter**
**(415) 781-5155**
Expensive

Campton Place is an exceptional culinary landmark where the elite come for very serious dining and very intense romancing. Its elegance and refinement are quite dazzling. I would think fast after dropping a fork or napkin at this establishment—better to kick it under the table next to yours than admit to a faux pas. (Well, perhaps I'm exaggerating just a bit.) The American cuisine is sublime and, as you would expect, rather costly.

If you wish, you can also visit Campton Place for a regal morning repast, with the same dazzling setting and service. The atmosphere is less stuffy in the morning: you could drop your napkin twice and no one would blink an eye.

◆ **Romantic Suggestion:** For the same formal style in accommodations, consider splurging by making reservations at the very posh, very deluxe **CAMPTON PLACE HOTEL**, (415) 781-5555, (Very Expensive to Unbelievably Expensive). Imagine a valet service that unpacks your baggage, brings fresh bouquets to your room, and provides shoe shines Each room boasts plush carpets and handsome antique furnishings. One wouldn't call Campton Place Hotel cozy; the only word for this place is aristocratic.

## THE CARNELIAN ROOM AND BAR
**555 California Street, at Montgomery Street,
in the Bank of America Building
(415) 433-7500**
Very Expensive

Fifty-two floors above it all, the distinctive glass-enclosed lounge at The Carnelian Room offers a mesmerizing view of San Francisco. For this stellar experience, you will want to arrive just before sunset. The last light of day will cast striking shadows across the city. Lights from the buildings at first shimmer in the dusk, and later sparkle brilliantly against the black velvet sky. All this heavenly grandeur serves as a poignant backdrop to the posh interior. The view is accessible from both the restaurant and the bar, with the bar being an economical kissing windfall. Over an espresso or a glass of wine, the wonder of the city spreads out before you with a radiance that needs to be shared.

The Carnelian Room's service is, to say the least, gilt-edged and the food is very good. Sunday a sumptuous brunch is served.

◆   **Romantic Indulgence:** For $50, you can have your own private room, complete with a table for two, a cushy love seat, and a green/red light outside of the room that you control, summoning your own personal waiter only when you require service. Other than that, this is your place alone, for the entire meal, suitable for proposals of any kind.

## THE CLIFF HOUSE
**1090 Point Lobos Avenue
(415) 386-3330**
Moderate

*Take Geary all the way to the ocean, where it dead-ends at The Cliff House.*

All right, I know this is a tourist attraction. I know it is hard to ignore the busloads of tourists that arrive here almost hourly to take in the stunning view from this landmark. But note that word "almost." In late afternoon or early evening, the place may be practically empty. It is worth the risk because The Cliff House offers an unparalleled view of the forceful, roaring ocean and the prolific sea life on Seal Rock below—a feast for the soul and eyes. The weather conditions won't affect anything adversely either. Whether the sun is boldly sizzling above the sea or hiding behind a curtain of fog, the waves colliding against the jagged black rocks at the base of the restaurant will compose a rhapsody you can call your own.

◆ **Romantic Note:** By the way, the food is good. The Sunday buffet brunch in particular is a good idea if you go early enough or don't mind waiting.

## CLUB 36
**345 Stockton Street, in the Grand Hyatt**
**(415) 398-1234**
Inexpensive to Moderate

This simple, elegant cocktail lounge hovers 36 airy floors above the city. Live entertainment begins at 5:30 P.M. nightly. The atmosphere, view, and music are a wonderful way to begin or end your evening out in San Francisco.

## THE COMPASS ROSE
**335 Powell Street, in the Westin St. Francis Hotel**
**(415) 774-0167**
Inexpensive to Moderate

The Compass Rose is a plush, stunning place for afternoon high tea. While a string trio performs, you can relax in this rich room of high ceilings, dark wood, Oriental carpets, and exquisite antiques. Tea service is from 3 P.M. to 5 P.M. daily, and includes finger sandwiches, scones, berries with Grand Marnier cream, and petit fours. Lunch and cocktails are also served, and the atmosphere is warm and sensuous any time of day.

## DOIDGE'S
**2217 Union Street, between Fillmore and Steiner**
**(415) 921-2149**
Very Inexpensive

Ask most people what their idea of a romantic meal is, and they will probably tell you it takes place at night in a wonderful restaurant glowing with candlelight. They might even mention violins. But those who believe romance can be found only in the evening are missing out on a fabulous opportunity. A leisurely breakfast with your loved one can be quite compelling.

You won't think much of Doidge's as you enter. The first thing you'll see is a diner-style counter, complete with cooks in the background flipping pancakes. But you'll also notice the music—classical, maybe even violins. Inside the dining room, you won't find candles, but crisp linens and fresh flowers do adorn the tables. That's all. That's plenty. Doidge's serves up big, bountiful breakfasts and leaves the romance up to you. Usually, customers are happy to oblige.

Doidge's is open seven days a week, between 8:00 A.M. and 1:45 P.M. Monday through Friday, and 8:00 A.M. to 2:45 P.M. Saturday and Sunday. On the weekends, it's crowded, but the restaurant does accept reservations in advance.

◆ **Romantic Option: JUDY'S**, 2268 Chestnut Street, (415) 922-4588, (Very Inexpensive), is another neighborhood restaurant with a reputation for delicious breakfasts and romantic morning encounters. It's a cute storefront cafe with a big window onto Chestnut Street. Expect a wait on weekends, because the food is good and the restaurant is small. It's worth the wait, though, especially if you're passing the time with someone you enjoy.

## DONATELLO
**501 Post Street, between Taylor and Mason**
**(415) 441-7100, (800) 227-3184**
Expensive to Very Expensive

The Italian Renaissance seems to be alive and well and thriving in glittering, noble style at Donatello. Superior in every respect, this striking dining room with its stately decor and subdued lighting lends itself to a sensual evening of culinary delights. The food is remarkable and the presentations artful. The only other place you are likely to find meals prepared as expertly as this would be in northern Italy. Thank goodness, Donatello is in San Francisco, because dining here will make you feel like Romeo and Juliet with a happy ending. Breakfast is also served in this same intimate atmosphere.

◆  **Romantic Note:** The Donatello is also a European-style hotel with 95 attractive rooms. More business oriented then affectionate, they are still very nice and comfortable.

◆  **Romantic Alternative:** There are several **UMBERTO RESTAURANTS** in the world, but the one at 141 Stewart Street, (415) 543-8021, (Expensive), happens to be the most beautiful. Reminiscent of an Italian villa on a hill overlooking the Mediterranean, this is a lofty setting for a pasta extravaganza. Arched doorways, terra-cotta-tiled floors, provocative artwork, and soft lighting create an eye-catching environment for conversation and *amore*.

## EMPRESS OF CHINA
**838 Grant Avenue, between Clay and Washington**
**(415) 434-1345**
Moderate

Those who know the Chinatown area understand that it can be too noisy and too crowded, with too much traffic. But there is romance to be found here, so don't overlook the possibilities of an intriguing evening in Chinatown.

When you step off the elevator at Empress of China (the restaurant is six stories above the hustle and bustle), you step into a distinctly mysterious setting. The soothing sound of Oriental music wafts through an interior fashioned after ancient Oriental architecture. The restaurant boasts a priceless assortment of antiques and temple artifacts that are coveted by museums. Big windows along the exterior walls look out onto the lights of the city after dark.

Empress of China is a frequent award-winner for its cuisine. The chefs highlight fragrance, color, and flavor in their preparation Chinese favorites such as almond chicken, Mongolian lamb, and lobster in garlic sauce. The opulent atmosphere, great food, and gracious service make dining at Empress of China an exciting adventure. The restaurant is open for lunch and dinner seven days a week.

◆  **Romantic Warning**: Parking in San Francisco, and especially in Chinatown, can be a real hassle. Don't let the frustration of searching for a space spoil the evening before it begins. If you are downtown or nearby, do yourselves a favor and catch a cab.

◆  **Romantic Option: THE IMPERIAL PALACE**, 919 Grant Avenue, (415) 982-4440, (Moderate), is known worldwide for its lavish interior design, quiet elegance, and superb cuisine. Its reputation has attracted dignitaries, celebrities, presidents, and royalty.

## ERNIE'S
**847 Montgomery Street, between Pacific and Jackson**
**(415) 397-5969**
Expensive to Very Expensive

Ernie's is the kind of restaurant you save for special occasions, a birthday, Valentine's Day, or maybe just because you are spending the evening out with the one you love. This restaurant is one of the most elegant dining establishments in the city. The lobby looks like a parlor in a Victorian mansion. The lounge is built around a dark wooden bar with mirrors and stained glass behind it. The main dining room is rich with tapestry, exotic flowers, and exquisite silver and crystal gleaming in the candlelight.

Ernie's serves fine French cuisine. The wine list is considered among the best in the country and the service is very accommodating. But the most compelling thing Ernie's offers is a feeling, a warm, sentimental kind of feeling that you might call inspiration. Ernie's puts you in the mood for romance, and provides the perfect atmosphere for reveling in it. Lunch is served Tuesday through Friday; dinner is served daily.

## FLEUR DE LYS
**777 Sutter Street, between Jones and Taylor**
**(415) 673-7779**
Expensive to Very Expensive

There are some illustrious explanations why Fleur de Lys is consistently recommended as one of the most romantic restaurants in San Francisco. Legend would have us believe that Gypsies are romantic nomads, colorful wanderers who lead lives of passion and excitement. Whether or not the legends are correct, Fleur de Lys is one place where couples can enjoy the Gypsy spirit for an enchanted evening.

Fleur de Lys evokes the festive mood of a Gypsy encampment—like something you could find in the French countryside. Hundreds of yards of hand-printed red floral fabric drape the ceiling and walls of the main dining room, giving you the feeling you are under a big, beautiful tent. In the center of the room, a tall arrangement of exotic flowers is spotlighted by a Venetian chandelier hanging from the pinnacle of the fabric. The food here completes the evening. It is fabulous! Fleur de Lys serves contemporary French cuisine with a flirtatious touch of Mediterranean flavor. Every dish is prepared to perfection, artistically presented, and served by a staff that truly wants you to delight in your dining experience. Dinner is graciously presented Monday through Saturday.

## FOURNOU'S OVENS
**905 California Street, between Powell and Mason,**
**located in the Stouffer Stanford Court Hotel**
**(415) 989-1910**
Moderate to Expensive

Breakfast, brunch, lunch, or dinner, you can always expect a culinary treat and an appealing atmosphere ar Fournou's Ovens. The restaurant is really a series of small dining rooms, and depending on your mood, you can select a setting that matches the kind of experience you hope to have. The enclosed atrium overlooking Powell Street and the cable car line is lovely for breakfast or lunch. At dinner, choose between the Mediterranean-style dining rooms decorated with antiques and art, or the lower level where tables surround an open wood-burning oven. The chefs prepare continental cuisine described as hearty and flavorful. The restaurant's wine cellar contains 20,000 bottles from all over the world, with an emphasis on California vintages. The service is always amiable. I'll admit Fournou's Ovens is extremely elegant, but it isn't really intimate. It is, however, a very good place to kiss.

◆   **Romantic Suggestion: THE FRENCH ROOM**, in the Four Seasons Clift Hotel, 495 Geary Street, (415) 775-4700, (Expensive), is probably one of the prettiest dining rooms in San Francisco. The provocative setting is adorned with stunning chandeliers, attractive seating arrangements, and rich wood paneling. The food is consistently good and the atmosphere unceasingly heartwarming.

## GAYLORD'S                                          ◆◆◆
**900 North Point Street, in Ghirardelli Square**
**(415) 771-8822**
Expensive

Gaylord's is an impressive setting for excellent East Indian food. The ornate interior and attentive service are highlighted by huge bay windows that overlook the harbor and wharf below. The view is what lends magic to Gaylord's, and when an affectionate evening is at stake, a dramatic stroke may be what's required. Perhaps it's too touristy to be considered totally romantic, but all the right ingredients are here for an intimate dining experience.

## LA FOLIE
**2316 Polk Street, between Green and Union**
**(415) 776-5577**
Expensive

The minute I saw it, I knew I'd like La Folie. A soft glow illuminates the mullioned windows and the boxes of flowering plants hanging from the second story. Inside, white billowy clouds are painted on the sky blue ceiling; the coral-colored faux-marble walls provide a backdrop for some wonderful artwork; lots of little tables for two fill the room; and yellow curtains with exotic animals complete the decor. It is an eclectic, yet charming mix that truly exhibits the "folly" expressed in the restaurant's name. The food is fabulous French with a striking flavor. The family-run restaurant exudes a friendly spirit and is open Monday through Saturday for dinner only.

## LA NOUVELLE PATISSERIE
**2184 Union Street, at Fillmore**
**(415) 931-7655**
Inexpensive

Now and then, rather than having a romantic destination, it's better to have a starting point and an open mind. If you find yourself feeling somewhat adventurous one morning and you decide to venture out on a romantic excursion, in search of new places to kiss, may I suggest you begin at La Nouvelle Patisserie. You can't miss this French bakery. The front window is filled with delectable sweets. Inside, the strong aroma of fresh brewed coffee complements the wide variety of pastries, breads, fresh fruit tarts, truffles, cakes, and chocolates waiting for you. Later in the day, lunch specials, salads, sandwiches, pates, and crepes are also offered. Eat at one of the little tables or take your treats with you on the next leg of your journey. Either way, La Nouvelle Patisserie will put you in the mood for more romance while it satisfies you with gourmet delights.

◆ **Romantic Option:** Delicious pastries and fresh baked goods can also be found at **LA SEINE BAKERY**, 2150 Chestnut Street,

(415) 921-8833, (Inexpensive). The chocolate eclairs filled with Bavarian creme can't be beat! La Seine also serves breakfast, lunch, and early (until 6:30 P.M.) light dinners in a lovely dining room with vaulted ceilings, art deco decor, and two large windows along the back wall that let in lots of light on sunny days and frame pretty trees that sway in the breeze outside.

## LASCAUX
### 248 Sutter Street, between Grant and Kearney
### (415) 391-1555
Moderate to Expensive

It seems fitting that you must descend a flight of stairs to reach this wonderful underground dining room. Lascaux is named for the famous cave in France that contains some of the world's oldest paintings, reproductions of which grace the textured walls. Arched ceilings, resplendent hues, soft lighting, and a blazing fire in the huge stone hearth complete this present day cavern.

The rustic theme continues in the food served at Lascaux. Many of the selections are based on old European recipes. Most prove to be treats, but those in the know here always order the chicken or veal, spit-roasted on the rotisserie. The desserts are decadent, and certainly delicious enough to justify the temptation. And share—there's something very sweet about one plate and two forks.

After dinner, a nightcap at the lively bar is a gratifying way to end the evening. A pianist or jazz ensemble provides the music. The rest of the evening's entertainment is left to your discretion. Lunch is served Monday through Friday, and dinner Monday through Saturday.

◆    **Romantic Option: BUCA GIOVANNI**, 800 Greenwich Street, (415) 776-7766, (Moderate), also has a cellar entrance and a cavelike setting. This brick-walled restaurant is more rustic in appearance than Lascaux, but that's part of the romance. The dining room reminds me of some places I've eaten at in Italy and the food does too. One thing you should be aware of is that the tables are very close to each other, so plan on sharing your romantic mood with others nearby if you dine here during prime time.

## LE CASTEL
### 3235 Sacramento Street, on Sacramento near Masonic
### (415) 921-7115
Expensive

Located in a renovated home in the very fashionable Presidio Heights neighborhood, Le Castel is a lovely place to dine on incredible French food in a romantic atmosphere that offers a welcome change of pace and temperament from the Nob Hill crowd. That doesn't mean this isn't a thoroughly chic or posh dining experience, but the words "ultra-chic" and "ultra-posh" don't apply. Our dinner was remarkable, the presentation impeccable. Don't forget dessert; they are some of the most sinful in town.

◆ **Romantic Alternative: CHEZ MICHEL,** 804 North Point Street, (415) 771-6077, (Expensive), has a lovely, seductive ambience. The interior holds a simple array of tables, shuttered windows, Renaissance-style tapestries draped from the ceiling, brass railings, and long-stemmed candles atop each table. The food is superior in every respect in spite of the location. (My theory is that the closer a restaurant is to Fisherman's Wharf, the farther away it is from serving a decent meal.) Wonderful things happen here: one of them is food, the other will be you two once you arrive.

## LEHR'S GREENHOUSE
### 740 Sutter Street, between Taylor and Jones
### (415) 474-6478
Moderate

In San Francisco, a continually capricious climate keeps most restaurants from offering outdoor dining. To compensate, one restaurant has brought the beauty of nature inside. Lehr's Greenhouse is a lovely spot in full bloom. The dining room is filled with lush, green plants; fresh flowers add an accent of glorious color and sweet fragrance. Dining at Lehr's is truly like being served in a garden. Some of the tables are even located in their own, private gazebos. The food is standard fare, steaks and seafood for dinner, salads and sandwiches for lunch, and eggs or pancakes for breakfast. On Sundays, Lehr's offers a wonderful buffet brunch. You can count on a good meal at Lehr's, but the real reason to come is for the splendid surroundings—pretty, pleasant, and perfect for a respite from everything and everyone except your sweetheart. Breakfast, lunch, and dinner are served seven days a week.

## L'ESCARGOT                                           ◆◆◆
**1809 Union Street, between Laguna and Octavia**
**(415) 567-0222**
Moderate to Expensive

Given the choice between a large restaurant, fine as it might be, and a small, intimate dining room, I'll take the cozier alternative every time. So while the crowds are gathering at larger establishments on Union Street, those in the mood for a quiet interlude opt for L'Escargot.

Candlelit tables for two (and only a few for four) are draped in pastel pink linen, adorned with a red rose, and set in elegant style. There are only 14 tables in the restaurant and most nights all of them are occupied; if you plan to share one with somebody special, be sure to make reservations. A cordial staff caters to your every need without ever seeming intrusive. And the food, fabulous French cuisine, is prepared with great pride.

◆  **Romantic Alternative**: A few blocks down Union Street, another "little" place is a big success with couples looking for a choice rendezvous. **RISTORANTE BONTA**, 2223 Union Street, (415) 929-0407, (Moderate to Expensive), is a cozy storefront restaurant with a warm and inviting interior. The dining room is reminiscent of a trattoria in a small Italian town. Abstract art, fresh flowers, and candlelight combine to create a comfortable atmosphere. The food is superb and the service is very amiable. Ristorante Bonta can accommodate only about 30 fortunate diners, and sometimes the restaurant seems a little crowded and noisy, but not so much that you can't focus your attentions on each other.

## LE ST. TROPEZ
### 126 Clement Street, between Second and Third
(415) 387-0408
Moderate

If you know anything at all about San Francisco, you know this is the city for dining out. Trouble is, everyone else who knows anything at all about San Francisco is competing with you for a reservation. That's what makes Le St. Tropez such a great treasure, because Le St. Tropez offers everything you expect from a good French restaurant— romantic ambience, sumptuous food, and attentive service—and one thing more: you can usually get a reservation within a day or two of your dinner plans. (Sometimes even on the same day!) The dining room has a homey feeling. It's warmed by a large wood-burning fireplace, copper kettles hang from the walls, and a table by the ivy-lined window is especially nice. Even if you haven't waited until the last minute to make reservations, you'll be pleased with Le St. Tropez. It's a pleasant change of pace from the better-known San Francisco dining establishments, but that won't last long. Dinner is served Tuesday through Saturday.

## L'OLIVIER
### 465 Davis Street, half a block south of Jackson Street
(415) 981-7824
Moderate to Expensive

By day, L'Olivier is popular with the business set, and seems to lose some of its appeal and charm. But by night, L'Olivier is altogether a different restaurant. After dark, it is an engaging setting for an evening of fine food and courtship.

The small, two-tiered dining room, aglow with candlelight, can be likened to a manor you might find in rural France. A floral print paper covers the walls, fresh flowers are placed on every table, there's always a large centerpiece arrangement in the middle of the room, French antiques add extra appeal, and chandeliers crown the room with soft light. All of these quaint touches combine to create an atmosphere that is inviting and intimate.

The traditional French menu includes favorites such as frog's leg soup, escargots de bourgogne, sauteed scaloppine of veal, and bouillabaise, the house specialty. The wine list, devised to please connoisseurs, is a compilation of popular California wines, well-known French vintages, and a few surprises that may be worth sampling. And if wine is among your indulgences, partake, because you'll find L'Olivier inspires a night of romance that can be best described as intoxicating. Lunch is served Monday through Friday, and dinner Monday through Saturday.

## THE MAGIC FLUTE
**3673 Sacramento Street, between Spruce and Locust**
**(415) 922-1225**
Inexpensive to Moderate

This angelic restaurant is a refreshing contrast to the affected style of many formidable, highbrow dining establishments where you sense that if you were to drop your napkin or fork, a waiter might reprimand you. The blue walls covered with a white trellislike pattern, the white filigree chandeliers, and the simple country tables and chairs create a light and airy setting. Your sentiments will easily blend with this engaging atmosphere as the evening slowly unfolds toward dessert. It would be an error not to mention the dedication this restaurant has to serving health-aware meals chosen from a diverse group of international cuisines.

## MAI'S
**1838 Union Street, between Laguna and Octavia**
**(415) 921-2861**
Inexpensive

I enjoy the unexpected, so when my husband suggested Vietnamese food one sunny Saturday afternoon, I prepared my taste buds for exotic cuisine. When we pulled up to Mai's, it was an additional pleasure to find the restaurant has a charming section outside that's set up like a sidewalk cafe. Pale pink tablecloths and single red roses adorn each table. The interior dining room is also romantic during cooler weather or for dinner.

We ordered spicy prawns and coconut chicken and, while we were waiting for our meal, sipped some wine and enjoyed the lively street scene. (Union Street is always a busy mix of shoppers and diners on warm weekends.) By the time our food arrived, we were holding hands, we had exchanged several smiles, and romance was on our minds. The fact that the food was good and the service courteous added to the experience, although I'm not sure we would have noticed if there had been anything wrong with either. We were concentrating solely on each other. Perhaps because there are no "expectations," these kinds of romantic interludes are by far my favorite. They just happen.

## MASA'S
**648 Bush Street, between Powell and Stockton**
**(415) 989-7154**
Very Expensive

Masa's is as formal as a French restaurant can be, and that's exceedingly formal. What the restaurant might lack in charm and coziness, it certainly makes up for in the stupendous quality of its cuisine. Masa's is, in the opinions of many, the best restaurant in San Francisco. From the foie gras with truffles and spinach to the white-and-dark-chocolate mousse with raspberry sauce, Masa's makes every dish a masterpiece. The restaurant is handsomely decorated in rich, dark tones with an occasional accent of soft color and low lighting. Each table is elegantly appointed with crystal, china, and silver. The room is small and the staff is large, so each guest is assured the personal attention Masa's is famous for. If you find romance is best when you are catered to in every way, you will find Masa's very romantic. Dinner is served Tuesday through Saturday.

## McCORMICK AND KULETO'S
**900 North Point Street, in Ghirardelli Square**
**(415) 929-1730**
Moderate to Expensive

The fact that McCormick and Kuleto's is located in touristy Ghirardelli Square didn't much interest me—personally or for purposes of this book either. But the wonderful view and showcase interior are worth a closer look. Huge picture windows accented with stained glass look out onto the bay. On a clear evening the water sparkles as the sun begins to slip away, and ships roll by on their way to destinations unknown. You can easily disregard the tourists with a view like this. Inside, the restaurant is large and airy, with dark wood, brass accents, and abundant green plants. It's often crowded, but the tables are situated far enough apart that in some ways your dining experience here can be more intimate than in a smaller, more crowded restaurant. The menu offers an incredible selection of fresh seafood and an extensive wine list. The restaurant is open seven days a week for lunch and dinner.

◆ **Romantic Extra**: If it's already too late for the view or you haven't planned far enough in advance to have reservations by the window, try the **CRAB CAKE LOUNGE AND BAR** attached to McCormick and Kuleto's. A glass case presents ocean delicacies for your inspection. The chefs will prepare these or other snacks, including individual pizzas and baby back ribs cooked in an open oven. Booths and a counter are available.

◆ **Romantic Alternative**: Next door to McCormick and Kuleto's, **CAFE ORITALIA**, 900 North Point Street, (415) 749-5288, (Inexpensive to Moderate), also offers a stunning view of the bay. The restaurant is decorated in art deco style. The menu is innovative, combining Oriental cuisine with Italian favorites. I liked the wilted spinach salad with mushrooms, red onions, pickled ginger, and cilantro; the Korean barbecued beef wrapped in lettuce; and the angel-hair pasta with crab and shrimp in garlic, tomato, and white wine sauce. The portions are small so you can order several items and enjoy all the benefits of sharing. Oritalia's second location, at 1915 Fillmore Street, (415) 346-1333, (Inexpensive to Moderate), is more formal, and the food just as interesting.

## NEW ORLEANS ROOM
950 Mason Street, in the Fairmont Hotel
(415) 772-5259
Moderate

The reasonably priced musical rhythms of the New Orleans Room make for a wonderful evening of tripping the light fantastic. This is swing at its best, with smoothness and intoxicating renditions that will make you sway and move to the beat like never before.

## NIEMAN MARCUS ROTUNDA RESTAURANT
150 Stockton Street, at Geary
(415) 362-3900
Inexpensive

When I began to research this book, I had a good idea about where to look for places that people would like to kiss. I knew that I would include quaint inns, charming restaurants, and pretty parks. If someone had suggested, way back then, that I could find a great place to pucker up in a department store, I would have smiled, said, "Now there's an idea," and moved right on to the next bed and breakfast. But, believe it or not, I have found a wonderful kissing place in Nieman Marcus. On the fourth floor, under a spectacular stained glass dome, the Rotunda Restaurant provides a respite from the shopping crowds and an invitation to romance. The dining room serves lunch and light meals from 11 A.M. to 5 P.M. Monday through Saturday, but for me, afternoon tea at the Rotunda is the ideal interlude. Select a table, draped in white linen and accented with a pale pink rose, near the floor-to-ceiling windows overlooking Union Square.

You'll be served a choice of brewed teas, finger sandwiches, pastries, muffins, scones with cream and preserves, and an assortment of cookies. In a world where late-afternoon romance is too often overlooked because of busy schedules, you'll discover tea time can be a leisurely treat!

## 1001 NOB HILL
**1001 California Street, between Taylor and Mason**
**(415) 441-1001**
Expensive

We'd been sitting at our little table by the window for about five minutes when a cable car rolled up California Street. Now this is what I call authentic San Francisco dining. You can watch the cable cars pass by from the California Room, one of several small dining rooms that flow together to form this lovely restaurant. Next to the California Room, in the Dome, six tables are surrounded by festive, pastel wall paintings that depict Renaissance themes. Next to the Dome, the most intimate tables in the restaurant are in the Fireplace Room by a warming hearth. Each room is slightly different in decor and ambience; all of them offer the right nuances to help create a special evening.

The continental cuisine is superlative. The oven-roasted Pacific salmon with garlic potatoes is highly recommended, as are the pork loin medallions with Watsonville apples and onion marmalade. Be sure to save room for dessert: the souffles are perfectly done. On weekends you will want to linger awhile to take in the jazz pianist and vocal performances. Dinner is served Monday through Saturday.

## NOB HILL RESTAURANT
**Number One Nob Hill, at the corner of California and Mason**
**(415) 392-3434**
Expensive

Normally, the Nob Hill Restaurant is not the kind of place I'd include in this book. Please don't misunderstand—it's a wonderful restaurant with outstanding continental cuisine, fine service, and a great wine list. It's just that this dining room is a bit too masculine for my taste. The dark wood paneling, flat lighting, and very formal atmosphere more closely resemble an executive board room than an intimate restaurant. So the Nob Hill Restaurant had to do something very special to win my approval. It did, and won my heart as well. On Friday and Saturday evenings, the center of the restaurant is cleared of tables, and a three-piece ensemble plays the kind of music that makes you want to be cheek-to-cheek with the one you love. I'm not sure when dinner and dancing went out of style, and I'll never understand why, but it seems to be a rare combination these days. Whether it has been a while since you last took a spin around the floor, or you've never tired of this romantic twosome of fancy food and fancy footwork, the Nob Hill Restaurant is a premier destination.

## PANE E VINO
**3011 Steiner Street, between Union and Filbert**
**(415) 346-2111**
Moderate

There's much more to Pane E Vino than the bread and wine its name salutes. Not the least is an enchanting atmosphere that invites devoted hearts to partake in the pleasures of an evening together. This charming restaurant comprises two small dining rooms. The one in the back is more romantic, with a brick fireplace, a sideboard adorned with fresh flowers and aged cheeses as the room's centerpiece, low lights, a wood-beamed ceiling, and a clay tile floor. Accommodating waiters, most with thick Italian accents, are always happy to make recommendations if you're having difficulty deciding. The food is delicious (especially the pastas), the wines are wonderful, and the atmosphere is certainly for lovers. The restaurant really should be renamed Pane E Vino E Amore!

## PIANO ZINC SUPPER CLUB
**708 14th Street, at Market Street**
**(415) 431-5266**
Moderate to Expensive

There's something seductive about a softly played piano. When the piano is a white baby grand, it's especially exciting. And when you're hearing jazz, well, you'll be in the mood!

This chic brasserie is small and cozy, sometimes crowded, but always comfortable. Banquettes line the mirrored walls, giving the illusion of more space than actually exists in the restaurant. If you plan to dine here, plan to sit close. (Personally, I consider that an attraction, not a drawback.) The proximity will allow you to easily sample each other's dinner selection, something you really should do. The French food at Piano Zinc can compete with any other restaurant in the city.

Dining here is a delightful change of pace from the more formal restaurants of San Francisco—fun, festive, and, for the romantically inclined, truly satisfying. Dinner is served Tuesday through Sunday.

### PIAZZA LOUNGE
**55 Cyril Magnin Street, at Fifth and Market,**
**in the Park 55 Hotel**
**(415) 392-8000**

The competition between large downtown hotels in San Francisco is apparent in their progressively more elaborate interiors, ranging from futuristic to flashy to opulent. The intention, of course, is to impress business travelers or out-of-towners with the hotel's image and design. From the older hotels, with their baroque, florid interiors, to the prodigious, ultramodern design of the newer hotels, "impressive" isn't exactly the word—"exaggerated" is probably more applicable. All this can indeed be fascinating, but having a meal or drink in that kind of setting is more like touring a museum than relaxing in a romantic respite.

One of the few exceptions is the Piazza Lounge in the Park 55 Hotel. It ingeniously unites conspicuous, contemporary extravagance with beautiful, intimate comfort. Sink back into a billowy chair as the sounds of the grand piano drift through the room. The intriguing artwork and the crystal chandeliers that dangle from the four-story ceiling will help give your afternoon or evening a sultry start.

### THE PLUSH ROOM
**940 Sutter Street, between Hyde and Leavenworth**
**(415) 885-6800**
Expensive

Remember those late-night black-and-white movies from the 1940s, where hearts were lost, found, broken, and mended, all at a quiet table in the corner of a jazz club? There was always moving music in the background that would reach a crescendo just in time for the lovers to join in a torrid embrace. The Plush Room keeps alive this tradition of steamy jazz and soothing contemporary ballads in an appropriately classy, intimate setting. Whether or not you are a jazz connoisseur, you'll find this place a tempting spot to share with your partner. You may be surprised to discover that words will be of no practical use all evening long.

## POSTRIO
**545 Post Street, between Taylor and Mason**
**(415) 776-7825**
Moderate to Expensive

Postrio is drama. Others might consider this just another tres chic San Francisco restaurant, which it is, but everything about Postrio reminds me of a theatrical production. Make an entrance down a unique staircase of sculptured iron and copper to the main dining room. This "set" is an artistic array of hues, textures, and lighting designed to stimulate the senses. Plush, fabric-finished booths alternate throughout the room with striking tables draped in white linen and accented with black chairs. Modern art hangs on the walls, lamps hang from the high ceiling, green plants and exotic flowers add even more color. The "producers" are in the large, open kitchen turning out flavorful California cuisine, and the dishes are served by a "supporting cast" that wants to enhance your performance, so it's up to you to decide how to play out the evening. As for my suggestion, the best shows always include a kissing scene! Breakfast and lunch performances are Monday through Friday, and dinner is served daily.

◆ **Romantic Extra:** The upstairs bar at Postrio serves gourmet pizzas and lighter fare until 1:30 A.M. It's the perfect place for a bite to eat and a quick kiss or two after a real night at the theater! And if you have trouble getting a reservation for lunch or dinner (they are difficult to come by), breakfast or Saturday and Sunday brunch are also possibilities.

## SILKS
**222 Sansome Street, between Pine and California**
**(415) 986-2020**
Moderate to Expensive

To arrive at Silks, pass through the Mandarin Oriental Hotel's lovely lobby and ascend an elegant sweeping staircase. The centerpiece of this dining room is a splendid copper-and-brass table plumed with a lavish floral bouquet and displaying a copious amount of fruit, breads, and liqueurs. Encircling it are tables set far enough apart to provide each with a considerable amount of intimacy. The food at Silks is imaginative, combining French techniques with Oriental ingredients and California zest. As its name suggests, Silks has a soft atmosphere that makes it a comforting place for tender time together.

◆ **Romantic Option: THE MANDARIN ORIENTAL HOTEL,** 222 Sansome Street, (415) 885-0999, (Unbelievably Expensive), is an outstanding, albeit business-oriented, place to stay while you are in San Francisco. The guest rooms are located on the top 11 floors of the 48-floor twin towers of the California Center. Every room has an unbelievable view, and some have marble bathtubs with the same celestial perspective of the city.

## SHADOWS RESTAURANT—See Telegraph Hill
**(Outdoor Kissing)**

## SQUIRE
**950 Mason Street, between California and Sacramento**
**(in the Fairmont Hotel)**
**(415) 772-5211**
Moderate to Expensive

There are a few secrets in my life, and until the publication of this book, Squire was one of them. This particular place is one I'd prefer to share only with my significant other. But when I considered excluding it from the book for such selfish motives, guilt got the better of me. There are few restaurants in San Francisco, or anywhere else, that can equal Squire for romance.

Squire is located just off the lobby of the Fairmont Hotel in a rotunda-style room with a domed ceiling. A huge chandelier descends from the high point of the dome, and a gorgeous floral arrangement sits under the illumination of the chandelier. The tables are positioned around this centerpiece, and walls with large, arched, mirrored windows encase the room. Soft colors and subdued lighting add to the elegance of the decor.

Squire specializes in seafood, but also offers poultry and beef dishes. The food is exquisite. The wine list is extensive and well chosen. The waiters are very attentive, but never overbearing. The atmosphere is absolutely captivating.

The truth is, even if I wanted to keep Squire a secret, I couldn't. Many people, looking for romantic places, have already discovered this impressive restaurant. So, if you too decide to try it, make reservations in advance. Enjoy the experience, but do me a favor, don't tell too many others how fabulous Squire is!

◆   **Romantic Alternative**: If you can't get reservations at Squire, try **MASON'S**, 950 Mason Street, (415) 392-0113, (Expensive). The Fairmont's other romantic restaurant is more formal in its decor and more refined in its ambience, but Mason's does offer wonderful window tables that look out on the cable cars of California Street, the beauty of brass and blond oak furnishings, the allure of low lights and fresh flowers, and delicious entrees like champagne-braised salmon or roasted breast of duck on a bed of spinach with shallots. Another attraction is the grand piano in Mason's lounge. It's played nightly in the center of a room that's surrounded by small tables and overstuffed sofas. Now that's romantic!

## TOMMY TOY'S                                    ◆◆◆◀
**655 Montgomery Street, between Washington and Clay**
**(415) 397-4888**
Moderate

There are no chopsticks at this ambrosial location. That's because Tommy Toy's is different—it serves Chinese cuisine with a French flair. There aren't many restaurants I know of where you can find Peking duck served with crepes for the main course, and a fluffy, smooth chocolate mousse for dessert. Elaborate is the only word to adequately describe the decor. The restaurant is patterned after the 19th-century Dowager Empress's reading room, and she obviously knew how to live. These ornate surroundings are subdued by candlelight and fresh, fragrant flowers. If you're just looking for a good Chinese dinner, you'd do best to go elsewhere. Here at Tommy Toy's you will find a unique dining experience that should be shared with your special someone.

## VICTOR'S
335 Powell Street, between Post and Geary,
in the Westin St. Francis
(415) 956-7777
Very Expensive

One of the most scintillating views of San Francisco is to be found at Victor's, 32 stories above the city. An outside, glass-walled elevator takes you to the restaurant, on the top floor of the Westin St. Francis Hotel. Here, floor-to-ceiling windows disclose what sitting on Cloud Nine is really like. The continental cuisine (the baby salmon in dry vermouth and caviar cream sauce is amazing) is excellent and the service superior. If Victor's has any drawback, it's popularity and tourists, but watch the view and you'll only see the city and each other.

# Outdoor Kissing

## ALAMO SQUARE—See Archbishop Mansion
(Hotel Kissing)

## ANGEL ISLAND
Ferries from San Francisco, Vallejo, or Tiburon
(415) 546-2810 (San Francisco and Vallejo)
(415) 435-2131 (Tiburon)
$5 to $10.50 for ferry

Become castaways for a day on this angelic island in the midst of San Francisco Bay. The ferry ride alone is worthy of a windswept kiss. On the island, romance rises as you leave the lively little marina and ascend primitive trails to your private panorama of the San Francisco skyline or forested Marin hills. Bring along a picnic lunch to enjoy in a sun-soaked meadow. With its six-mile perimeter trail and rugged climb up to a 360-degree view of the Bay Area, you're sure to find a secluded kissing spot where you can dream of sailing ships and solitude on some sensual South Sea isle.

## GOLDEN GATE BRIDGE

*Lincoln Boulevard, Park Presidio Boulevard, and Lombard Street all merge onto the Golden Gate Bridge. There is a parking area just east of the toll booths, where you gain entrance to the walkway across the bridge.*

Walking over the venerable, symbolically soaring Golden Gate Bridge is an exhilarating, unforgettable journey. This monumental structure offers views that can only be described as astonishing. From this vantage point you can survey the city's physique while you balance high above it, unencumbered by buildings or earth. The Pacific Ocean, 260 feet below, is an endless blue apparition framed by the rugged curve of land north to Marin and south to San Francisco. As unbelievable as it sounds, the gusts of wind up here can cause the reinforced, herculean steel cables to sway to and fro. This is the time and place where, without even kissing or touching, you can really feel the earth move—and it won't be from an earthquake, either. On a clear, sunny day, just once in your life, put on your walking shoes and discover this one for yourselves.

◆ **Romantic Option: GOLDEN GATE PROMENADE** wraps three and a half miles around one of the most astounding scenic routes the Bay Area has to offer. This walkway extends from **AQUATIC PARK** at Fisherman's Wharf to **FORT POINT** under the Golden Gate Bridge. If there is a lover's lane to be found anywhere in San Francisco, it would be the projection of land at Fort Point. As you gaze out to the golden rocky hills, the vast lengths of the Golden Gate and Bay bridges, the glistening blue water, and the formidable cityscape, there is little else to do but nuzzle close and kiss.

## GOLDEN GATE PARK

*Between Lincoln Way, Fulton Street, Stanyan Street, and the Pacific Ocean.*

For those who know this vast acreage of city woodland and gardens, it is possible to imagine that Golden Gate Park and Romance are themselves an adoring couple. There is so much to see in this diverse three-mile-long park that even in a day, you can only scratch the surface. Nevertheless, any of the park's varied attractions can provide a prelude to an enchanting day together. You can start at the **STRYBING ARBORETUM**, a horticultural wonderland of plants and trees from all over the world. Another remarkable city escape is the **JAPANESE TEA GARDEN**, where an exotic display of Japanese landscaping gives you a tranquil reprieve from anything having to do with urban life. While school is in session, the **CHILDREN'S PLAYGROUND**, with its extraordinary carousel, offers adults a grand backdrop for playtime. The **CONSERVATORY OF FLOWERS** is a stunning structure that houses many of the earth's most brilliant colors and plant life. Wherever you find yourselves, this magical San Francisco park is the foremost outdoor spot of the city.

## PALACE OF FINE ARTS

*Bordered by Lyon, Bay, Baker, and Jefferson streets.*

On a sunny day in San Francisco, no place can compare to the Palace of Fine Arts. Pack a picnic, bring a blanket, and prepare to spend a carefree hour or so in this tranquil setting. When you arrive, you will probably spot ducks and swans gliding across the glistening lagoon. Spread your blanket and lunch in the grassy park in front of the water and watch the birds while away the day. From this vantage point, you can also admire the majestic Palace, an ornate domed structure supported by a circle of columns and flanked by colonnades. The Palace of Fine Arts was erected in 1915 for the Panama-Pacific International Exposition, but it was not built to last. In the late 1960s, when the structure began to crumble, San Franciscans, who had come to cherish the Palace, raised enough money to restore it, making it a permanent landmark for people who love romantic places. Chances are good that you too will be captivated by the ethereal setting, and picnics at the Palace will become an enduring part of your romantic ritual.

◆ **Romantic Note:** In 1991, the city of San Francisco lit up the Palace of Fine Arts. Now this stunning structure can be enjoyed after dark. If you're planning a romantic evening drive, be sure the Palace is on your route.

◆ **Romantic Option:** A few blocks away, on Marina Boulevard, between the Yacht Harbor and Fort Mason (Cervantes and Buchanan streets), you'll find a grassy stretch of land called **MARINA GREEN** that hugs the bay. On warm weekends, if you don't mind crowds, it's a good place from which to watch sailboats, fly a kite, or simply sit and enjoy the sunshine.

## PIER 39

*At the foot of Beach Street at Embarcadero.*

OK, call me a kid, I won't be insulted. After all, sometimes it is easier to see the joy of life through the eyes of a child. In the case of Pier 39, if you don't use a younger viewpoint, all you're likely to see is a sizable tourist attraction. Try my approach and spend your time eating cotton candy on the carousel or riding the bumper cars. Or you can investigate the teddy bear store, home to more than 2,000 of these huggable creatures. Or watch mimes, magicians, and musicians perform while you wrinkle your nose at the smell of the sea and squint at the sparkling reflection of the sun on the ocean. On a nice day, you're sure to see sailboats whipping across the water with the wind.

On the tourist side of things, more than 100 specialty shops line the two-story boardwalk. There are at least a dozen eating spots for every taste and budget, and as an extra incentive many of the restaurants have views of the bay. Pier 39, if you're willing to adjust your biases and be young at heart, can be a pretty neat place.

◆ **Romantic Suggestion:** Take a cruise on exquisite San Francisco Bay. **THE BLUE AND GOLD FLEET,** (415) 781-7877, is docked at Pier 39's west marina; scenic, very touristy tours depart frequently. You won't be alone, but if you concentrate on the scenery the crowds will be much less apparent.

## THE PRESIDIO

*Bordered by the Pacific Ocean, San Francisco Bay, Lyon Street, West Pacific Avenue, and Lake Street.*

It started in the 1700s with the Spanish settlers. Then, the Presidio was their northern military post. Now, the Presidio is home base to the U.S. Army's Sixth Division. Fortunately for those who are inclined to kiss in the great outdoors, the Presidio is not just a military installation. This beautiful corner of San Francisco contains hundreds of acres of lush lands, and is open to the public. There's much more to the Presidio than you can see on foot, so start by driving around the grounds on roads that are lined with redwood and eucalyptus trees. Then, do yourself a favor, and park the car, take your companion's hand, and go for a walk. You might choose to stroll by some of the historical sites and displays. Maybe you'll opt for an open area with views of the Golden Gate Bridge and the Pacific Ocean. Or perhaps you'll select the residential area, where old, yet immaculate base houses (still occupied) evoke the nostalgic feeling of a time gone by. The Presidio, itself, is like that: a place where memories of the past linger while new ones are waiting to be made!

## TELEGRAPH HILL

*From Union Street, head east up Telegraph Hill.*

If you live in or visit San Francisco regularly, there is probably one place that symbolizes for you what this city is all about. For some it's Fisherman's Wharf, for others it's Union Square, for some eccentrics it may be Alcatraz. For kissing, I nominate Telegraph Hill.

The top of Telegraph Hill is where the famous Coit Tower presides over the city. From this vantage point you get a sense of the city's passionate personality, its pulsating energy as well as its orderly, well-contained physique. You will also be exposed to a lot of other sightseers, who may obscure the view and reduce your hope for a romantic measure of time. But then again, when you actually witness the sights and sounds from this pinnacle, you may find that the crowds around you don't seem to matter. It's worth the risk!

◆ **Romantic Suggestion**: When you've finished admiring this hallowed view, be sure you have made dinner reservations at **THE SHADOWS RESTAURANT**, 1349 Montgomery, (415) 982-5536, (Expensive), which sits on the easternmost flank of the hill, just a stroll's length down from Coit Tower. Here the crowds will seem to melt away as your emotions and taste buds come alive. This pastel, high-beamed restaurant overlooking the bay has floor-to-ceiling picture windows, high-backed wicker chairs, apricot-colored tablecloths, pine paneling, and an open, airy atmosphere. As you relish the California cuisine, watch the mosaic patterns of water and sky alter as day makes its transition into night.

◆ **Romantic Option**: At the foot of Telegraph Hill is the North Beach area, overflowing with Italian restaurants and Italian bakeries that tantalize the senses. In the midst of this ethnic paradise is the **MILLEFIORI INN**, 444 Columbus Avenue, (415) 433-9111, (Moderate to Expensive), where you can feel connected to the unique city life of San Francisco. This European-style bed and breakfast has an artistic blend of chandeliers, rich wood paneling, stained glass windows, polished brass, and graceful antiques in every room. The Millefiori is a find, not only because of its location, but because of its inviting personality and diligent attention to service.

> "*Press yourself into a drop of wine, and pour yourself into the purest flame.*"
>
> Rainer Maria Rilke

# EAST BAY

## Oakland and Berkeley

### Hotel/Bed and Breakfast Kissing

**BOAT & BREAKFAST, Oakland**
77 Jack London Square
(510) 444-5858, (800) BOAT-BED
Moderate to Unbelievably Expensive

*From Highway 880 south take the Jackson Street exit and turn right at the first light onto Jackson. At the second stop sign, turn right onto Third Street. In one block, turn left onto Alice Street. Jack London Square will be on your right.*

Imagine smooching on your own half-million-dollar yacht as the sun sets behind the San Francisco skyline across the shimmering bay. Fantasies can become reality on the quiet Oakland waterfront. Whether you fancy sailboats or luxury motor yachts, you can kiss like a millionaire, at least for an evening. The selection changes, depending on which boats are in port. As enthusiastic day sailors, kissing on our own 35-foot sailboat was like a dream come true, but many would find the accommodations confining and a bit too rustic. Some larger yachts cruise into the Unbelievably Expensive category, but you can share the romance of the evening with another like-minded couple, then retire to the seclusion of your private stateroom, complete with private bath. Color televisions, top-quality stereos, and spacious living rooms and bedrooms are de rigueur. Dive in headfirst and indulge in a candlelit catered dinner on board, or stroll hand-in-hand through the picturesque marina to one of the many diverse restaurants clustered along the waterfront. In the morning, awake to the melody of lapping waves and quacking ducks. A continental breakfast, packed in a picnic basket, is delivered to your boat.

## THE CLAREMONT HOTEL
## AND TENNIS CLUB, Oakland
**Ashby Avenue and Domingo Avenue**
**(510) 843-3000**
Expensive to Very Expensive

*From San Francisco, take the Bay Bridge to Highway 24 East. Exit at Claremont Avenue, turn left onto Claremont, and then right on Ashby.*

We almost always prefer a small, intimate hotel or bed and breakfast to a large flashy resort, even when the large flashy resort has everything we want. The problem with resorts is that they lend themselves to conventions and tour groups. There's something about feeling like part of a software association's annual meeting that doesn't quite feel intimate. Besides, the facilities often tend to be crowded and the hot tub overflowing with people instead of water. As you may have already guessed, though, this famous hotel and tennis club is an exceptional exception to that rule.

As we drove up Ashby Avenue, this majestic white stone mansion reminded us of villas we had seen in Europe. The exterior is epic in scale and style. The castlelike structure is surrounded by the Berkeley Hills and literally acres of deftly cultivated gardens and endless rows of palm trees. Gracing the horizon in the distance beyond the resort is one of the most impressive views of the San Francisco skyline to be seen anywhere.

Here at the Claremont, guests are encouraged to engage in any and all of the available outdoor activities. Tennis courts, an Olympic-size swimming pool, and a nearby golf course offer invigorating ways to spend the day. Your personal energy level may benefit immensely by knowing that saunas and a hot tub are waiting for you inside. Following a full day of athletic playtime, you can indulge your whims again, this time at the **PAVILLION RESTAURANT**. This four-star dining room (we rated it a four-kiss experience), with a spectacular view of the San Francisco Bay, will seem even more satisfying after your long workout.

So where, you might wonder, is the romance in all of this athletic activity? We found it in the old-world architecture of the building, and in the cozy, yet grand accommodations that took us a lot farther away from home than we expected. We felt it in the warmth of the sun as we tested our skills and took our time relaxing after a match or race. At the Claremont, romance is what you find in the physical workout of playing together.

## GRAMMA'S ROSE GARDEN INN, Berkeley
**2740 Telegraph Avenue**
**(510) 549-2145**
Moderate to Expensive

*From San Francisco, take the Bay Bridge east and then stay on Interstate 80 to the Ashby Avenue exit. Turn right on Ashby and then make a left on Telegraph Avenue.*

Sometimes you want a place to stay that's comfortable and cozy, a place designed for cuddling, without pretense or affectation. Gramma's Inn is one of those places. It's not what I would call a notably amorous-sounding name, but then what's in a name—beside letters?

This Tudor-style bed and breakfast is actually five skillfully restored buildings in a neighborhood that should take the hint and renovate itself. All of the rooms have been lovingly enhanced with antique furnishings and thick hand-sewn quilts. Some of the suites overlook the garden, others have private decks or fireplaces, and one has stained glass windows that encompass the entire room. It is likely that "Gramma" will spoil you beyond repair. Milk and cookies are set out in the afternoon, along with wine and cheese, and a respectable full breakfast of egg dishes, baked breads and homemade preserves is served in the morning.

◆ **Romantic Option:** Gramma's Inn is so close to the **UNIVERSITY OF CALIFORNIA AT BERKELEY** that you shouldn't miss the opportunity to see this beautiful campus. It is a lovely place for a picnic, particularly in the summer, when the student population dwindles significantly.

## THE SHATTUCK HOTEL, Berkeley
**2086 Allston Way**
**(510) 845-7300**
Inexpensive to Moderate

*From San Francisco take the Bay Bridge east; stay on Highway 80 to University Avenue and turn right. When you reach Shattuck Avenue turn right again. The hotel is on the corner of Shattuck and Allston Way.*

If you are spending time in Berkeley and want a peaceful place away from the hustle and bustle of this town's quaint but busy streets, choose The Shattuck Hotel. It is located in the midst of all the activity, but once inside you'll feel as if you've entered a refuge where matters of the heart are tended to with style and care. The attractive lobby is decorated with Victorian furnishings, dark wood paneling, white columns, and subtle lighting. The guest rooms are comfortable and stately. This historical landmark has been renovated with just the right balance of modern amenities to make it a tasteful blend of two opposing worlds.

◆ **Romantic Note:** Plan to have at least one meal at **SEDONA'S**, (510) 841-3848, a Southwestern-style restaurant connected to the hotel. The food is outstanding, and the room itself has architectural flare and smashing decor.

## WATERFRONT PLAZA HOTEL, Oakland
**10 Washington Street at Jack London Square**
**(510) 836-3800 or (800) 729-3638**
Expensive to Very Expensive

*Call for directions.*

A romance package designed just for kissing is the year-round specialty at this recently opened luxury hotel. Champagne and chocolate-dipped strawberries are the prelude to an amorous adventure in your spacious waterfront view room. For a little extra, you can indulge in a suite with a gas fireplace. Bleached pine furnishings, televisions, VCRs, mini-bars, hair dryers, coffee makers, a fitness center, a sauna, and a pool are all provided to ensure that the only thing you need to make the scene complete is your love. In the morning, a continental breakfast is delivered to your bed. You're also given two complimentary nightshirts, which, in this setting, are most likely to go home with you unworn.

◆  **Romantic Note:** The hotel's restaurant, **JACK'S**, (510) 444-7171, serves basic American cuisine in a romantic atmosphere overlooking the water.

## *Restaurant Kissing*

**CHEZ PANISSE, Berkeley**
**1517 Shattuck Avenue**
**(510) 548-5525**
Expensive

French restaurants are not always rated as romantic by the same standards we use for other restaurants. Granted, their lighting and mood are often right, but we expect more than linen tablecloths, French accents, fine china, and a Julia Child wannabe in the kitchen. Having explained all that, suffice it to say that Chez Panisse is as stellar a dining experience as any two hearts with gourmet appetites could want.

Many restaurant reviewers say that if you eat out only once in San Francisco, Chez Panisse should be the place—even though it just happens to be in Berkeley. Well, far be it from me to argue with the edible truth. If unsurpassed French cuisine is your idea of a fabulous romantic meal and you happen to be on the other side of the bridge (and you can get reservations), the food and atmosphere are indeed the best ever.

◆  **Romantic Warning:** Did I mention that you may have to book your reservations a month in advance, particularly if you want to dine on a weekend? Also, the staff tends to be a bit on the stuffy side—although they wouldn't call it stuffy, they'd call it professional. I suppose it depends on your point of view.

◆  **Romantic Option:** If you find there is no way you can get into Chez Panisse, you will not be disappointed if you try **RESTAURANT METROPOLE**, 2271 Shattuck Avenue, Berkeley, (510) 848-3080,

(Moderate). The Metropole has the warm ambience of a French country inn and the food is beautifully prepared. Fresh flowers grace the room; and a pianist plays classical music. This place is hard to pass up, even if you do get reservations for the above-mentioned culinary extravaganza.

**CUTTERS BAY HOUSE, Oakland**
**1 Franklin Street, Jack London Square**
**(510) 835-8600**
Moderate

*Call for directions.*

A veritable waterborne parade passed by on the estuary outside our window as we dined in this sunny lunch spot perched on the end of a wharf. Sailboats, tugs, motor yachts, even a seal drifted by while we enjoyed yakisoba noodles with grilled chicken. Both the menu and decor are ultra-modern and eclectic, a blend of East meets West meets Caribbean, cooked with flair in the exhibition kitchen.

◆   **Romantic Warning**: After dark, the loud music and singles atmosphere in the restaurant's swinging lounge seem to overwhelm the quiet waterfront ambience. I found it too distracting for a romantic dinner for two.

**IL PESCATORE, Oakland**
**57 Jack London Square**
**(510) 465-2188**
Moderate

*Call for directions.*

While the harbor lights wink on the water and marina yachts rock just outside the window, this Italian eatery serves up a touch of magic in the evenings. White linen cloths and crystal wine goblets add a whisper of elegance, while the friendly, down-to-earth service reaffirms that a waterfront restaurant should remain refreshingly unpretentious. The tender carpaccio (slices of raw beef served with sauce) proved the perfect start to our dinner. One creative pasta dish was topped with a scrumptious ground veal and prosciutto sauce. Calamari steak, salmon, and scallops are just a few of the seafood selections that tease your appetite for more waterfront romance.

## THE LOBBY, Oakland
**5612 College Avenue**
**(510) 547-9152**
Inexpensive

*From San Francisco, take the Bay Bridge east to Highway 24, then take the Claremont Avenue exit and cross over Claremont. Turn right onto Hudson and then left on College Avenue.*

In my well-researched opinion, a piano bar can put you in the mood for something more than just listening to music. Not that table-side swaying to the rhythms isn't rousing all by itself, but somehow, when all the right details are right, a visit to a piano bar such as The Lobby can be one of the best romantic escapades you'll ever have. This hideaway is filled with lots of Tiffany lamps, Victorian love seats, and, of course, a grand piano. Dulcet tunes and more boisterous sing-alongs offer a little something for every musical taste. It's the kind of place that puts the finishing touches on a night out on the town.

## SKATES ON THE BAY, Berkeley
**100 Seawall Drive at the University**
**(510) 549-1900**
Moderate

*From San Francisco take the Bay Bridge east and stay on Interstate 80 north to the University exit. Make a (legal) U-turn at the first stoplight and head back in the opposite direction. You will come to a fork in the road at the marina. Stay to your left, and where the road dead-ends, turn right into the restaurant's parking lot.*

San Francisco has one of the world's most stunning skylines. One way to really appreciate it is to go east and look back across the water, taking in the entire view. From Skates on the Bay, you can observe the city's dazzling profile, defined by the expansive blue bay and steep urban hills lined with steel-and-glass skyscrapers. Thank goodness the food is good and the interior is a respectable blend of modern and quaint. You'll be tempted to stay for dessert so you can linger over the city's lights and each other's company a little longer.

## Outdoor Kissing

### BERKELEY ROSE GARDEN, Berkeley

*From San Francisco, take the Bay Bridge east and stay on Interstate 80 going north. Take the University exit and turn right. Go straight to Shattuck Avenue and turn left. At Hearst Street, turn right. From here your last turn is a left onto Euclid, which you follow to the top of the hill.*

The Berkeley Rose Garden is an enchanting realm filled with color and fragrance. From its upper level, you can gaze over an amphitheater of nature's glory. As you make your way down the stairs, passing one rosebush after another, the sweet air rises to meet and surround you. This is prime kissing territory, acre after flawlessly beautiful acre. The sedate setting is so expansive that even when others are around, you can almost always find an empty bench waiting for just the two of you. Here you can sit very close together and spend a few moments (or hours) in a location that feels like paradise.

### LAKE MERRITT, Oakland

*From San Francisco, take the Bay Bridge to Highway 880 south, then take the Broadway exit east. From Broadway, turn right onto Grand, which eventually winds its way into the park.*

Ask anyone in the East Bay area if downtown Oakland has any amorous potential and you'll probably hear the same answer: "No!" During my research, one person said, "Oakland is a pit," a response that was brief but to the point. If you ask about Lake Merritt, however, people tend to whistle a different tune. Surrounded by 155-acre Lakeside Park, Lake Merritt is located in, yes, downtown Oakland. Its surprising setting is ideal for picnicking, strolling, canoeing, or any of myriad outdoor activities. When the leaves slowly change and frame the lake in vibrant shades of gold and orange, autumn is perhaps the best time to discover this city oasis.

Start an afternoon here with a picnic near the water, then try a sailing lesson or maybe take a tour on a miniature stern-wheeler. At **CHILDREN'S FAIRYLAND**, which attracts just as many adults as kids, puppet shows, a baby zoo, amusement rides, and scenes from your favorite fairy tales come alive and provide an ebullient diversion. Don't be too disappointed when you find the afternoon has slipped away while many sections of this domain remain unexplored. You'll have to return a few times to see it all, but that leaves you with something to look forward to next time you happen to be near downtown Oakland.

## TILDEN REGIONAL PARK, Berkeley Hills
## (510) 525-2233

*From Highway 24 east, exit at Claremont Avenue and turn left onto Claremont. Follow it all the way up to the top of the hill and turn left onto Grizzly Peak Boulevard. Look for entrance signs to Tilden on the right; several entrances are located along Grizzly Peak.*

Kissing amidst nature's majesty is always close at hand in the Bay Area. Tilden is one of the most expansive and convenient of the region's earthy getaways. It encompasses more than 2,000 acres of forested trails, gardens, picnic grounds, and fun family activities. A hand-in-hand stroll at the park's Botanic Garden is a fine first step to romance. Peaceful trails wind through terraced plantings of native California blooms and trees. Picnic spots abound throughout Tilden; just drive until you find one that suits your fancy. Ardent hikers will find private paradises along the park's paths, romantic respites from nearby civilization.

# Lafayette and Walnut Creek

## *Hotel/Bed and Breakfast Kissing*

**LAFAYETTE PARK HOTEL, Lafayette**
**3287 Mount Diablo Boulevard**
**(510) 283-3700, (800) 368-2468**
Moderate to Expensive

*From San Francisco take the Bay Bridge east to Highway 24, then take the Pleasant Hill Road exit to Mount Diablo Boulevard and turn right.*

From the freeway it looked like a Swiss chalet, which was impressive, but because it was visible from the freeway I was worried. After all, a love nest that borders a highway or a busy road is potentially a pigeonhole when it comes to romance. In this case, however, my skepticism was unfounded. The moment our weekend at Lafayette Park Hotel began, I forgot the freeway even existed.

High above the lobby, skylights illuminate a hand-carved staircase that winds its way down three stories. A profusion of fresh flowers brought soft color and life to the elegant decor. Our brightly appointed room had a vaulted ceiling and a wood-burning fireplace. We were thoroughly pleased. Exploring further, we found three charming court-yards: one built around an Italian marble fountain, another surrounding a stone wishing well, and the third with a large swimming pool and a whirlpool spa. Adjacent to the lobby is the **DUCK CLUB RESTAU-RANT**, offering an admirable dining experience. After dinner, a latte or cappuccino in the lounge, near the cobblestone fireplace, is a wonderful way to round out the evening.

**THE MANSION AT LAKEWOOD, Walnut Creek**
**1056 Hacienda Drive**
**(510) 946-9075**
Moderate to Very Expensive

*From Highway 680, exit at Ygnacio Valley Road. Continue through seven signals to turn right onto Homestead. About two blocks up, turn left onto Hacienda.*

I felt as though heaven awaited me when the grand, immaculately white wrought-iron gates opened majestically to allow passage into this mansion's inner sanctum. On the lawn, whimsical deer crafted of grapevines seemed real enough to raise their heads and watch as I made my way up the low-rise staircase to the front door. Inside, the dream continued in the grand Victorian parlor with its plush settee and side chairs before a wood-burning fireplace; an impressionistic portrait of the inn hangs above the mantel. Romantic details highlight the commodious guest rooms, from billowing canopies to intricate white brass beds, from private balconies to a cupid fresco. The Terrace Suite is warmed by a white brick hearth. The french doors of the Summer House open to a flowery porch where you can sink into a bubble bath in the claw-foot tub. In the irresistible Estate Suite, climb a small platform to reach the majestic four-poster bed with its bridal white comforter; the suite is warmed by a wood stove and has an immense bath with double whirlpools and fluted brass fixtures. Even the glasses are etched in delicate gold, just as your memories will be after dreaming here together.

# Restaurant Kissing

**TOURELLE'S, Lafayette**
**3565 Mount Diablo Boulevard**
**(510) 284-3565**
Moderate

*From San Francisco take the Bay Bridge east and turn onto Highway 24. Take the Central Lafayette exit and make a right at the end of the off-ramp, then another right onto Mount Diablo Boulevard.*

A stone path takes you past the garden to an ivy-covered tower and two brick homes that surround a charming courtyard with a pond at its center. Here is an engaging place for lunch on a warm, leisurely afternoon. On one side of the courtyard is an informal bistro with a big, open kitchen; on the other is a beautiful dining room with towering vaulted ceilings, brick walls, and delectable French food. Dining at Tourelle's can make you feel as if you are in the south of France, a terrific feeling to share with someone special.

**LE VIRAGE, Walnut Creek**
**2211 North Main Street**
**(510) 933-8484**
Expensive

*From San Francisco take the Bay Bridge east, turn onto Highway 24, and take Highway 680 north. Take the North Main Street exit and turn left. The restaurant is a few blocks ahead on your left.*

Driving down the streets of Walnut Creek, you may be surprised to find a charming little farmhouse at *le virage* ("a bend in the road"). Surrounded by glass and cement, this oasis is a startling contrast to its many officious neighbors. Le Virage serves excellent continental cuisine in a setting that whisks you away from modern-day business life and its hectic pace. The mood is one of nostalgic, unhurried romance.

◆ **Romantic Option: MAXIMILLIAN'S**, 1604 Locust Street, Walnut Creek, (510) 932-1474, (Moderate to Expensive), has two dining rooms, each sporting its own menu and decor. Upstairs, oak paneling and bricks blend to create a handsome, formal atmosphere for classic continental dinners. The downstairs, done in softer shades of dusty rose and mint green, offers contemporary California nouvelle cuisine. Both are congenial spots for an evening interlude.

# SOUTH OF SAN FRANCISCO

## Woodside

### *Restaurant Kissing*

**BELLA VISTA, Woodside**
13451 Skyline Boulevard
**(415) 851-1229**
Moderate to Expensive

*From Highway 101 or Interstate 280, take Highway 92 west to Skyline Boulevard. Turn left and follow the road about five miles to the restaurant, which is on your left.*

Bella Vista is rustic on the outside and perhaps a bit too formal on the inside, but an abundance of floor-to-ceiling windows helps to create an environment that blends refreshingly with the expansive wooded exterior. The view seems to go on and on, with a rolling procession of redwood trees ending at the blue outline of the bay. It is best to plan an evening here to take full advantage of all that this location has to offer. Arrive before sunset so you can have dinner while darkness begins to veil the area in velvety black. If you've timed things just right, dessert will be served as the lights of the towns below begin to twinkle in the distance.

## Outdoor Kissing

**FILOLI GARDENS AND ESTATE, Woodside**
**Canada Road**
**(415) 364-2880**
$8 per person

*Filoli Gardens is about 25 miles south of San Francisco. From Interstate 280, take the Edgewood Road exit west, then turn right onto Canada Road and drive 1.2 miles to the entrance.*

This magnificent garden evokes passion in all who visit. Its sheer beauty reminds us that life is precious and ever so special when shared with the one we love. The gardens are laid out in a sumptuous Italian-French design, with parterres, terraces, lawns, and pools forming a succession of garden rooms. More than 20,000 plants are added annually to ensure year-round splendor. The Chartres Cathedral Garden recreates a stained glass window with roses and boxwood hedges; the Woodland Garden is Eden revisited. The wisteria-draped mansion is akin to a European summer palace. Original furnishings and items from the Getty and de Young museums recall an era of grand luxury. If you feel a sense of deja vu, it may be because you have seen Filoli portraying the classy Carrington estate on television's *Dynasty*, or perhaps you kissed here in your most pleasant dreams.

◆    **Romantic Note:** Filoli is one of California's best-loved gardens. Reservations should be made as far in advance as possible.

# Campbell

## Restaurant Kissing

**CAMPBELL HOUSE, Campbell**
**106 East Campbell Avenue**
**(408) 374-5757**
Moderate to Expensive

*Call for directions.*

This cozy restaurant provides a homey atmosphere, attentive service, and delicious food, all in just the right proportions. Located in a 60-year-old home adorned with a lovely fireplace, a sun porch, and only 12 very intimate tables, it is a pretty setting for a leisurely, intimate meal. Lunch is served Tuesday through Friday, and dinner is served Tuesday through Sunday. Campbell House is considered one of the better restaurants in the South Bay area; even if you don't want to kiss, the atmosphere and dining pleasures will help change your mood to a more amorous one.

# San Jose

## *Restaurant Kissing*

**LA FORET, San Jose**
**21747 Bertram Road**
**(408) 997-3458**
Moderate to Expensive

*From Highway 101, take the Capitol Expressway to the Almaden Expressway and head south until you reach Almaden Road. Turn right and watch for the La Foret sign on the left.*

Just a short drive away from the high-tech world this area is famous for, La Foret is known as one of the prettiest restaurants in the South Bay. Located in the historic village of New Almaden, the restaurant sits next to a brook in what was the first two-story adobe hotel in California. The original wood paneling frames sizable windows that look out onto a wooded landscape. The French food is very good and the service outstanding. Soft candlelight will cast a gentle glow on the interior as you lovingly share your evening here.

# Saratoga

Our weekend in Saratoga began with a visually stirring yet relaxing drive on a Sunday morning in early spring. A typical San Francisco fog shrouded us for about two-thirds of the way, but in the distance we could see that sultry sunshine would greet our arrival.

Everything about Saratoga was picture-perfect: the surrounding forest and parkland, the tall shade trees lining residential streets where much pride seems to be taken in well-tended gardens and homes, and the Victorian storefronts in the tradition of country shopping. The main street, Big Basin Way, is best described as petite, but we still had no trouble finding a fair number of award-winning restaurants that scored as high on the kissing-rating scale as they did on the culinary one. Saratoga has more then enough to fill a superlative afternoon or weekend interlude.

◆    **Romantic Warning:** Due to the growing popularity of the Paul Masson concert season, there are times when Big Basin Way is a traffic bottleneck the likes of which are not supposed to happen outside the city. (At least not when I'm there.) Keep your schedule loose if you happen to be here at the end of a concert. Simply park your car and have a snack or cappuccino at any of the dining spots along Basin Way.

## Hotel/Bed and Breakfast Kissing

**THE INN AT SARATOGA,** Saratoga
**20645 Fourth Street**
**(408) 867-5020**
Expensive to Unbelievably Expensive

*One block north of Big Basin Way on Fourth Street.*

If the idea of a bed and breakfast strikes you as a little too casual or informal, The Inn at Saratoga is much slicker than that. Or if a hotel seems too cold and practical, this inn is much warmer than that. It has the best of what makes some hotels distinctive and most bed and breakfasts quaint and cozy, with attractive, bright suites that have all the amenities seasoned travelers require and romantics yearn for. For the purposes of this book, one of the most appealing details here is the balcony that comes with each room. These private viewpoints face a small forest of sycamore, maple, and eucalyptus trees, with a creek flowing through the center, butterflies breezing by, and birds serenading you with melodic songs. As you stand on your balcony watching the sunlight flirt through the branches and pinery, it is impossible not to feel the glory of a summer or autumn day. Imagine what a composed setting like this can do for those in need of heartfelt moments alone!

## *Restaurant Kissing*

**BELLA MIA, Saratoga**
**14503 Big Basin Way**
**(408) 741-5115**
Inexpensive to Moderate

*Two blocks west of Sunnyvale-Saratoga Road on Big Basin Way.*

A gentle breeze swirled across the porch at Bella Mia, brushing our cheeks with cooling relief from the intense sun overhead. The air rustled the leaves that shade the table-clad deck where couples sat and dined on designer cuisine, sipping steamy cups of espresso and sharing decadent-looking desserts. This historic Victorian mansion has been beautifully renovated, which makes the ambience inside and out notably romantic.

I strongly recommend the salmon ravioli, with its ever-so-smooth and creamy sauce, while my partner insists the lasagne he so stubbornly refused to share is the best he ever had. After a few cajoling remarks he eventually gave in and let me have a savory, cheesy taste. My only regret after leaving Bella Mia was that I had not insisted on having a few additional nibbles of his lasagne. Looking forward to the remainder of the evening, I restrained my interest in what was on his plate and concentrated on him and the atmosphere we were sharing.

## LA MERE MICHELLE, Saratoga
**14467 Big Basin Way**
**(408) 867-5272**
Moderate to Expensive

*One block west of Sunnyvale-Saratoga Road on Big Basin Way.*

When making reservations at La Mere Michelle, which you absolutely must do if you want to dine here, you will also have to make a delicate romantic choice: do you want to eat indoors or outdoors? Inside you will find a refined restaurant, highlighted by crystal chandeliers, fine art, and mirrored walls. Outside is an entirely different atmosphere that is equally enticing. The wooden deck is encircled by a short brick wall blooming with periwinkle blue flowers. Candles softly light the patio, which is decorated with blue-and-white accents. Whichever you choose, you won't be disappointed, because the food will be traditionally French, and the enchanting atmosphere will be right for an evening of conversation and looking deep into one another's eyes.

## LE MOUTON NOIR, Saratoga
**14560 Big Basin Way**
**(408) 867-7017**
Moderate

*On Big Basin Way, between Fourth and Fifth.*

Le Mouton Noir is anything but "the black sheep" of Saratoga's restaurant row. The decor, a combination of pink and dusty rose paisley and Laura Ashley prints, gives a light and airy country feel to this classic Victorian dining room. French-inspired California cuisine is served with care, and the food is delectable. Whether you have lunch here, with sunlight streaming through the many windows, or bask in the glow of a lovely candlelight dinner, Le Mouton Noir is a delightful discovery for two hearts desiring to feast on fine food and romance.

## THE PLUMED HORSE, Saratoga
## 14555 Big Basin Way
## (408) 867-4711
Expensive

*On Big Basin Way, between Fourth and Fifth.*

Only dinner is served in this extremely romantic location. Inside, you'll find a series of exquisite dining rooms, each with a personality all its own. One is outfitted with Victorian antiques and opulent, red velvet furniture, another has weathered wood walls encircled by stained glass windows. The fine French food is rarely disappointing. Venison, pheasant, quail, and delectable fresh fish are often on the menu. Afterwards, you can go dancing in the Crazy Horse Saloon next door.

# Outdoor Kissing

## HAKONE JAPANESE GARDEN, Saratoga
## 21000 Big Basin Way
## (408) 867-3438

*Take Big Basin Way through town; about a mile up the road you will see a turnoff sign on the left side of the street.*

We missed it the first time we visited Saratoga, but after several friends who had been there admonished us for not checking out the Hakone Garden, we returned for what they said would be an unbelievable outing. We searched valiantly for the turnoff sign. Finally we saw it and followed it to one of the most serene settings I've ever seen, a horticultural utopia, pure and simple and sublime.

Righteous redwood trees stretched to the sky, sheltering a sculptured landscape of exquisite flora and fauna. In the center of the garden is a blue pond where sleepy carp, a Japanese symbol of love and longevity, languish in the still water, white water lilies float effortlessly over the surface, and a cascading waterfall fills the air with mild, tranquilizing music. The garden is edged with wood-fenced walkways adorned by delicate, sweet-smelling flowers. The contemplative mood of the area makes it prime territory for a walk with the one you love.

◆    **Romantic Note:** Food is not allowed in the garden, so a picnic is out. But if you truly want to experience the flavor of this exotic place, authentic Japanese tea ceremonies are performed on weekends. Reservations are required, so call ahead if you want to be served.

### MOUNTAIN WINERY, Saratoga
### 14831 Pierce Road at Highway 9
### (408) 741-5181

*From Big Basin Way turn left onto Pierce Road and follow the signs to the main gate.*

Spread above the idyllic town of Saratoga, up a steep and winding country road, the Paul Masson Vineyards cover some of the most august, sun-drenched earth in the entire South Bay. Everything here seems almost too picture-perfect. Graceful trees rustle in the soft, billowing breezes. Grapevines arc across the mountainside, disappearing from sight as the land curves to meet hill after hill. The panoramic view is a joy to behold day or night. Perhaps the only flaw in this majestic setting is that the Paul Masson Vineyards are not open to the public except during special events. Then again, for most of the spring, summer, and part of fall, that's not a problem. Every year, the winery presents a spectacular summer concert series featuring entertainers who appeal to almost every audience. Past concerts have showcased the soulful sounds of Ray Charles, classy jazz vocals from the legendary Ella Fitzgerald, the country-influenced stylings of Ricky Skaggs, and the soothing instrumentals of the talented Kenny G. Regardless of what you choose to hear, there is something miraculous about listening to music in the mountains with a clear sky and the sweeping countryside as the only backdrop.

◆    **Romantic Warning:** On a summer day, sitting in an unshaded spot can be a melting proposition. Try to find protected seats or bring a sun visor, sunglasses, and towels. On the other hand, at night the mountain breezes can be cooler than you might expect. An extra sweater will keep shivers at a minimum.

# SOUTH COAST

## Moss Beach

### Hotel/Bed and Breakfast Kissing

**SEAL COVE INN, Moss Beach**
221 Cypress Avenue
(415) 728-4114
Expensive to Very Expensive

*Call for directions.*

All the nuances are here for an enamored escape from city life, only 25 minutes away from San Francisco. Seal Cove Inn's adobe-colored stucco exterior with green trim is very attractive. Inside everything is first-class and immaculate. Each room has its own fireplace with a nearby sitting area, private deck or terrace, step-up four poster bed, TV with VCR, and plenty of space; two of the rooms have Jacuzzis. The decor and furnishings are simple yet comfortable. Full breakfast in the morning may include cinnamon French toast and fresh pastries, and complimentary wine is to be found in your room when you arrive.

◆ **Romantic Suggestion:** Unlike Half Moon Bay, Moss Beach is in a small neighborhood setting, minus the development. Just around the corner from the inn, explore the fascinating natural tidal pools at **FITZGERALD MARINE RESERVE.** Diminutive **MOSS BEACH** is the perfect place to observe the sun's nightly glissade into the ocean. My only hesitation in recommending Seal Cove Inn is that the rooms are a bit formal and there is a conference room next to the dining room. The "corporate retreat" feel here is great for executives, but for the purposes of this book a little cozier would be nicer. However, other than that you won't be disappointed with your stay at this beautiful getaway.

# Princeton-by-the-Sea

## Hotel/Bed and Breakfast Kissing

PILLAR POINT INN, Princeton-by-the-Sea                ◆◆
380 Capistrano Road
(415) 728-7377
Moderate to Expensive

*Head south of San Francisco, on Highway 1. In about 25 miles, turn right off Highway 1 at the traffic light for Capistrano at Princeton-by-the-Sea. Then turn right, toward the harbor down by the water. The inn will be on your right.*

A short 25-mile journey south of San Francisco will place you at the front door of a seaside lodging where you can immerse yourselves in quiet, carefree time together. The 11-room inn is not quite a bed and breakfast, and it is not a typical hotel either. Pillar Point Inn looks like a New England-style home. In every room you can sit back and evaluate the profile of the harbor, ocean, and coastline, leisurely reviewing the movement around you. The boats anchored close to shore will rock in rhythm with the waves, and the fishing boats will come and go, increasing your expectations of a fresh fish dinner. Accompanying this tableau are a fireplace, downy European featherbed, private steam bath, and, if you prefer, breakfast in bed. New England was never this warm or this close to San Francisco—till now, that is.

Breakfast in the morning is a delicious combination of homemade granola, fresh muffins, coffee cake, waffles, and egg dishes. There are two fireplaces in the bar and one in the dining room, which makes your morning meal even more satisfying.

◆ **Romantic Note:** For a momentary change of pace from the solitude of Pillar Point Inn, be sure to stop across the street at **THE**

**SHORE BIRD RESTAURANT**, 390 Capistrano Road, Princeton-by-the-Sea, (415) 728-5541, (Moderate). The building closely resembles a Cape Cod-style cottage and is surrounded by cypress trees and a flower garden. Inside, the rustic furnishings and low ceilings create a friendly, easygoing environment in which to enjoy locally caught fresh fish. Outdoor dining in the garden, with the ocean as backdrop, is also an option these days. Romancing may not be the primary reason to visit The Shore Bird, but the food and relaxed pace certainly are something you can get accustomed to.

# Miramar

## Hotel/Bed and Breakfast Kissing

**CYPRESS INN, Miramar**
**407 Mirada Road**
**(415) 725-6002, (800) 83-BEACH**
Expensive to Very Expensive

*From Highway 1, 26 miles south of San Francisco, turn right onto Medio Avenue and then north onto Mirada Road.*

This newly built contemporary structure sits on five miles of dreamy, white sand beaches. Every room is endowed with a seductive seaside view, fireplace, private deck with louvered doors, and down comforters. Some have generous sitting rooms and one has a Jacuzzi. The emphasis here is on beachside living—a few steps from the front door is the boundless blue Pacific Ocean. Extended walks along the shore here will happily influence your feelings and desires. The only sound you will hear, besides your own voices, will be the roar of the waves rolling onto the shore.

In the morning, breakfast on an unforgettable cornucopia of gourmet delights, such as peaches-and-cream french toast, a roasted-red-peppers-and-Brie omelet, or crab crepes. Lunch and dinner are available on request, and it is well worth your while to do so: the presentation and preparation are lavish. At night, when you retire to your lavish room, with the fireplace glowing against the darkness and the sound of the surf caressing the air, you will have a perfect prelude to time together.

# Half Moon Bay

## Hotel/Bed and Breakfast Kissing

MILL ROSE INN, Half Moon Bay
615 Mill Street
(415) 726-9794
Expensive to Very Expensive

*Two blocks west of Main Street, at the corner of Mill and Church.*

From the moment we saw it, we knew Mill Rose Inn would be an affectionate place for a not-so-out-of-town sojourn. We entered through a classic white picket fence that wrapped around a slightly overgrown garden bursting with a beaming array of color. Sleeping in the sun on the front porch was the inn's cat, who conveyed the notion that here was a carefree, easy place. Here we could soothe our frazzled city nerves and find serenity and quiet.

There are seven suites in this spacious home, and each is subtly different. Two of my favorite rooms are the Briar Rose and the Bordeaux Rose. The snug and homey Briar Rose has a hand-painted tile fireplace, a large bay window big enough for two, and an ample bathtub (also big enough for two). The Bordeaux Rose is intimate and inviting: shades of peach and ivory accent a lace-covered canopied bed framed by a hand-sculpted stained glass window. If you get tired of your room, which hardly seems possible, visit the flower-shielded gazebo that encloses a Jacuzzi spa. Don't worry about finding a crowd in the spa—you can reserve time here for a private, hot steamy soak of your own. After a good night's sleep, enjoy a champagne breakfast in the dining room or, if you prefer, have it delivered to your suite. I think that last option is definitely preferable.

## OLD THYME INN, Half Moon Bay
### 779 Main Street
### (415) 726-1616
Very Inexpensive to Moderate

*Four blocks east of Highway 1 in Half Moon Bay.*

Sometimes "cute" can spark even the most skeptical among us to expose our amorous, snuggly side; at other times it can do just the opposite. The Old Thyme Inn is careful to make sure its cute touches are only warmhearted, not trite or corny. The well-behaved puppy looking up at me with eyes pleading for attention, and the stuffed animals in every room captured my heart. This handsomely renovated home, built in 1899, packed with a sense of history, feels warm and affable. The seven rooms are simple, but each is outfitted with something distinctive that makes it welcoming and delightful: a fireplace, a four-poster bed, a whirlpool bath built for two, or a stained glass window, for example. The Garden Suite is by far the most romantic room. It has a private entrance, a double Jacuzzi tub under a large skylight, vaulted ceilings, and breakfast brought to your room at your leisure.

In the evening, wine and sherry are served around a wood-burning stove in the parlor. Breakfast in the morning is always a plentiful offering of fresh scones, muffins, quiches, and fresh fruits. The garnishes are all from the inn's overproductive herb garden, which contains more than 80 aromatic varieties, all available for tasting by inquisitive guests. This may not be the most luxurious place you'll ever stay, but it could be one of the more interesting.

## *Restaurant Kissing*

### SAN BENITO HOUSE, Half Moon Bay
### 356 Main Street
### (415) 726-3425
Very Inexpensive to Moderate

*Three blocks south of Highway 92, at the corner of Main and Mill.*

The aroma of freshly baked bread caught my attention as I happened past the San Benito House Restaurant one extremely lazy, sun-drenched summer afternoon. Unfortunately, it was not open for lunch that day. I continued on, but found nothing else particularly interesting. As the day progressed, that tempting fragrance lingered in my memory and I couldn't resist the idea of returning for dinner. We called for reservations and went that same evening.

This French country dining room is adorned with a fanciful blend of dried and fresh flowers, wicker baskets, and original oil paintings. The impression is one of charming sophistication. Guests who know the restaurant call first to see what the chef has prepared for dinner. The prix fixe meal consists of several courses and a choice of three entrees. Almost always, fresh fish brought in by local fishermen and fresh produce from local farmers are included. Our dinner that evening was delicious, the service professional and helpful, and the homemade bread tasted as good as I thought it would.

◆    **Romantic Warning**: The hotel attached to San Benito House is not as expensive as some of the other places to stay in Half Moon Bay, but be forewarned: it is not anywhere near as nice, either.

# Outdoor Kissing

## HALF MOON BAY COASTLINE
*Take Highway 1 or Highway 280 south from San Francisco, and then Highway 92 into town.*

When the rest of the world is heading north of San Francisco to Stinson Beach and other points along the exquisite Marin County and Mendocino County coastlines, you can be winding your way south to Half Moon Bay. This quintessentially quaint little hamlet by the water feels literally a hundred miles away from big-city life (it's actually about 25 miles from San Francisco) and, in comparison to its northern counterparts, is relatively unpopulated.

Half Moon Bay lovingly hugs the seaside along the rocky Pacific Coast Highway. It is replete with miles of sandy beaches, equestrian trails, and bicycle paths; adventurers can arrange fishing charters, sailing sessions, and whale-watching expeditions. Combine all of that with epic scenery and, believe me, it is difficult to find a place that isn't suitable for hugging and kissing. Local wineries, charming little lunch spots, and plenty of parks will help round out your day. At night, visit one of the restaurants serving up an eclectic assortment of cuisines, or a club featuring classical and jazz music. Both can keep you busy well into the wee hours of morning, unless, of course, you can find something better to do.

# Santa Cruz

## Hotel/Bed and Breakfast Kissing

**BABBLING BROOK INN, Santa Cruz**
**1025 Laurel Street**
**(408) 427-2437**
Moderate

*From Highway 1 head west on Laurel Street to the inn.*

If you could transport the Babbling Brook Inn to a quiet neighborhood or a wide stretch of beach, it would be superb. Unfortunately, it is located on a busy, rather noisy street. Nevertheless, the setting will help you ignore the traffic, because an acre of redwoods, pines, flowered gardens, tumbling waterfalls, a graceful babbling brook, and covered footbridges highlights this delightful bed and breakfast. The landscaping is impeccable from every perspective. Inside, a French country atmosphere is evident throughout the guest rooms and cottages. There are 12 units here, some with private entrances, private decks, fireplaces, Jacuzzi bathtubs, and sturdy canopied beds. A short stroll away are the beaches and sparkling waters of the Pacific Ocean. In the early evening, after a long day of building sand castles, you will find wine and cheese waiting for you. In the morning, a generous country breakfast will give your day a good start.

## Restaurant Kissing

### CASA BLANCA INN RESTAURANT, Santa Cruz
**101 Main Street**
**(408) 426-9063**
Moderate

*Take Highway 1 to Bay Street, proceed to West Cliff Street, and turn left. Drive half a block to Beach Street and turn right. The inn is at the corner of Main and Beach, a half block east of the Santa Cruz Wharf.*

If you're looking for a restaurant with a view, you need look no further. This renovated 1918 mansion is directly across the street from the beach, and the dining room's tall, stately windows overlook this wonderful sight. You'll glimpse boats rocking on the bay and the surf rolling onto the shore. Just beyond, the wooden pier seems to change moods as the sun sets and the lampposts begin to brighten the scene. The interior feels like a small country inn, and the menu offers classic continental steak and seafood dishes. A wonderful brunch is served on Sundays, and dinner is served nightly. After an enjoyable meal, don't be surprised if the one you're with reaches for your hand and says something like "I think this is the beginning of a beautiful friendship."

◆ **Romantic Note:** Attached to the restaurant is the **CASA BLANCA MOTEL**, (Inexpensive to Expensive). The 27 rooms here are spacious and attractive. Most rooms have spectacular views of the water and boardwalk, many have their own private deck, and some have a fireplace. Rooms 18, 19, and 22 have more privacy than the others (meaning no view of the boardwalk) and are cozier and more romantic. The other rooms are also quite nice, but if you look past the boardwalk and focus your attention on the Pacific Ocean in all its endless blue glory, your stay will be more mellow and intimate.

## Outdoor Kissing

**NATURAL BRIDGES STATE PARK, Santa Cruz**
**West Cliff Drive**
**(408) 423-4609**
$6 per day per car

*From the Santa Cruz boardwalk, follow West Cliff Drive north along the shore to the park entrance.*

Once upon a time, a beautiful orange and black monarch butterfly came to court in a wooded canyon near the seashore. Before long, other wooing butterflies discovered this lovers' lure. Today, hundreds of thousands of monarchs return to this spot each winter, creating a kaleidoscope of color among the sweet-scented eucalyptus. The two of you can stroll hand-in-hand into this storybook setting along a wooden walkway that leads down into the woods to a platform nested in the monarchs' winter home. The best time to visit is midday, when the butterflies are most active and flit about as you kiss. Or you can simply lie on the platform and watch them flutter above you like so many stars touched with life. The beach and tide pools nearby welcome additional kissing before you reach the ocean.

# Aptos, Soquel, and Capitola

Capitola has been described as "what Carmel was like 30 years ago." This quaint seaside hamlet has just enough handicraft stores and clothing boutiques to make it interesting, but not enough to steal an entire afternoon away from kissing to the melody of the Pacific surf. Though it is farther north than its affluent seaside neighbor, Carmel, Capitola has a decidedly Southern California feel. Brightly clad surfers skim through the waves, students from the nearby college play beach games, and couples picnic on the sand. A promenade stretches along the shore, and the view stretches even farther north and south along the coastline. Benches face out over the ocean, so you can sit, embrace, and daydream.

# Hotel/Bed and Breakfast Kissing

**BLUE SPRUCE INN, Soquel**
**2815 South Main Street**
**(408) 464-1137**
Inexpensive to Moderate

*From Highway 1 take the Capitola/Soquel exit, go east to the first stop sign,*
*and turn right onto South Main Street.*

With the nearby Pacific as inspiration, it's no wonder that the Blue
Spruce Inn indulges its guests with a Jacuzzi built for two, a four-jetted
massage shower, or a shower that couples can't resist getting wet in
together—in addition to the hot tub in the garden. Even with these
luxuries, this renovated 120-year-old home is as fresh and unpretentious
as a sea breeze. The colorful Amish quilts that warm each bed are the
focal point of each guest room's decor. The innkeepers commissioned
local artists to echo the hues and motifs of the quilts in the paintings
adorning each room. A private entrance opens to Seascape, with its
ocean blues and greens, wicker chairs, featherbed, gas stove, and bow-
shaped double Jacuzzi. Two Hearts is a cozy hideaway with a deep red
heart-motif quilt, touches of white eyelet, dormer ceilings, and a full-
body shower. In the Carriage House, skylights just above the headboard
of the raised bed invite kissing beneath the stars.

**INN AT DEPOT HILL, Capitola**
**250 Monterey Avenue**
**(408) 462-3376**
Expensive to Unbelievably Expensive

*From Highway 1, take the Capitola/Soquel exit to Bay Avenue and turn*
*toward the ocean. Bay becomes Monterey Avenue. The inn is two blocks up*
*from the ocean and the town center.*

If ever an inn deserves to enter the annals of romance, this one does.
I wish I could extend my kiss rating, because it would surely rate 10 lips.
Opulently decorated rooms evoke the world's most romantic destina-

tions. Imagine kissing your love in a Parisian pied-a-terre, a Mediterranean retreat on the Cote d'Azur, an English cottage in Stratford-on-Avon, or an Italian coastal villa in Portofino: the guest rooms truly do reflect the visual essence of these locales.

All the spacious rooms have unbelievably luxurious furnishings, private marble baths, wood-burning fireplaces, stereo systems, televisions with VCRs (concealed unobtrusively in cabinets), coffee makers, hair dryers, fabric steamers, and fresh flowers to match the decor. Five have private Jacuzzis. Cuddle with your love before the blue-and-white Dutch tile hearth in the Delft Room; or embrace beneath the full, white linen-and-lace canopy on the billowing featherbed; or daydream on the window seat while gazing upon your private garden; or indulge in a private whirlpool surrounded by tulips; or splash together in a double-headed shower—and this is just one room! Each room description could fill a book, and we haven't even told you about the private red-brick patios with their own gazebos. Full breakfasts, afternoon wine with appetizers, and evening desserts ensure energy for continuous kissing, because if you can't kiss here, you can't kiss anywhere.

**MANGELS HOUSE, Aptos**
**570 Aptos Creek Road**
**(408) 688-7982**
Moderate

*Call for directions.*

During the Victorian heyday, the elite vacationed in fabulous country homes, far from the cares of the city but complete with all the luxuries. The Mangels House, built in the 1880s by California's sugar beet king, is one of the most secluded and best restored of these homes. To reach it, you must drive (carefully!) down a one-lane, woodland road. Just when you would expect to see a rustic campground, this whitewashed mansion with a wraparound veranda looms above the forest. Enter the door to a ballroom-size parlor, where the grand piano seems dwarfed. Comfortable, contemporary sofas are clustered around the massive stone fireplace. The recently redecorated guest rooms preserve the feeling of spaciousness. Delicate color schemes and lush florals reflect today's luxury in the grand tradition. The Jungle Room is decidedly different, with dark furnishings and animal prints. Right outside the door are some of the area's best hiking trails, perfect for an afternoon stroll back to nature.

◆    **Romantic Alternative**: If you're looking for something more old-fashioned than elaborate, **THE APPLE LANE INN**, 6265 Soquel Drive, Aptos, (408) 475-6868, (Inexpensive to Moderate), is a charming 1870s Victorian farmhouse perched on a knoll overlooking orchards. A fire warms the Victorian parlor, the breakfasts will content hearty gourmets, and guest rooms are pleasantly decorated with antiques. The dormer ceilings may cramp the style of taller kissers.

## Restaurant Kissing

### CAFFE LIDO BAR AND RISTORANTE, Capitola
**110 Monterey Avenue**
**(408) 475-6544**
Moderate

*From Highway 1 take the Capitola/Soquel exit to Bay Avenue toward the ocean. Bay becomes Monterey Avenue. The restaurant is the last building on your left before the beach.*

Somebody had actually left a kiss mark on the window near my table at the Caffe Lido. This contemporary Italian cafe is *perfetto* for fun romance and good food topped off with special liqueur-laced coffees. Classic Italian music and opera set the mood. In the afternoon, as the sun pours in, you can gaze out over the beach and watch couples strolling by, monarch butterflies flitting on the bushes, and surfers searching for the endless summer (it's right here!). Pasta with seafood, grilled Mediterranean chicken dishes, and hearty coppa or prosciutto sandwiches with cheese will delight the palate. Lunch and dinner are served daily.

## CHEZ RENEE, Aptos
9051 Soquel Drive
(408) 688-5566
Expensive

Chez Renee is synonymous with exquisite dining in the Santa Cruz area. This cozy, unpretentious little restaurant, situated off a small business area, serves traditional and not-so-traditional French cuisine. The award-winning dining you will find here is a very serious affair for your palate, but never let it be said that French chefs don't have a sense of humor. The night we were there, we had the "Maui Wowee" entree: pan-grilled fresh Hawaiian ono, served with pineapple salsa and macadamia nuts. It was excellent.

## COUNTRY COURT TEA ROOM, Capitola
911-B Capitola Avenue
(408) 462-2498
Inexpensive

*On Capitola Avenue, just off Soquel Drive.*

A restaurant that specializes in fireside breakfasts and authentic English-style high teas may seem out-of-place on a busy surburban street, but here it is and it is charming. The interior is simple, with only a handful of tables (the ones near the fireplace are the most desirable). The food is excellent. Due to pressure from loyal fans, the chef offers a Friday-night dinner with a choice of two main courses. When we were there the ambrosial entrees were lamb stuffed with feta and pesto and salmon perfectly broiled in lemon butter. I don't think the English ever had it this good.

## FIORELLA'S, Capitola
911 Capitola Avenue
(408) 479-9826
Moderate

*On Capitola Avenue just off Soquel Drive, behind the Country Cottage Inn.*

The location, next to an apartment complex, is a bit peculiar for a romantic spot; nevertheless Fiorella's is an enchanting place. Subtle and refined, small and intimate—all the right ingredients combine to create an attractive setting for dinner. And speaking of ingredients, the food is absolutely delicious. The pasta dishes are beautifully presented, and the service is polite but casual. Weather permitting, there is garden seating outside in a pretty courtyard. By the way, on your way in, be sure to notice the reproduction of the Sistine Chapel's ceiling on the wall in the bar. It was painted by a local high-school boy and is an amazing facsimile.

### SHADOWBROOK, Capitola

**1750 Wharf Road**
**(408) 475-1511**
Moderate

*Four miles south of Santa Cruz on Highway 1, take the 41st Street exit and head west. In a half mile, turn left on Capitola Road. Proceed a half mile to Wharf Road and turn left to the restaurant.*

Shadowbrook is probably the most often recommended romantic restaurant in the Santa Cruz area. Access to this unique dining room located on the banks of the Soquel River is gained via a winding footpath or a little red cable car that creaks over its tracks to a stop by the bar. Covered by dense, lush foliage, this Swiss-style chalet has a storybook appearance that is totally enchanting. Dinner is served seven nights a week, lunch on Saturday and Sunday only. The traditional California cuisine is usually quite good, especially if you order what's fresh. The cocktail lounge is a particularly romantic destination, and worth a visit for a quiet after-dinner tete-a-tete.

◆ **Romantic Suggestion:** GREENHOUSE, 5555 Soquel Drive, Soquel, (408) 476-5613, (Inexpensive to Moderate), offers a garden setting for lunch or dinner. You can choose between dining in the atrium next to a glowing fireplace or on the wooden deck surrounded by knotty oak trees or in the dining room of the original farmhouse. The only drawback to romance is the family atmosphere, but if you focus on the farm setting and each other, no one else will exist but the two of you.

THE VERANDA, Aptos
8041 Soquel Drive
(408) 685-1881
Expensive

*From Highway 1 South: Take the Seacliff Beach exit. Turn left over the freeway to the first light (Soquel Drive). Turn right onto Soquel; The Veranda is about a half mile down on the left. From Highway 1 North: Take the Rio del Mar exit. Turn right, then left onto Soquel Drive. The Veranda is about a half mile down on the right.*

You may be surprised to find a grand Victorian hotel in the little town of Aptos. You'll be even more pleasantly surprised at the elegant restaurant that adorns its first floor. Its series of spacious dining rooms are decorated in delicate peach and accented with dried flower wreaths. Creative American dishes with a gourmet twist are the house specialty. Try the salmon cooked in a mustard-herb crust, or the filet mignon in a Roquefort-pecan crust with a Kentucky bourbon demi-glace. Pick a table on the glass-enclosed veranda and hold hands across the table on a sunny afternoon. In the evening, one dining room glows with the warmth of an old Victorian hearth.

◆ **Romantic Note: THE BAYVIEW HOTEL**, 8041 Soquel Drive, Aptos, (408) 688-8654, (Inexpensive to Expensive), offers charming bed-and-breakfast accommodations upstairs from The Veranda. High ceilings, antiques, and rich florals add a touch of romance, but the rooms are on the cozy side, as the hotel was built in 1878. The small parlor downstairs, with velvet furnishings and a Victorian gas hearth, is for guests, but shares the same entrance as the restaurant.

◆ **Romantic Alternative:** Across the street from The Bayview Hotel is a small, appealing restaurant called **CAFE SPARROW**, 8042 Soquel Drive, Aptos, (408) 688-6238, (Inexpensive to Moderate). For lunch and dinner, you will be served savory traditional country French cuisine with a flair you would expect to find in a more sophisticated setting. But the casual ambience is more than appropriate. This kind of romantic dining can be cherished without any affectation. Breakfast (weekends only) is also very French and superb. Try the omelet with sauteed chicken livers, served with smoked bacon, apples, and creme fraiche.

# Monterey

Monterey was once a part of Mexico, and that heritage is reflected in its venerable adobe homes and the meticulously maintained parks bursting with flowers. Many of the surviving historical landmarks now house museums, and you can almost touch the past as you stroll by them. The main signatures of this well-known romantic destination are the cypress forests, rolling hills, and spectacular rugged coastline. Because of Monterey's position at the edge of the Pacific, it offers those who stop here some of the same nuances that a small (relatively crowded) waterfront town would supply; almost everything you'll want to see and do is within walking distance. There are intriguing restaurants and hotels that take full advantage of the almost year-round mild weather, and many are blessed with bewitching views of the clear aqua bay and vivid blue sky. Of course, there are also the concomitant tourist attractions, such as Fisherman's Wharf, Cannery Row, and the Monterey Bay Aquarium, which means Monterey can also be dreadfully crowded. Fortunately, that can easily be dealt with by allowing yourselves to concentrate on the stunning location and architecture.

Speaking of popular destinations, **CANNERY ROW** is a bustling reminder that the more things change the more they stay the same. This building complex once thrived on the business of catching and canning sardines. Now it is a series of shops and restaurants in the business of catching tourists. Why would you want to kiss here? Well, actually you probably won't want to kiss here. What you could do, though, is browse, laugh, hold hands, stroll, and have a leisurely meal by the sparkling blue bay. Cannery Row is not what you would call romantic, but it can be fun, and that's a good prelude to just about anything—including kissing— any time.

## HOTEL PACIFIC, Monterey
**300 Pacific Street**
**(408) 373-5700**
Expensive to Very Expensive

*On Pacific Street, one block south of Del Monte.*

With so many bed and breakfasts and small inns to choose from on the Monterey Peninsula, it's hard to believe anyone would want to stay at a big hotel. Hard to believe until you see a handful of the very chic, very lavish hotels that have been developed in this area. Hotel Pacific is one of them, and it seems more like a retreat than a traditional hotel. The approach to this genteel escape reveals a flowing fountain at the entry, ring-necked doves serenading in the lobby, courtyards trimmed with weathered wooden furnishings, and dense flowering vines lining the pathways and walls. Terra-cotta and Sante Fe print fabrics accent the guest rooms, where a wood-burning fireplace, a thick, cushy featherbed, a separate living area and private patio or balcony overlooking the ocean all feel appropriately luxurious. The hotel is located in the heart of historic Old Monterey, close to all of the things you will want to see in this town. But don't be surprised if you find yourselves staying in your suite.

◆ **Romantic Alternative: The MONTEREY PLAZA HOTEL**, 400 Cannery Row, Monterey, (408) 646-1700, (Expensive to Very Expensive), is located in the heart of Cannery Row, which would be a romantic problem if it weren't for what happens once you step inside the foyer. Your eyes will scan past the polished marble floor, the cozy lounge, and the balcony, to the horizon, most of it filled with ocean. Water is the focal point of the Monterey Plaza Hotel. Waves break underneath the building and the sound of the surf swells through its chambers and corridors. Many of the rooms and suites have views of the bay. If yours doesn't, be sure to return to the hotel's main balcony in time for sunset. Later, dinner at the hotel's restaurant, **DELFINO'S**, will be a pleasurable interlude. From its windows you'll admire the shimmering moon dancing across the bay and the sparkle of city lights twinkling in the distance.

◆   **Second Romantic Alternative:** On a downtown street, **THE MONTEREY HOTEL**, 406 Alvarado Street, Monterey, (408) 375-3184, (Moderate to Expensive), is small enough to be charming yet large enough to offer all the amenities of a larger resort. Some of the rooms and suites have views of the harbor and bay. Be sure to ask for a description of the room you are booking; while all of them are handsomely furnished, some are too small for even the most intimate of couples.

**OLD MONTEREY INN, Monterey**
**500 Martin Street**
**(408) 375-8284**
Expensive to Very Expensive

*From Highway 1 South: Take the Soledad/Munras exit. Cross Munras Avenue, then turn right on Pacific Street. Go a half mile to Martin Street, on the left. From Highway 1 North: Take the Munras Avenue exit. Make an immediate left on Soledad Drive, then turn right onto Pacific Street. Drive a half mile to Martin Street, on the left.*

This is the kind of place you fall in love with from the moment you enter the garden gate. It is Eden with all the extras. The gardens are opulent in a natural way, with pots of flowers hanging like jewels from the gnarled branches of old trees; paths meander to secluded niches where you can kiss to your heart's delight. In the warmer months, breakfast is served on brick patios surrounded by a profusion of pink and white impatiens, roses, wisteria, and boxwood hedges. Inside this 1929 English Tudor, every detail spells romance. Eight of the 10 guest rooms have fireplaces. An antique book of poetry placed upon a shawl in each room sets the mood for old-fashioned cuddling. In the Garden Cottage, a bridal white linen-and-lace crown canopy is draped above the bed, while a fireplace with tile hearth warms the white wicker sitting room. Even the Dovecote, despite dormer ceilings, feels bright and spacious, with a skylight overhead and a wood-burning fireplace. Rich florals, antiques, gourmet breakfasts, billowing floral draperies, rich colors— this is Monterey's piece of paradise.

**SPINDRIFT INN, Monterey**
**652 Cannery Row**
**(408) 646-8900**
Expensive to Very Expensive

*On Cannery Row, between Hoffman and Prescott.*

In the midst of Cannery Row, right on the ocean, the Spindrift Inn is an elegant, ultra-chic, architecturally beautiful place to stay. The setting makes it even more attractive. Waves roar up onto the rocks below, and the smell of salt water turns the aesthetic suites into a sanctuary for interpersonal introspection. On the ocean side, there are window seats in each room to nestle in while you feel the surf's magnetism vibrate in the air. Behind you, a crackling fire bathes the hardwood floors, Oriental carpets, canopied beds, and down comforters in an amber glow. If it's a warm evening, only one irresistible option could tempt you away from all this newfound comfort: a stroll along the silvery moonlit beach. In the morning, a continental breakfast awaits you at your door; in the afternoon, high tea is served in the inn's rooftop garden, where there's a magnificent view of Monterey Bay.

# Restaurant Kissing

**CAFE KIEWELS, Monterey**
**100-A Heritage Harbor**
**(408) 372-6950**
Inexpensive

*Heritage Harbor is located at the corner of Pacific and Scott.*

Dusk—that lovely limbo between day and night—is a majestic event in Monterey. The water over Monterey Bay turns dark blue as sunset shadows cover the ocean in a blanket of darkness. A few late-returning boats, with their wind-filled sails, make their way back to the harbor as the last rays of light paint the horizon golden and the sun slips out of view into the sea. How we love early evening! And Cafe Kiewels may be the best place to go after you've indulged this love. Besides, at this hour most of the other tourists have either left for the day or won't be arriving until later. We were lucky enough to have this charming outdoor cafe almost to ourselves. The food was satisfying and we were happy, because as the sunset ended we knew the night was just beginning.

**FRESH CREAM, Monterey**
**Heritage Harbor, 99 Pacific Street**
**(408) 375-9798**
Expensive to Very Expensive

*Across from Fisherman's Wharf, on the second floor of the Heritage Harbor building.*

One of the most revered French restaurants in Monterey, Fresh Cream is anything but pretentious. Its vitality invites laughter and discourages whispers. The dining room is refreshingly bright, with colorful reproductions of early California art highlighting the simple, modern architecture. The service is refined yet down-to-earth. The food, artfully presented yet served in hearty portions, is so delicately scrumptious that you will want to savor every bite. The subtle spices of the veal sausage en croute were enhanced by Madeira and white wine sauces, the rack of lamb was perfectly roasted, and the chocolate cake Celestine was sinfully delicious. Not surprisingly, this is a popular meeting place for friends as well as lovers, ideal if you're in the mood for light-hearted romance rather than a quiet dinner for two.

**BINDEL'S, Monterey**
**500 Hartnell Street**
**(408) 373-3737**
Moderate to Expensive

*At the corner of Hartnell and Madison.*

This meticulously renovated old house was built back when Monterey was still a part of Mexico, and the bright salmon-colored adobe exterior seems to bring that era alive. A wheelbarrow filled with flowers stands by the front door and potted plants hang down from the second-story terrace. As you approach the restaurant, you might want to linger a moment or two on the front lawn, where a kiss under one of the old cypress trees will be the perfect appetizer for your upcoming meal. When appetizers no longer suffice, step inside, where several dining rooms, upstairs and down, are warmed by burnished fireplaces and the soft pastel decor is subtly lit by handmade chandeliers. The food, according to the owners, is Monterey Regional, but I think they are confused, because the servings are much larger than that description would imply. Bindel's prepares substantial portions of fresh fish and wild game. When your cravings are satisfied, stop once again, on the veranda outside, where a kiss in the darkness will still be something to savor.

## SARDINE FACTORY, Monterey
**701 Wave Street, on Wave at Prescott**
**(408) 373-3775**
Expensive

The Sardine Factory has the reputation of being one of the more romantic dining spots in Monterey, and as wary as we are about places with that kind of reputation, we agree—this is an illustrious choice. The centerpiece of the lounge where we waited for our table to be ready is a stunning 120-year-old hand-carved bar. Friends had told us to request seating in the Conservatory, one of the restaurant's five dining rooms, and they were right. Covered by a glass dome and surrounded by a garden, this lovely room makes a prime setting for inspirational conversation and loving thoughts. Like the atmosphere, the menu is also impressive. The fresh seafood was delicious and the desserts were among the best we've ever tasted.

◆ **Romantic Warning**: We waited in the lounge about 20 minutes for our table. Often, glowing reputations also mean delays, even when you have reservations.

# Outdoor Kissing

**ADVENTURES BY THE SEA, Monterey**
**299 Cannery Row**
**(408) 372-1807**
Kayak rentals $20 per day

*In the Alvarada Mall at the Doubletree Hotel. Shop is located in the back of
the building, next to the bike bath.*

Kayaking side by side on the gentle waters of the Monterey Bay is a
special experience you'll remember long after you return home. Pelicans
skim the water's surface. Seals laze on the rocks. Playful otters loop in
and out of the kelp, sometimes even plopping coquettishly on the front
of your kayak. Beneath you, myriad colors and textures flow by, punctuated with bright orange and gold starfish. These stable boats are made
for laid-back drifting, interspersed with unhurried paddling. Far from
the crowds of Cannery Row, you can hold hands and, perhaps, steal an
adventurous kiss. You'll even stay nice and dry, with special coveralls
that pull over your clothes. If you pack a picnic before heading out, you
can pull up onto a beach or share it right on the water.

**FISHERMAN'S WHARF, Monterey**
*At the intersection of Scott and Olivier Streets.*

Like Cannery Row, this is a location worth visiting for an hour or two
on a sunny afternoon. Actually, it's not the facility that makes it
worthwhile, it's the oceanfront location. Ambling down the boardwalk,
your senses tickled with the smell and taste of the swirling, salty ocean
currents, you will pass souvenir shops, stands selling OK-to-mediocre
seafood, and lots of restaurants boasting views of the bay. Be sure to stop
in at **RAPPA'S**, Fisherman's Wharf #1, Monterey, (408) 372-7562,
(Inexpensive), at the end of the pier. From the moment you enter, you
will feel that the restaurant is floating. From tables near the window you
can watch pelicans and sea gulls skim over the water as they rush to feed
on the fish piled high by the fishermen returning with their daily catch.

## MONTEREY BAY AQUARIUM, Monterey
### 886 Cannery Row
### (408) 648-4888

At the end of Cannery Row is another of the city's tourist attractions, but this one presents a not-to-be-missed opportunity to view the marine life that abounds below the water's surface. This aquarium is one of the world's largest and best, housed in an unbelievably realistic underwater setting.

## RENT-A-ROADSTER, Monterey
### 756 Foam Street
### (408) 647-1929
About $30 per hour

*Two blocks from the Monterey Bay Aquarium, next to the Sardine Factory.*

We never knew driving could be this much fun. With a toot of the *"ah-ooga"* horn, we were off to tour the coastline in our reproduction of a 1929 Model A roadster. The top was down, the sun was shining in, waves were crashing, and people waved to us as we trundled by—we hugged each other with the delight of it all. This unusual company offers five Model A's and one two-door deluxe phaeton for rent, all very easy to drive, with modern engines capable of 55 mph (but why hurry?). Be sure to allow enough time to stop by the seashore along Lovers Point near Pacific Grove, which is only a few minutes away from Rent-A-Roadster. Or plan on doing the 17-Mile Drive in style. If another couple you know is romantically inclined, they can join the fun in the Model A's rumble seat.

◆    **Romantic Alternative:** Another fun way to tool around Monterey is to rent a pedal surrey or a bicycle built for two at **BAY BIKES**, 640 Wave Street, Monterey, (408) 646-9090. The surreys have two sets of pedals and a brightly striped, fringed roof, but you can pedal them only on Monterey's bike path along Cannery Row: the surreys aren't allowed on streets. Energetic kissers can pedal their bicycle built for two along the 17-Mile Drive or all the way to Carmel (about 14 miles). If you're tuckered out, you can leave the bike at **BAY BIKES II**, on Lincoln between Fifth and Sixth in Carmel.

# Pacific Grove

For now the developers have left the oceanfront of Pacific Grove alone, which for them might be a disappointment, but for you is a delightful kissing advantage. Pacific Grove is the most overlooked town on the Monterey Peninsula. Whereas Monterey and Carmel are often crowded to overflowing, you can still find a measure of peace and solitude along the Pacific Grove shoreline and in the town of Pacific Grove. The bed and breakfasts and restaurants here are some of the most wonderful I've encountered anywhere in my travels.

## *Hotel/Bed and Breakfast Kissing*

**THE CENTRELLA, Pacific Grove**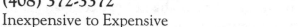
**612 Central Avenue**
**(408) 372-3372**
Inexpensive to Expensive

*From Highway 68 take Forest Avenue to Central, turn left, and continue two blocks to the inn.*

It is evening, and the logs in the fireplace are just beginning to burn. What's left of the daylight filters through the beveled glass windows that line an entire wall of the parlor. Freshly baked cookies and a carafe of cream sherry sit on an old oak table. We decided to pour ourselves a glass of sherry and nibble on a cookie or two while we went over the details of the fantastic places we had seen that day. This is a homey, warm place to come back to after a long, unhurried afternoon of meandering through the streets of Monterey and Pacific Grove. There are 26 guest rooms, some with shared baths. The best rooms are the garden cottages. A brick walkway bordered by camellias and gardenias connects the inn to these separate dwellings, which all have private entrances, fireplaces, and attractive sitting areas.

In the morning, we stirred to the scent of freshly brewed coffee as the innkeepers set out a breakfast buffet. The cool, crisp air tempted us to pull the covers close for just a few more minutes. We succumbed to the temptation and decided to get a slightly later start on the day than originally planned. When we finally made our way down to breakfast, the coffee was still fresh and the baked goods still warm. After this, anyone would feel pampered enough to survive until the next special outing.

### THE GATEHOUSE INN, Pacific Grove
### 225 Central Avenue, at Second Street
### (408) 649-1881
Moderate to Expensive

Built as a "seaside cottage" in 1884, this imposing but gaily restored Victorian has all the trappings of an elaborate home enhanced with amenities that its original builders would envy. Elaborate, custom-designed, hand silk-screened wallpapers adorn the walls and ceilings. In some rooms, you'll want to lie in bed together just to admire the intricate patterns above you. In the Langford Suite, a lacy canopy hangs cloudlike above the bed while a gas fire glows in the white, very feminine cast-iron stove. The Sun Room feels almost like an indoor garden with its white wrought-iron bed and view of the ocean. The black-and-pink art deco Hollywood Room was a bit too garish for my taste, but some insist that it's their favorite. Fresh home-baked cookies, fresh fruit, and tea and coffee are served all day, and you can help yourself to the fully stocked refrigerator of juices, sodas, milk, cheese, and yogurts. We also enjoyed the afternoon wine and appetizers, including delicious homemade cheeses. In the morning, a full breakfast of specialties such as pumpkin-cornmeal pancakes or cheese strata with bacon was the perfect start to a romantic day by the sea.

**GREEN GABLES INN, Pacific Grove**
**104 Fifth Street**
**(408) 375-2095**
Moderate to Expensive

*From Highway 1, take Highway 68 west to Pacific Grove. Follow Forest Avenue to the ocean, then turn right on Ocean View Boulevard, and drive to Fifth Street. The inn is at the corner of Ocean View and Fifth.*

From the street the exterior is striking; from the front gate the surroundings look like a fairy tale come to life; and from the moment you step inside this Queen Anne-style mansion, you'll know you are about to begin an enchanting experience. The inn, as its name suggests, is a multigabled structure with leaded glass windows that accord a dreamy view of Monterey Bay. The parlor houses a collection of antiques, where a brightly painted carousel horse sits behind a sofa, stained glass panels frame the fireplace, and freshly cut flowers are arranged about the room. Halfway up the stairs that lead to some of the guest rooms, a pair of teddy bears keep company on a small wicker chair.

Most of the 11 rooms are decorated in paisley and floral prints. Some have sloped ceilings, others have bay windows, fireplaces, and scintillating views of the water. Regardless of which corner is yours, all entreat you to indulge yourselves in this soothing setting. At first sight, the Green Gables Inn will capture your imagination, and before you leave it will certainly capture your hearts.

◆ **Romantic Warning:** Some of the rooms share bathrooms, which in the opinion of the editors is not conducive to uninterrupted kissing. Be sure to request a room with private facilities, unless your ability to partake in uninterrupted smooching is contingent upon lower-priced accommodations.

**THE GOSBY HOUSE, Pacific Grove**
**643 Lighthouse**
**(408) 375-1287**
Inexpensive to Moderate

*At the corner of Lighthouse and 16th.*

This stunning Victorian bed and breakfast has all the charm you will need to feel at home during your stay in Pacific Grove. The guest rooms are sumptuously appointed with fireplaces and down comforters. No detail is left unattended. The generous buffet breakfast and late-afternoon high tea will be highlights of your stay. In fact, the only thing that's missing here is the ocean view.

## LIGHTHOUSE LODGE, Pacific Grove
**1249 Lighthouse Avenue**
**(408) 655-2111**
Moderate to Very Expensive

*Follow Lighthouse Avenue toward the ocean. Lighthouse Lodge is on the left just before the shore.*

Even those of us who love Victorian decor sometimes grow weary of intricately patterned wallpapers, antique knickknacks, and, yes, claw-foot tubs. The Lighthouse Lodge is a delightfully romantic change of pace that combines modern luxuries with the friendly hospitality of a bed and breakfast. All the rooms have private entrances, vaulted ceilings, refrigerators, microwaves, wet bars, large Jacuzzis, gas fireplaces, plush robes, and color televisions, but my favorite touch was the bedside dimmer switch for uninterrupted mood setting. Full, cooked-to-order breakfasts are served in the spacious common room, which has fireplaces at either end. In the afternoon, a hearty variety of complimentary appetizers and local wines invite quiet conversation after a busy day of touring together. All this is a pebble's toss away from one of the Monterey Peninsula's most beautiful seaside settings. Waves crash majestically against the craggy rocks and the sunset washes a rosy glow across the Pacific as couples stroll hand-in-hand along a wooden walkway that meanders along the beach, pausing now and then to drink it in and seal the moment with a kiss.

## THE MARTINE INN, Pacific Grove
### 255 Ocean View Boulevard
### (408) 373-3388
Moderate to Very Expensive

*Call for directions.*

This towering, light pink mansion resides on the cliffs overlooking Monterey Bay. The exterior is classic Mediterranean in style and the interior is entirely Victorian. The 19 rooms here are spacious (some border on huge), furnished with authentic, massive antiques, and handsome wood detailing. Some have fireplaces and views of the water. Although the bathrooms tend to be simple, the other comforts more than make up for this failing. The best rooms—other than those with a view—are the spacious garden cottages. In the morning, hearty breakfasts are served in the dining room, with the spectacular view of the bay featured as the main course.

## PACIFIC GROVE INN, Pacific Grove
### 581 Pine Avenue, at Forest Avenue
### (408) 375-BUCK
Inexpensive to Expensive

If you prefer more cosmopolitan kissing, this 1904 national historic landmark has the feel of a San Francisco inn. A classic Queen Anne, its decor is that of an elegant Victorian-era home, but it has added modern amenities such as private baths with towel warmers, in-room refrigerators, and televisions tucked away in cabinets. You may feel like the Victorian elite while relaxing with a book in the sedate parlor. A buffet breakfast is served in the dining room by the hearth. The Robert C. Gass suite is a favorite for romance, with a sunny hexagonal sitting area where you can sip wine together while watching the sun set over the ocean on the horizon.

◆   **Romantic Warning:** The Pacific Grove Inn is just five blocks from the ocean, but it is on a busy street and just a few doors down from a fire station.

◆ **Romantic Alternative: The Jabberwock**, 598 Laine Street, Monterey, (408) 372-4777, (Moderate to Expensive), has a much more lived-in ambience than the Pacific Grove Inn, which can feel friendly to some and frumpy to others. Its wraparound sun deck in back looks over a delightful lawn and gardens. Romantic touches like The Toves' cathedralesque, carved wooden bed or The Borogrove's spacious sitting area by a hearth will make you forget this was once a convent.

## SEVEN GABLES INN, Pacific Grove
**555 Ocean View Boulevard**
**(408) 372-4341**
Moderate to Expensive

*From Highway 1, take Highway 68 west and follow the signs to Pacific Grove. Once in Pacific Grove, stay on Forest Avenue to the ocean. Turn right on Ocean View, continuing two blocks to Fountain Avenue. The inn is at Ocean View and Fountain.*

There is no other word for this celestial bed and breakfast than perfection. Every detail, every appointment is sheer luxury. Once you've spent time here, every other accommodation in the area will pale next to this one. The Seven Gables Inn is a prodigious, yellow mansion trimmed in white that sits on a rocky promontory in Pacific Grove. From every plush, stately room you have dramatic views of the glistening ocean and coastal mountains. This grand house, painstakingly renovated, is filled with an extensive collection of fine art and antiques. Tiffany glass windows, Persian carpets, 18th-century oil paintings, marble statues, and crystal chandeliers are just some of the collector's items that adorn the inn. The interior is formal and polished, yet it is a place where you will feel at ease and comfortable.

Each guest suite is an extraordinary, spacious, ultimately cozy private retreat. Broad windows draped in lace and balloon valances make the rooms bright and sunny by day. The bathrooms are contemporary and beautiful. At night, the classic lighting fixtures give each room a soft, warm glow. It must be the elegance and warmth that draw so many honeymooners to the Seven Gables Inn. On most weekends you will find couples spending their wedding night here. And even if it's not your honeymoon, all that romance is sure to rub off!

   Breakfast is a grand affair of freshly made muffins, croissants, special egg dishes, tortes, homemade fudge, and a large assortment of pastries. A generous, proper high tea is also served in the exquisite dining room with a stunning view of the water.

## Restaurant Kissing

**CAFE BELVEDERE, Pacific Grove**
**The Penthouse, Ford's Department Store**
**(408) 372-7131 ext. 2920**
Inexpensive

*In Pacific Grove's small town center, on the top floor of Ford's. Enter Ford's through the back door, by the parking lot. Pass the candy counter to the penthouse elevator and ride it up four floors to the penthouse level.*

   This may be the strangest romantic recommendation we'll make, but that is what makes this local favorite so special. Ford's is an old, 1950s-style department store, making Cafe Belvedere even more unexpected. Once upstairs, you will lunch while gazing out at one of the best views on the Monterey Peninsula. There aren't any bad tables in this cozy cafe with a gray-and-rose art deco flair. Husband-and-wife team Steve and Nico Bishcoff greet most of the diners by name, but will make you feel right at home with classy but unpretentious service. Sandwiches, such as smoked salmon and cream cheese, are made with homemade breads. Salads, quiche, cheese blintzes, wiener schnitzel, and delectable pastries round out the lunch menu. The Bishcoffs introduce dinner service soon.

**FANDANGO, Pacific Grove**
**223 17th Street**
**(408) 373-0588**
Moderate

*On 17th Street, just south of Lighthouse Avenue.*

This engaging Mediterranean-style restaurant is a potpourri of options. Flowers and sunshine engulf a festive patio where outdoor brunch
is a gratifying repast. Indoors, a crackling fire and just a few tables in each
of the three front dining rooms provide a more intimate eating experience. If you step down a curved stone staircase, you'll find a wine cellar
set up for special occasions. In the glass-domed terrace, the scent of
mesquite from the open grill mingles with the sounds of laughter to
create an informal setting. Lunch and dinner are served daily and there
is a reasonably priced, incredibly well-done Sunday brunch here too.
There is only one thing more difficult than deciding where to eat here,
and that is deciding what to eat. The food is flavorful and the menu
traditional. Once the tough decisions are out of the way, though (all
decisions should be this tough), you can sit back and unwind. After all,
isn't that what this evening is all about?

## GERNOT'S, Pacific Grove
**649 Lighthouse Avenue**
**(408) 646-1477**
Moderate

*On Lighthouse Avenue and 19th Street.*

Gernot's is special. The stately Victorian mansion houses a polished,
plush interior where every aspect of your evening will be wonderful. The
small menu, with a handful of specials every evening, includes such
delicacies as simple broiled salmon with angel-hair pasta, and wild
boar. The moderate prices add to the pleasure, but regardless, the setting
is priceless.

## OLD BATH HOUSE, Pacific Grove
**620 Ocean View Boulevard**
**(408) 375-5196**
Moderate to Expensive

*At the edge of Lovers Point, on Ocean View Boulevard.*

The Old Bath House provides a beautiful oceanside dining experience. The fact that it's located at Lovers Point Park makes it even more

romantic. Waves roll up onto the rocks right below your table. After the sun ebbs into the sea, only city lights in the distance compete with the flickering flames of candles alight all over the restaurant. Little can compete with the intimacy this place sparks, except the food, which is a blend of French and northern Italian cuisine. The desserts are created by the kitchen's own pastry chef and worth every sinfully rich calorie.

# Outdoor Kissing

### PACIFIC GROVE SHORELINE

*Take Highway 1 to Highway 68 heading west. Highway 68 becomes Forest Avenue. Take it all the way to the ocean.*

The major activity here is relaxing and savoring the majestic scenery. Take time to saunter arm-in-arm along **OCEAN VIEW BOULE-VARD**, where a whisper of salt water gently sprays over you as the waves thunder against the rocks at water's edge. Here you can watch sea otters splashing in kelp beds, pelicans perching in a sunny spot, and, if the time of year is right, maybe a whale or two swimming by as they migrate south for winter. If you expect your walk to take you to **LOVERS POINT PARK**, at the southern tip of Monterey Bay, consider packing a picnic to share in the shade of a tree or in the warmth of a gloriously sunny day.

For an even more isolated stroll, be sure to traverse the glorious, windswept sands along **ASILOMAR BEACH**.

### 17-MILE DRIVE

*From Highway 1, take Highway 68 west to Sunset Drive, and go west again to the Pacific Grove entrance gate. There is a $6 entry fee.*

This drive is so awesome and resplendent that you will take much longer traveling this unspoiled terrain than its 17-mile length suggests. That's because you will want to stop several times along the way to observe the infinite variations as ocean and land meet along the Monterey Peninsula. White, foamy waves wash up on black rocks, sending a spray of sea into the crisp, clean air; sea gulls cry out as unruffled pelicans perch near the water's surface.

As you round one spiral of road, you'll spy a crescent-shaped, sandy cove that provides a calm place to pause. Here, sunlight shimmers on the vast Pacific, and in the distance a sailing vessel slowly makes its way across the horizon. Many other turns in the road will reveal undulating sand dunes, violently frothing sea currents, and abundant marine life sanctuaries. Watch for the stark beauty of a lone cypress clinging to the side of a cliff, swaying effortlessly in the wind, and be sure to stop at **SEAL AND BIRD ROCK** to witness a multitude of marine beasts and birds basking in the sun and frolicking in the water.

As you continue on your passage up a hill, turning to the east, you will enter a deeply wooded area that shelters palatial homes and estates and the occasional world-class golf course. Unless watching the rich and famous is your idea of an intimate interlude, continue on and in a few more turns the natural beauty of the peninsula will be yours again. If you are hungry or would like to pause, you can visit any of the three restaurants at the **INN AT SPANISH BAY; THE DUNES, THE BAY CLUB**, and **THE CLUBHOUSE BAR AND GRILL** (all open to the public) overlook the stunningly profound landscape below, and the food almost equals the view.

# Carmel

After spending a great deal of my time looking for kissing places, I take some pride in knowing that I've been to (probably) all of the most romantic places in Northern California. From that perspective, when I say no other place I've seen is quite as quaint or as charming or as crowded as Carmel, I'm saying a lot. Much of that allure I attribute to what Carmel lacks—namely billboards, neon signs, tall buildings, parking meters, and high heels. (There is actually a law on the books stating that it is illegal to wear high heels on the sidewalks, but don't worry, I assure you that it is not enforced!)

Carmel is home to some of the most colorful shops, interesting galleries, adorable inns, and finest restaurants in the state. Since these are clustered in a very small area, discovering all of Carmel is an outstanding way to spend the day. A few blocks away from the center of town are enviable seaside homes, and white sandy beaches lie just in front of them, proffering a more restful way to while away the hours. Without question, you will find yourselves captivated by the town's charm and flawless setting.

◆     **Romantic Note:** Part of Carmel's appeal is its small size; most of the establishments don't even have numbers on their doors. Therefore, most of the entries in this section of the book do not include formal addresses, only street junctions. Once you are in Carmel, these will be more than enough to find your destination. Because of Carmel's popularity, be warned that most weekends during the entire year are disturbingly crowded, and the entire summer season goes beyond crowded to the point of bursting.

## Hotel/Bed and Breakfast Kissing

**CARMEL VALLEY RANCH RESORT, Carmel**     ❤❤❤❤
**1 Old Ranch Road**
**(408) 625-9500, (800) 4-CARMEL**
Very Expensive to Unbelievably Expensive

*From Highway 1, take a left onto the Carmel Valley Road. Drive six miles past ranches and rolling hills to Old Ranch Road on the right. Look for the gated entrance to Carmel Valley Ranch Resort on the left.*

Alas, the limits of a four-kiss system, for even the memory of the Carmel Valley Ranch Resort makes us long for an embrace. Once through the gated entrance of this 1,700-acre estate, we were greeted by name, then led to a secluded suite nestled in the branches of old, sculpted oak trees. Although the buildings are contemporary and new, they seem right at home in this stunning natural setting. For one magical evening, this was our private retreat. The sun was setting over the valley below and a small herd of deer pranced by our window as we settled before the wood-burning fireplace in the living room. A cathedral ceiling soared above, soft floral watercolors set the mood, and a second wood-burning fireplace in the bedroom promised late-night romance. Before dinner, we indulged in a romantic soak beneath the stars in our private hot tub on a wraparound deck set up high in the trees, a nest for lovebirds.

As if this were not enough, we headed to the resort's restaurant, reserved exclusively for guests, for a meal that was impeccable. The food filled the senses like the kiss of true love, from the home-baked whole wheat hazelnut bread to the shiitake mushrooms with cream in filo to the veal medallions with prosciutto to the chocolate marquise cake. Artfully presented and flawlessly served, this masterpiece was complemented by an award-winning wine list, a warm fire, and the clear tones of a grand piano that we felt was being played just for us.

## CARRIAGE HOUSE INN, Carmel
**Junipero, between Seventh and Eighth**
**(408) 625-2585**
Expensive to Very Expensive

This attractive country inn has 13 rooms, all with wood-burning fireplaces, king-size beds, down comforters, and comfortable detailing. The upstairs rooms have open-beam ceilings and sunken tubs. In our room, touches of blue accented the large, white-quilted brass bed, and an exposed beam ceiling towered over head. There are plenty of logs available for building a glowing fire so you can cuddle up in the bay window and admire the pastoral view. If you prefer to explore, all that Carmel has to offer is right outside your door. In the morning a continental breakfast is delivered to your room for your convenience and privacy.

◆ **Romantic Option: THE SUNDIAL LODGE,** Monte Verde at Seventh, Carmel, (408) 624-8578, (Moderate to Expensive), is cordial and cozy. The rooms are done in an assortment of French country, wicker, and Victorian. The red brick courtyard, surrounded by multicolored flowers, is a nurturing place to spend time outdoors on a sunny afternoon.

## COBBLESTONE INN, Carmel
**Junipero, between Seventh and Eighth**
**(408) 625-5222**
Moderate to Expensive

*Call for directions.*

The common rooms at the Cobblestone Inn are hardly what anyone would call common: you cross a cobblestone courtyard to enter a living room that is also covered in stone. This is where a lavish breakfast buffet and afternoon hors d'oeuvres are served in front of a massive stone fireplace. (You can also have breakfast served to your room if that is your romantic preference.) All of the 23 guest rooms have the same cozy, rustic feel. This is reputed to be one of Carmel's best-run bed-and-breakfast establishments, and in this part of the world that's saying a lot.

## THE HAPPY LANDING, Carmel
**Monte Verde, between Fifth and Sixth**
**(408) 624-7917**
Moderate to Expensive

You may feel like Prince Charming and Sleeping Beauty in this whimsical fairy-tale inn. Each guest room is a cozy little cottage with high peaked ceilings that are quaint without being too cutesy. Each has a private entrance: a rounded, gabled door opening to a delightful inner courtyard that consistently wins blue ribbons in the Carmel Garden Fair. Romantic touches include Victorian fringed lamps, hand-painted floral sinks, and a decanter of sherry with glasses for two. If you splurge on a suite, which is the same price as many standard hotel rooms in Carmel, you can warm your toes by a fire. If not, you can cuddle up by the fire in the Victorian common room and nibble on cookies with tea in the afternoon. In the morning, after the Prince has awakened his Beauty with a kiss, a breakfast of home-baked muffins or scones is delivered to your door. Another kiss and the memory of your stay here will live happily ever after.

## HIGHLAND INN, Carmel Highlands
## Highway 1
## (408) 624-3801
Very Expensive to Unbelievably Expensive

*Just south of Carmel, on the east side of Highway 1. Look for a small sign on your left that indicates where to turn in to the inn.*

When discussing the encapsulated world of the Monterey Peninsula, the subject of elite, posh places to stay (and the area has several) just may come up. Less opulent than some, the Highland Inn is a captivating series of rooms and restaurants with a fairly captivating accompanying price tag. Money aside, you really need to see this location to appreciate what a rare romantic stay you are in for.

Highland Inn sits on an incredibly breathtaking expanse of coastline. From this prominence, windswept trees, white surf breaking over outcroppings of rocks, and the occasional pod of spouting whales are all showcased. The glass-enclosed view from the formal **PACIFIC'S EDGE** restaurant alone is worth the price of Sunday brunch ($25) or dinner. Even if you opt for drinks alone, the fireside lobby is just as formidable a place to watch sunset, when the sky explodes in a riot of intoxicating, evocative colors.

All of the contemporary-style rooms here share this four-lip view, and all have fireplaces and lanais. The one- and two-bedroom suites (including townhouse-style apartments) have spa baths, fireplaces, and fully equipped kitchens. Everything here is very first-class, very California, and very wonderful.

## LA PLAYA HOTEL, Carmel
## P.O. Box 900, Camino Real and Eighth Avenue
## (408) 624-6476, (800) 582-8900
Moderate to Unbelievably Expensive

*Take Highway 1 to Ocean Avenue and continue into Carmel. Turn left on Camino Real and drive to Eighth Avenue, where you will find the hotel.*

The sun is setting in Carmel-by-the-Sea and the azure sky is brushed with shades of pink and lilac. Two blocks away, the Pacific Ocean peers at you through pine and cypress trees, and the sound of the surf against the shore echoes in the distance. From somewhere overhead, every now and then, a sea gull lets out a piercing, haunting cry that fades in the wind. Here you are at La Playa, and the world is dazzling. In spite of its "hotel" appellation, this is the place to stay if you long for a graceful setting that also has all the luxury of a larger establishment.

La Playa's lobby is warmed by an enormous fireplace and decorated with hand-loomed area rugs and antiques. The 75 guest rooms are filled with hand-carved furnishings reflecting a Spanish influence, and some have incredible ocean views and fireplaces. Surrounding this handsome Mediterranean-style villa are neatly manicured lawns awash with flowers. There is even a heated pool encircled by lavender poppies swaying on slender stems. If you believe sheer beauty can conjure up romantic rapport, you will find just that at La Playa.

The cottages and suites at La Playa are even better places to find yourselves, but only if you have very deep pockets. These are some of the most expensive units available, but they are also the most enticing. Each has its own full kitchen or wet bar, terrace or garden patio, and most have fireplaces.

◆    **Romantic Alternative: PINE INN**, P.O. Box 250, Ocean Avenue, between Monte Verde and Lincoln, Carmel, (408) 624-3851, (800) 228-3851, (Inexpensive to Expensive), has a slow-burning fire in the hearth of the main lobby, beside which is a love seat of rich, red velvet. It would be easy to lose track of time here, were it not for the grandfather clock in the corner striking each hour. Upstairs, some of the 49 guest rooms have fireplaces and ocean views, and all have comfortable antique beds and choice Edwardian-style furnishings. The restaurant at the inn is nice, and the reasonably priced meals are quite good. Be sure to have breakfast or lunch in the restaurant's indoor/outdoor garden—on a sunny day, the domed glass ceiling rolls back to reveal a crystal clear blue sky. The Pine Inn is located in the heart of Carmel, close to the beach, shopping, and theater.

◆ **Second Romantic Alternative: THE CYPRESS INN**, Lincoln and Seventh, Carmel, (408) 624-3871, (Moderate), is inspired by the same Spanish influence as the La Playa Hotel, but it is a much smaller place. While the rooms here are not quite as elaborate, the simple beauty of the inn evokes the appropriate frame of mind for encounters of the heart.

◆ **Romantic Suggestion:** The **THUNDERBIRD BOOKSHOP AND RESTAURANT**, 3600 Barnyard, Carmel, (408) 624-9414, (Inexpensive), is not your typical romantic location, but I urge you to seek it out. After you've perused the aisles and selected a book together, you can sit around an open fireplace in one of the rooms and lose yourselves in your new literary find. The golden warmth from the fire helps set the mood for spicy reading while you sip a cup of coffee and nibble one of the Thunderbird's fresh pastries. All this can add up to a perfect expenditure of time. (Dinner is served here also.)

## LINCOLN GREEN INN, Carmel
**Carmelo, between 15th and 16th**
**(408) 624-1880**
Moderate

*Call for directions.*

I would love to change the name of this picturesque place, because there is nothing resembling an inn to be found here. Lincoln Green Cottages would be a much more appropriate moniker. Set in a quiet neighborhood, far away from Carmel's bustling town center, two blocks from the legendary Carmel shoreline, are four quaint country cottages encircled by immaculate gardens, venerable shade trees, and a white picket fence. Each cottage is painted white with forest green trim and shutters, much like you would expect to find in the English countryside. The only drawback is that the interiors are not as splendid as the exteriors. Even though the cottages are large, have beamed cathedral ceilings, and three have stone fireplaces and a full kitchen, they are more utilitarian than plush or charming. Still, they are a great secluded place to call home while you explore the Monterey Peninsula. And from this vantage point, you may never know that the summer crowds are only a mile down the street.

## ROBLES DEL RIO LODGE, Carmel Valley
**200 Punta del Monte**
**(408) 659-3705**
Inexpensive to Moderate

*From Highway 1, take Carmel Valley Road to Esquiline and follow the signs to the lodge.*

Perched high in the hills above Carmel Valley, this rustic resort has everything you need for a genuine getaway from the rest of the world. You will feel somewhat isolated up here in the hills and forest, but the privacy is part of what makes this escape so exciting. Robles del Rio means "oaks of the river," and branches from these old trees cascade over terraced guest rooms that look out onto the California countryside. The rooms are more comfortable than they are elegant, ranging from one with a board-and-batten look to another with a Laura Ashley motif.

The dense woodland is fitting for long, invigorating hikes or lazy walks. When it finally comes time to lie around and do nothing, try the mountaintop Jacuzzi or the heated pool. The pool is warm enough for swimming, and the breeze is cool enough to make you feel refreshed. If you dine at the **RIDGE RESTAURANT**, and you should, ask for a table on the glass-enclosed terrace. The menu offers excellent French cuisine and the view of the valley below is stunning.

## SAN ANTONIO HOUSE, Carmel
**P.O. Box 3683, San Antonio between Ocean and Seventh**
**(408) 624-4334**
Moderate to Expensive

*Call for directions.*

There are four generous suites here, each with its own entrance; comfortable, cozy antique furnishings; and radiant, wood-burning fire-place. Helping round out this intimate place are the gardens and stone terraces, plus it's one short block to the sun-clad beach. A generous continental breakfast of fresh pastries, egg dishes, and fresh fruit is brought to your room or served on the beautiful garden patios. This intimate home is a wonderful find in the Carmel area.

**STONEPINE, Carmel Valley**
**150 East Carmel Valley Road**
**(408) 659-2245**
Very Expensive to Unbelievably Expensive

*From Highway 1, take Carmel Valley Road east about 15 miles and watch for the sign on the right side of the road.*

When the wrought-iron gate opened for us at Stonepine, we instantly had the feeling that something unforgettable was waiting for us within its grounds. Our anticipation intensified as we drove up the mile-long access road to the main house. Just past the gate, we crossed a sturdy wooden bridge over a swiftly running creek. The entire way was lined with gnarled oak trees that sent streams of filtered sunlight through outstretched branches and fluttering leaves. Farther ahead, we noticed a couple touring the countryside in a horse-drawn carriage driven by a liveried coachman. In spite of our growing impatience to see what lay in wait at the chateau, we couldn't help but stop at the equestrian center we passed along the road. Vital, energetic horses galloped around the corral, making it difficult to pull ourselves away. But no doubt there would be plenty of time to saddle up two horses of our own and explore some of Stonepine's prodigious 330 acres of forest, meadow, and bridle trails.

When we finally reached the chateau, we embarked on a style of living that is hard to surpass. The spacious foyer and living room were filled with morning light that flowed in through a gallery of windows, enhancing the subtle elegance of the damask sofas and love seats. A handwoven Chinese rug, threaded with rose tones, stretched across the hardwood floor, and golden flames gently caressed each other in an oversize stone hearth. Throughout the evening this room was graced by the sounds of a string ensemble.

There are 11 suites at Stonepine, each one with the same lavish appointments and exquisite detail as the public area. We were thoroughly delighted at everything we saw and experienced. Even the restaurant was a cornucopia of superb food and courtly service. Our first kiss at Stonepine was only the beginning of a truly magnificent weekend.

**VAGABOND'S HOUSE INN, Carmel**
**Fourth and Dolores**
**(408) 624-7738, (800) 262-1262**
Inexpensive to Moderate

*From Highway 1, turn west on Ocean Avenue, continue to the heart of town, and turn north onto Dolores. Three blocks down is the inn.*

This English Tudor home is engulfed by oak trees rustling softly in the breeze. Each of the 11 rooms is ample, with a decanter of sherry beside the bed and a view of the inn's verdant garden; some have woodburning fireplaces. This is a great place to call home for a few days of time alone.

## Restaurant Kissing

**ANTON AND MICHEL, Carmel**
**Mission, between Ocean and Seventh**
**(408) 624-2406**
Expensive

As we walked by Anton and Michel one evening, we could see that there was something extraordinary about this restaurant. Impressive oil paintings hung on pastel walls; long, slender white columns separated one part of the dining room from another; and one entire wall of windows framed a patio that had a cascading water fountain at its center. Quickly we made reservations for the next night. The setting seemed to inspire intimate conversation and long loving looks at each other—that is, until the food arrived. We tried the house specialty, rack of lamb, and would recommend it to anyone. It's cooked to perfection and carved at your table. A little later, after turning our attention back to each other, we ordered a chocolate mousse that was sinfully rich and beautifully served. The focus of the menu is fresh meats carved at your table, but the fresh fish is equally good. This is a place where you can share a truly memorable evening. In fact, lunch here is also wonderful, and a romantic bargain. The restaurant is open daily for both lunch and dinner.

## CASANOVA, Carmel
**Fifth Street, between San Carlos and Mission**
**(408) 625-0501**
Expensive

When we asked a friend who grew up on the Monterey Peninsula for Carmel's most romantic restaurant, she immediately answered, "Casanova." This charming restaurant in an old home once owned by Charlie Chaplin's cook is tucked away on one of Carmel's quiet side streets. The unassuming entrance is a surprising threshold to old Europe. Inside, a series of cozy dining rooms invites intimacy. An inner courtyard offers dining beneath the stars, with the splash of a marble fountain and heaters that will keep you warm even in winter. One can hardly help but hold hands across the table and imagine a faraway honeymoon. Dinner, like linguine alla scapesce (pasta with lobster) and filet mignon bearnaise, comes complete with three courses, including antipasto, fresh mushrooms, homemade soup, and gnocchi verde.

◆ **Romantic Option:** Right around the corner from Casanova is a striking northern Italian restaurant called **GIULIANO'S**, Mission and Fifth Streets, Carmel, (408) 625-5231 (Moderate). This pocket-size, single-room dining establishment is outfitted in an array of mauve, cranberry, and rose cotton fabrics. The food is excellent and the atmosphere refined and polished.

## LA BOHEME, Carmel
**Dolores and Seventh Streets**
**(408) 624-7500**
Moderate

La Boheme is a small cafe with a festive European rural theme. The cottagelike interior has brightly painted walls and a pastel blue ceiling with hand-painted white fluffy clouds daubed here and there. Each table is covered by a floral print cloth and fresh flowers. Besides the amiable details of the interior, the creative chef serves a very French three-course prix-fixe meal that changes every night. The homemade desserts are delicious and worth lingering over with the one you love and two spoons. By the way, the diminutive size of the restaurant is such that you won't have to worry about sharing this place with too many other hungry diners. La Boheme is only open for dinner.

◆  **Romantic Option:** If La Boheme is filled, you may want to head over to **PATISSERIE BOISSIERE**, Mission Street, between Ocean and Seventh, Carmel, (408) 624-5008, (Inexpensive). This polished, choice French restaurant, open for lunch and dinner, has an eclectic menu with everything from quiche to extravagant fish dishes. The interior is European country with touches of Louis XV. By the way, if you don't want dinner, a cappuccino and one of their wickedly rich pastries would be wonderful too.

## SANS SOUCI, Carmel
**Lincoln Street, between Fifth and Sixth**
**Expensive**
(408) 624-6220

Locals have been renewing romance in this intimate restaurant for more than 30 years. Perhaps it's the crystal chandeliers, or the warmth of the fire, but this cozy restaurant feels more like a country French dining room than a commercial enterprise. The menu is classic French combined with innovative use of local seasonal produce and seafood. For those with a flair for the flamboyant, tuxedo-clad waiters will prepare several dishes at your table, including chateaubriand and rack of lamb. Desserts made only for two are the perfect finale: cherries jubilee or crepes with ice cream and fresh fruit, both flamed tableside.

### SHABU SHABU, Carmel
**Mission Street, between Ocean and Seventh**
**(408) 625-2828**
Moderate

This small, intimate (and intimate is an understatement) Japanese country restaurant is hard to find, but once you do, your senses and palates will be pleased. Traditional Japanese table cooking is the specialty of the house. The casual atmosphere, excellent food, and uncommon setting make it an international find.

## Outdoor Kissing

### Carmel Beach
*From Highway 1, turn west onto Ocean Avenue and follow it until it dead-ends at the beach.*

Carmel Beach is an awesome stretch of surf and sand. Those who have houses that border this mile-long parcel of heaven are in an enviable position. The landscape is an inspiring combination of surging waves, rolling hills, and endless ocean. A morning stroll (before the populace wakes up) or a walk at sunset when the sky is burnished with fire (and it doesn't matter who else is there) can renew the soul. All kinds of sparks can be kindled from this vantage point. Don't miss it.

### POINT LOBOS STATE RESERVE, Carmel
**(408) 624-4909**
$6 per car day-use fee

*Located on the ocean side of Highway 1, four miles south of Carmel.*

It's been called "the greatest meeting of land and water in the world." Where better to share a lasting kiss with your love? Point Lobos is one of my favorite spots in the Monterey area. I visit it often, but each time

I'm struck by that sense of experiencing something new and vibrant, like love itself. At the Sea Lion Point parking lot, the first sound you'll hear are the sharp barks of these robust creatures. Follow the short trail along a hillside blanketed with ice plants to the promontory and you'll see them crowded on the water-washed rocks. Nearby, you can explore the tidal pools together, searching out battling crabs and purple sea urchins. Or follow one of the less-traveled trails that hug the cliffs of this rugged coastline. Seclusion and spectacular scenery are yours to share.

## ROBINSON JEFFERS' TOR HOUSE, Carmel
**26304 Ocean View Avenue**
**(408) 624-1813**
$5 per adult

*From Highway 1, turn onto Ocean Avenue toward downtown Carmel. Turn left onto Scenic (the last street before Ocean). Turn left on Stewart, then left on Ocean View. Look for Tor House and its stone Hawk Tower on the left.*

A poet's home needn't be extraordinary to be considered a rendezvous with romance. This one is, but not in its size or architectural significance. The aura of love and romance is so strong here that even those who have never heard of Robinson Jeffers will be inspired. The Tor House ("tor" is an old Irish word for a craggy knoll) is a simple Tudor cottage, built in 1918, where Jeffers wrote all his major works and most of his poetry. More important, this is where he lived in splendid happiness with his wife, Una, and their twin sons. Throughout the home, loving epigrams are carved into the timbers. Jeffers built the Hawk Tower, making "stone love stone," by hand as a treasured retreat for Una and a magical playground for the children. In Una's room, at the very top of the tower, an epigram carved in the wooden mantel of the fireplace reads, "They make their dreams for themselves," truly reflecting Jeffers' life-style.

◆ **Romantic Warning:** The Tor House is open by guided tour only on Fridays and Saturdays, from 10 A.M. to 3 P.M. Reservations are advised.

> *"Kissing is a means of getting two people so close together that they can't see anything wrong with each other."*
>
> Rene Yasenek

*"You know I'd rather be lost in love than found."*
Michael Tomlinson

# GOLD COUNTRY

## Sacramento

### Hotel/Bed and Breakfast Kissing

**AMBER HOUSE, Sacramento**
**1315 22nd Street**
**(916) 444-8085, (800) 755-6526**
Very Inexpensive to Very Expensive

*From Interstate 80, take the N Street exit west. The inn is on the corner of N and 22nd Streets.*

Poets and artists inspired the decor at the Amber House. You, too, may be inspired to compose an ode to kissing while staying here. The inn encompasses two early-20th-century homes. The parlor of the Poet's Refuge, with massive exposed beams, a dark brick hearth, and hardwood floor, is the yin to the yang of the parlor in the Artist's Retreat, with its rose walls, white hearth, and overstuffed floral sofa. The poets' rooms pulse with romance, especially the double Jacuzzi in the Lord Byron Room and the antique tub beneath the skylight in the Longfellow Room, but my penchant for impressionists made me partial to the artists' abodes. The Van Gogh is stunning, a bright yellow bedroom that opens to a solarium bathroom. If not for the trees, even the immodest would blush, as the double Jacuzzi and shower are encased entirely in glass. In the Degas, the billowing floral canopy and curtains are as graceful as a ballerina. Double whirlpools surrounded by pink and gray marble in Degas and Renoir invite you to soak and fantasize about the dreamy world of the impressionists.

**AUNT ABIGAIL'S, Sacramento**
**2120 G Street**
**(916) 441-5007**
Very Inexpensive to Moderate

*From the Business 80 Loop, take the H Street exit. Cross H Street and turn*
*left onto G Street. The inn is near the corner of G and 22nd streets.*

A feeling of warm hospitality, generosity, and spaciousness embraced
us the moment we entered the grand foyer of this 1912 Colonial Revival
mansion. Aunt Abigail's may not be the most extravagant of Sacramento's inns (the only whirlpool is in the backyard garden), but it is
the most congenial, enhanced with antiques, Oriental rugs over hardwood floors, and nostalgic prints. In the evening, you can snuggle by the
fire in the parlor or choose a game to play after returning from dinner.
Or you may want to spend the wee hours tucked away in your room, as
we did, sipping herb tea and nibbling on the inn's scrumptious home-
baked cookies. Staying in the Solarium, with windows on three sides, is
like sleeping in a treehouse; a private door leads to a private deck.
Margaret's Room is like that of a refined Victorian lady, with soft tones,
an immense vanity with a hand-painted sink, and a claw-foot tub. Uncle
Albert's Room is decidedly masculine, with maroon and gray paisleys
and stripes. In the morning, guests join together for a hearty breakfast
that may include warm applesauce, vegetable-cheese strata, fresh fruit,
cinnamon muffins, and an assortment of teas and coffee.

**DRIVER MANSION INN, Sacramento**
**2019 21st Street**
**(916) 455-5243**
Inexpensive to Very Expensive

*From Business 80 east, take the 15th Street exit. At the foot of the ramp,*
*continue on X Street, parallel to the freeway, to 21st Street. Turn left onto*
*21st Street. The inn is about four blocks up on the right.*

This stately 1899 Colonial Revival crowning a grassy knoll is one of the capital's most formal inns. The spacious parlor nearly dwarfs the grand piano, which, one feels, serves more for decor than music as the ambience is far too imposing to allow any but a concert pianist to tickle the ivories. Still, those who want to go straight to kissing rather than small talk with strangers will find a delightful retreat here. The Carriage House in back offers cozy rooms to snuggle in before the warmth of a marble fireplace or corner wood stove. An unusual touch in the main house is the penthouse suite, reached by a narrow spiral stairway. Its modernistic black tables and pink sofas, a separate bedroom in black and pink, and a black tile double whirlpool make it a unique departure from Victorian lace and frills.

## HARTLEY HOUSE INN, Sacramento
## 700 22nd Street
## (916) 447-7829, (800) 831-5806
Inexpensive to Moderate

*From the Business 80 Loop, take the H Street exit. Cross H Street and turn left onto G Street. The inn is on the corner of G and 22nd streets.*

A certain manliness dominates this turn-of-the-century Italianate Victorian. Dark-stained woodwork, hardwood floors with distinctive Oriental carpets, leaded and stained glass windows, and the stately ticktocking of old clocks will appeal to many as a fresh retreat from the preciously feminine accoutrements of most bed and breakfasts. Although Hartley House caters to executives during the week, weekends are prime for romantic getaways. The man's touch is carried throughout the guest rooms' brass beds, antique wardrobes, converted gas fixtures, and dusky paisley bedcoverings. Brighton is the brightest room in the inn: daylight streams in through a dozen lace-trimmed windows in this former sun porch. In the morning, a full breakfast is served in the dining room.

## Restaurant Kissing

**FRANK FAT'S, Sacramento**
**806 L Street, between Eighth and Ninth Streets**
**(916) 442-7092**
Moderate

This venerable Chinese restaurant has been a Sacramento landmark for 50 years. Although it may be the stomping ground for government types at lunch, and even a few in the evening, the cozy tables, high-backed booths, and blend of modern and traditional Asian decor create a romantic ambience that isn't often found in Chinese restaurants. The menu offers all the traditional favorites, plus a selection of Mandarin, Cantonese, and Szechuan delicacies. We find Chinese restaurants perfect for sharing the spice of life together.

## Outdoor Kissing

**ADVENTURE LIMOSINE SERVICE, Auburn**              ◑◑◖
**(916) 878-8212**
From $325 per day

*Call for information about pickup and drop-off details.*

Although I'm not one to splurge capriciously, I would be remiss if I didn't tell you how much fun it can be to tour the gold country wineries in the backseat of your own private limo. Your driver will take you almost anywhere your heart, or your sweetheart, desires. One itinerary begins with a continental breakfast en route to a stop at **SOBON** and **SHENANDOAH WINERIES** for their tours, tastings, and on-site museums. Next would be a choice of lunch in Sutter Creek or a picnic at **MONTEVINA WINERY** and a return home via antique stores, photo shops, or more wineries, and one last golden kiss.

◆ **Romantic Note:** Adventure Limousine also will arrange tours of the Napa wineries, including lunch for two at one of the valley's fine restaurants.

## THE DELTA KING, Sacramento
**1000 Front Street, Old Sacramento Waterfront**
**(916) 444-KING, (800) 825-KING**
Moderate to Expensive

*Call for directions.*

The night was quiet and the river still as we boarded this grand old riverboat for an after-dinner cocktail. The ghosts of yesteryear seemed to whisper of dancing cheek-to-cheek in evening gown and tux. We swirled up a broad staircase to the fine saloon, with its rubbed mahogany and teak and its windows overlooking the water on one side and the vintage Western-style facades of Old Sacramento on the other. Time, it seemed, had stopped. This stern-wheel paddleboat, the kind so often connected with the Mississippi, plied the river between Sacramento and San Francisco from 1927 to 1940. It was a floating pleasure palace for flappers when Prohibition outlawed drinking in land-locked lounges. Today, the restored vessel is a dockside voyage into nostalgic romance. Its restaurant rates high on romantic ambience; unfortunately, the cuisine is only passable.

## OLD SACRAMENTO

*From Interstate 80, exit at Business Loop 80. From Business Loop 80 get on Interstate 5 heading north and exit on J Street. Get in the left lane and turn left onto Third Street and follow signs to the area.*

You can almost hear the swish of a woman's bustled, long skirt and the jingle-jangle of spurs as you stroll along Old Sacramento's boardwalks. The restored Western-style facades along narrow streets make you feel as though you should be planning a picnic together or a surrey ride to the back 40. Instead, you'll be enticed into the many fun boutiques, restaurants, and museums that inhabit this little village by the river. Invest in a special antique, indulge in old-fashioned chocolate fudge, or investigate the **B.F. HASTINGS MUSEUM,** where you can sit across the room from each other and telegraph "I love you" to your partner.

# Lodi

## Restaurant Kissing

**WINE AND ROSES, Lodi**
**2505 West Turner Road**
**(209) 334-6988**
Inexpensive to Moderate (Inn)
Moderate to Expensive (Restaurant)

*From Interstate 5, take the Turner Road exit. Head east 5.1 miles to the inn on the left.*

They seemed to glow with the warmth of the fire in this romantic dining room. He had filet mignon, she chose lamb chops in rosemary and garlic. For dessert, the piece de resistance: a diamond ring served on a silver platter. Who could refuse? Proposals are a specialty at Wine and Roses, as well as the weddings that follow. This 89-year-old estate is a pleasant surprise in lackluster Lodi. Its five-acre setting is landscaped with several shaded kissing spots favored by the guests. Of the guest rooms, Moonlight and Roses is the most romantic, with its fancy white brass bed, a sitting area before the windows, and a claw-foot tub enveloped by curtains that seems to whisper, "Come soak in me." The televisions in each room, a necessity for the midweek business clientele, can be removed on request so as not to distract from an evening of kisses.

◆ **Romantic Note:** The dining room is open for lunch Tuesday through Friday, for dinner Wednesday through Saturday, and for Sunday brunch.

◆ **Romantic Suggestion: LODI LAKE** is a five-minute walk down the road. In the summer, this is a lovely spot to rent paddleboats and kayaks, enjoy a picnic, or fish in the river.

# Ione

## Hotel/Bed and Breakfast Kissing

The Heirloom, Ione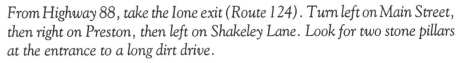
214 Shakeley Lane
(209) 274-4468
Very Inexpensive to Inexpensive

*From Highway 88, take the Ione exit (Route 124). Turn left on Main Street, then right on Preston, then left on Shakeley Lane. Look for two stone pillars at the entrance to a long dirt drive.*

I half expected to hear cicadas hum beneath a "Fiddle-dee-dee" from Scarlett as I approached The Heirloom. This beguiling antebellum mansion, built by a Virginian in 1863, is a world apart from anything else in gold country, or in California for that matter. Set back from the road, encircled by lawns bordered with thickly leafed trees, the inn feels completely secluded, a sanctuary for nostalgic romance. Two spry ladies keep the inn. Many of the extraordinary antiques that crowd the spacious parlor are family heirlooms, including the massive, 450-year-old carved wood table from Italy and the elaborate fans, now framed, that coyly cooled the cheeks of Melisande's great-great-grandmother from France. The square rosewood piano once belonged to the famous Gold Rush entertainer Lola Montez. You could settle by the wood-burning fireplace in this old manor home and spend the evening nibbling on appetizers and admiring the antiques.

More antiques fill the cozy guest rooms upstairs. Springtime opens onto the balcony, which drips with wisteria in its namesake season. Winter, warmed by a fire, holds a four-poster colonial bed with flouncy drapes above the headboard. Apart from the main house, an authentic rammed-earth adobe harbors two graciously rustic rooms warmed by a blend of cedar, redwood, and pine paneling and wood stoves.

## Outdoor Kissing

**GREENSTONE WINERY, Ione**
**Along Highway 88, across from Jackson Valley Road**
**(209) 274-2238**
*Call for directions.*

The setting of this majestic winery is as beguiling as its award-winning vintages. A long drive spills over vineyard-laden hills, past a serene duck pond, to a stately stone structure akin to a French country manor. In the modern tasting room, sun pours through multipaned windows set high near the cathedral ceiling, casting a golden glow over the wood paneling. Picnic tables, set amongst natural greenstone outcroppings and shaded by old oaks, overlook bucolic fields and Bacchus Pond, and, beyond them, a pastoral stretch of Miwok Indian land. Be sure to bring a picnic lunch with you to enjoy with a bottle of Greenstone's finest to complete this dreamy vision.

◆   **Romantic Alternative: WINTERBROOK VINEYARDS,** 4851 Buena Vista Road, Ione, (209) 274-4721, like most gold country wineries, is secluded and rural. You must seek it out to find its hidden riches. Picnic tables overlook vineyards and a slow-flowing brook. Winterbrook is only three miles from Greenstone.

# Amador City

## Restaurant Kissing

**BALLADS, Amador City**
**14220 Highway 49**
**(209) 267-5403**
Moderate to Expensive

*Just after the curve as you head north on Highway 49, about two miles north of Sutter Creek.*

A sterling restaurant like Ballads is as precious as gold in this neck of the woods. The cuisine is as scrumptious as many of San Francisco's finest. The ambience is unpretentiously romantic. A wood fire crackles and glows in the large stone hearth at one end of the dining room; local art and photographs are showcased on the wide-planked wood walls. Soft melodies, brass chandeliers, and petite flowering plants peeking from baskets on each table set the mood for creative California cooking. Although fritters are coming back into vogue, I hadn't eaten them in years, and was delighted with this unusual appetizer served with a sprightly pineapple chili sauce. The pork tenderloin with tomatillos, jicama, and poblana peppers was the perfect coupling of sweet and spicy. Everything on the menu was appealing, from the smoked duck tortellini with pesto sauce appetizer to the beef tenderloin with shiitake mushrooms, artichokes, and thyme. Discover Ballads together and you'll know you've struck gold.

# Sutter Creek

Set like a pearl deep in the green velvet folds of the surrounding hills, Sutter Creek's whitewashed overhanging balconies, balustrades, and Western-style storefronts lend a freshness to this old gold rush town. Beyond the history that whispers from every building, the boardwalks are hemmed with antique shops, gift boutiques, and casual cafes that invite a relaxing stroll together. This is the spot to wonder what it would have been like had you met a century before.

**THE FOXES, Sutter Creek**
**77 Main Street**
**(209) 267-5882**
Moderate to Expensive

*In the center of town along Highway 49.*

A plush fox lay curled on my bed when I checked in. It looked serene, warm, and naturally luxuriant, just as I felt from the moment I entered The Foxes. This beautifully restored 1857 Victorian is one of the best inns in gold country. The Victorian furnishings in the parlor and the formal dining room are elegant but not at all pretentious. Intricate silver tea services shimmer in the large country kitchen, promising indulgent gourmet breakfasts served to your room in the morning. Wood-burning fireplaces warm three of the six guest rooms. Kiss by the light of the flames in the spacious Honeymoon Suite's half-tester bed, then indulge in a bubble bath in the claw-foot tub or take a stroll through the delightful garden outside your private entrance. Cuddle by the hearth in the cozy private-library atmosphere of the Foxes Den, or sleep like royalty in the Victorian Suite's bed with its magnificent nine-foot, carved wood headboard. Let your imagination of times past soar. Romance is brushed on with gentle strokes—a petite bowl of potpourri, a shelf with a motif of carved lovebirds, a sunburst of sheer fabric above your bed—that blend to create the perfect canvas for kissing.

### GOLD QUARTZ INN, Sutter Creek
**15 Bryson Drive**
**(209) 267-9155, (800) 752-8738**
Inexpensive to Moderate

*On the crest of the hill to the south of town. Bryson Drive is off Highway 49, just to the north of the intersection with Highway 88.*

If you're weary of staying in century-old homes but love the romance of the Victorian era, check into the Gold Quartz Inn. A brand-new hotel with a Queen Anne motif, it enhances the tenderness of yesteryear with the deluxe appointments of today. The spacious parlor is akin to the lobby of a refined hotel. Several sitting areas are filled with graceful wing chairs and plush sofas accented with floral needlepoint pillows. Beyond the lobby, a sunny breakfast room overlooks the inn's lawns and gardens. Throughout these rooms, lace-curtained french doors open onto the wraparound veranda. Guest rooms are spacious and feminine in soft blues and pinks that are echoed in the sunset you can watch from your porch.

## THE HANFORD HOUSE, Sutter Creek
**61 Hanford Street**
**(209) 267-0747**
Inexpensive to Moderate

*On Highway 49, at the north end of town.*

It looks like a restored historic hotel on the outside, but inside you'll find pleasant, modern accommodations without all the froufrou of so me bed and breakfasts. Early pine furnishings, white walls, and high ceilings lend an air of clean spaciousness. One oversized room invites you to kiss by the corner fireplace or on the fancy white brass bed with its white eyelet comforter. You'll find plenty of room for outdoor kissing on the sunny redwood deck above Sutter Creek's jumble of rooftops or on the sun-dappled patio on the west side of the inn. A continental breakfast buffet is served in the cheerful breakfast room, where guests have left their names and appreciative comments on every inch of wall and ceiling.

# Jackson

## *Hotel/Bed and Breakfast Kissing*

## WINDROSE INN, Jackson
**1407 Jackson Gate Road**
**(209) 223-3650**
Inexpensive to Moderate

*From Highway 49, turn east on Jackson Gate Road (look for the Buffalo West trading post on the corner). The inn is about one mile down on the right.*

The gurgling brook seemed happy to greet me as I crossed the arched footbridge and headed up the garden path to this charming Victorian farmhouse. Once inside, I could have sworn I heard the parlor whisper "Come on in and set a spell." Setting is what guests do best here, kicking off their shoes by the wood stove in the cozy parlor, savoring afternoon wine and hearty hors d'oeuvres such as sausages and oven-baked potatos. Some take their evening treats out to the garden gazebo and kiss in the country air. Two guest rooms carry on the gentle simplicity of the inn, while Sterling Silver exhibits an unusual art deco black-and-plum motif. For privacy, some prefer the rustic miner's cabin in back of the home, which is secluded but somewhat slumping.

# Murphys

## Hotel/Bed and Breakfast Kissing

**DUNBAR HOUSE, Murphys**
**271 Jones Street**
**(209) 728-2897**
Moderate

*From Highway 49, exit at Route 4 east, then take the Murphys exit. The inn will be on the right, set back from Main Street, across from the Milliaire Winery tasting room.*

The crown jewel of one of gold country's most charming towns, this 1880 Italianate Victorian indulges you with generous hospitality and old-fashioned romance. The moment you walk into the dining room, you're treated to chocolate macadamia nut cookies, along with coffee, tea, and cocoa. A full country breakfast is served here by the wood stove, in your room, or in the lovely garden with its brick patio and white porch swing. Wood stoves warm your body as you toast each other with the complimentary bottle of wine provided in each guest room. In the Sequoia Room, settle into a bubble bath in the claw-foot tub, with its hand-painted flowers, set next to the wood stove. In the Cedar Room, lie down on the white brass bed before the warm flames or relax on your private sun porch in the late afternoon. A fireplace also warms the parlor, akin to an indoor garden of delicate, softly hued florals.

◆    **Romantic Suggestion:** Romantics will find a stroll around town a step back in time. Old Western-front buildings with raised wooden boardwalks now house boutiques, an intriguing mineral and fossil store, a historic saloon, and an ice cream shop. You can even bundle up together in a horse-drawn carriage for a ride down Main Street.

## Outdoor Kissing

**STEVENOT WINERY, Murphys**
**2690 San Domingo Road**
**(209) 728-3436**

*From the center of Murphys, follow signs for Mercer Caverns. Just before the road dead-ends at the caverns, turn right and follow a narrow, winding road down into the valley. Look for the Stevenot sign on the left at the bottom of a hill.*

You'll feel like an adventurer when wine tasting in gold country. Although this is one of the oldest wine-grape growing regions in California, wineries here are ensconced in secluded, rural areas, unlike Napa's domino set-up. Stevenot is one to discover together. In the rustic, sod-roofed tasting room, you can sample wines, specialty mustards, scrumptious chocolate sauce, and delectable kiwi jam, then choose one of each, add Brie and bread, and enjoy your repast at one of the picnic tables beneath the arbor. All you'll see around you are vineyards, unassuming winery buildings, and forested rolling hills.

◆   **Romantic Alternative: INDIAN ROCK VINEYARD**, Pennsylvania Gulch Road, off Highway 4, Murphys, (209) 728-2266, is located on a country road lined with small horse ranches. The tasting room is little more than a shack, but picnic tables are set by a small pond with horses grazing next door and old wagons set picturesquely in the grass.

◆   **Second Romantic Alternative:** Down a narrow lane past grazing cattle, **KAUTZ VINEYARDS**, Six Mile Road, Murphys, (209) 728-1251, is a vision in the making. The tasting room is set in the cool cave tunnels that harbor barrels of wine. When the winery is complete, it promises to be one of gold country's finest.

# Columbia

The small towns of gold country cast a magic spell on all who enter. As you walk along the narrow streets hemmed with Old West storefronts and overhanging balconies, each step takes you further away from the cares of today and into the romance of yesterday. **COLUMBIA STATE HISTORIC PARK** is the best restored and most unique of gold country's portals to the past. Only the Wells Fargo stage and ponies, no automobiles, are allowed to share Main Street with you as you stroll hand-in-hand or sneak a coy kiss in a shady corner. Shopkeepers and waitpersons in period costume greet visitors to their antique stores and old-fashioned restaurants. Fiddlers and banjo players enliven the street with their foot-stomping tunes. Children clamber onto the stage, lick ice cream cones, and pan for gold in a seeded wooden trough. You, too, may find gold here, in the memories you bring home together.

◆   **Romantic Option: THE CITY HOTEL DINING ROOM,** Main Street, Columbia, (209) 532-1479, (Expensive), with its high-backed leather chairs, burgundy velvet draperies, brass chandeliers with etched tulip glass, classical music, and elegant cuisine, is a refined departure from rough-and-ready Columbia. Established in 1856, this is where the wealthy celebrated their fortunes, away from the dusty hoi polloi. Today it is a training kitchen for hotel management students from nearby Columbia College. Chefs create such unusual entrees as sauteed veal with raspberry-mustard bearnaise served with crabmeat-stuffed mushrooms and wild rice pancakes, or a lobster souffle served on sweet potato straw.

◆   **Romantic Note: THE CITY HOTEL** rents rooms upstairs (Very Inexpensive to Inexpensive), with impressive carved wood antique beds in the Parlor Rooms, but I found that they felt too much like a public museum, as tourists come up to explore this vintage setting during the day. Also, nine rooms share two gymnasium-style shower stalls down the hall.

# Sonora

## Hotel/Bed and Breakfast Kissing

**BARRETTA GARDENS INN, Sonora**
700 South Barretta Street
(209) 532-6039
Inexpensive to Moderate

*Follow Highway 49 into Sonora. At the stoplight in the center of town, turn right onto Washington Street. Take Washington to Baretta Street and turn left. The inn is high on a hillside the on left.*

"Gardens" is an appropriate middle name for this recently refurbished turn-of-the-century inn. Perched on a hillside above the tumbling gold country town of Sonora, a wraparound veranda overlooks compact terraced gardens, while a back balcony faces western sunsets over rolling hills. The bright sun porch, like a Victorian conservatory, is filled with lush greenery, screening in secluded kissing spots on the wicker and rattan furnishings. A wood-burning fireplace glows in the comfortable parlor, although the television here may cool your warm kisses. The guest rooms are highlighted by elegant details such as the original crystal chandelier, ornate floor-to-ceiling gilded mirror, and silver vanity set in the Periwinkle Room. While antiques set the mood, sparkling new baths (including a whirlpool in the Dragonfly Room), ensure modern comfort.

**RYAN HOUSE, Sonora**
153 South Shepherd Street
(209) 533-3445
Inexpensive

*Follow Highway 49 into downtown Sonora. Turn left on Washington Street to continue on Highway 49. After one short block, turn right onto Theall Street. The inn is two blocks up, on the corner of Theall and South Shepherd.*

If you stop to smell the roses at the Ryan House, your senses will be more than satiated by the time you reach the front door. A long garden walkway hemmed with the blooming bushes is your first treat at this dainty 1850s Victorian. The interior, too, is pretty in its simplicity. The decor is clean and uncluttered, with soft lavenders or blues accented in patchwork quilts and dried flower wreaths. The emphasis is on old-fashioned comfort, from top-quality mattresses to the warm aroma of baking cookies for your afternoon sherry or scones for your breakfast. In the evening, you can share a favorite book on the love seat by the wood stove in the library or venture out for a kiss beneath the branches of the hawthorn tree.

◆    **Romantic Alternative**: If you want to make beautiful music together, **LULU BELLE'S**, 85 Gold Street, Sonora, (209) 533-3455, (Inexpensive), is the perfect accompaniment. Innkeeper Chris Miller is a musician, and a symphony of instruments, including a piano, organ, guitars, and clarinet, are provided for your use in the music room. Recent renovations have resulted in a sunny solarium in which to enjoy your full breakfast. Guest rooms are homespun and have private baths and entrances.

## Restaurant Kissing

**GOOD HEAVENS RESTAURANT, Sonora**
**49 North Washington Street (Route 49)**
**(209) 532-FOOD**
Inexpensive

*Follow Highway 49 into downtown Sonora and turn left onto Washington Street to the restaurant.*

Good Heavens! It's a delightful gourmet cafe in gold country! This unpretentious eatery is a favorite with the locals. Exposed brick lines one wall, and windows peek out to Sonora's small-town main street along another. In between, a cluster of cafe tables topped with country-style blue-and-pink floral cloths and linen napkins fanned in wine goblets invite diners to enjoy hearty brunch specials, quiches, and sandwiches. No frozen waffles here. The crepes Normandie are filled with sauteed apples, onions, garlic, capers with a hint of ginger, and country sausage; topped with rum raisin sauce; and served with mixed veggies in a Parmesan flan. With this, you have your choice of four homemade salads and soups. Rumor has it that their famous orange crunch cake was sought after by *Bon Appetit*, but the recipe remains secret.

◆   **Romantic Note**: Good Heavens is open for lunch and Sunday brunch only.

*"Our deepest feelings live in words unspoken."*
Flavia

# LAKE TAHOE AREA

## South Lake Tahoe

### Hotel/Bed and Breakfast Kissing

**CHRISTIANA INN
AND RESTAURANT**, South Lake Tahoe
3819 Saddle Road
(916) 544-7337, (800) 4-CAL-SKI
Very Inexpensive to Expensive

*From Highway 50, turn toward the mountains onto Ski Run Boulevard, then left onto Needle Peak, right on Wildwood, and left on Saddle Road.*

A fire flickers in the brick hearth warming the sunken sitting area of the lounge in this old Alpine-style inn. Low-slung couches invite you to relax with a warm drink to melt away the cool of the evening. You may want to sink in for the night, but the pleasures of the restaurant will soon beckon you. The fire blazes in an immense hearth here, framed by boulders and antique skis. Lace curtains, beams decorated with little white lights, and intimate booths set the scene for heartwarming dishes such as beef tenderloin in brown shallot cognac butter, veal with scallops in tomato saffron sauce, or sirloin with your choice of three delectable accompaniments. The menu is enhanced by more than 200 wines. Share a dessert for two—bananas flambe, cherries jubilee, or baked Alaska, all flamed tableside—and you'll be ready to discover the inn's ultimate pleasure. Six guest rooms await you upstairs, all beautifully appointed with a blend of contemporary and antique furnishings. Fireplaces warm four suites, and several are two stories. You can take a dry sauna in suite 5, a whirlpool in suite 6, or, in suite 4, lie together in a loft overlooking the ski runs at Heavenly, which is just the word for this dream of an inn

**EMBASSY SUITES, South Lake Tahoe**
**4130 Lake Tahoe Boulevard**
**(916) 544-5400, (800) EMBASSY**
*On the California/Nevada state line, adjacent to Harrah's Casino.*

This splendid new hotel would have ranked more than two kisses, but for the families who have discovered it. It is ideal for parents with munchkins—each room is a two-room suite with heavy doors in between—but couples, too, will find romance in this High Sierra high-rise. Rather than the clang and neon of a casino as in Tahoe's other luxury properties, you'll walk into this Bavarian-motif hotel to find a series of three soaring nine-story-tall atriums. In the first, water splashes over a paddlewheel and down a chute to a decorative pool surrounded by lush greenery. Umbrella-crowned cafe tables fill the patios of the other atriums, where complimentary cocktails and hor d'oeuvres are served each afternoon and a full buffet breakfast each morning. As the glass elevator lifts you to your room high above, so will it lift your vision of a night of lofty romance.

**INN BY THE LAKE, South Lake Tahoe**
**3300 Lake Tahoe Boulevard**
**(916) 542-0330, (800) 877-1466**
Inexpensive to Unbelievably Expensive

Mouthwatering truffles, imported cheeses, gourmet sausages, fresh fruits, and a bottle of bubbly with keepsake glasses all bundled in a basket—this is what awaits you as part of the Inn by the Lake's Romance Special. You may never want to leave your room, which is decorated in soft peaches and sands, like the dawn light glimmering on Lake Tahoe just across the street. But who can resist their two-tiered whirlpool, where you soak away the cares of today and just indulge in being together? The best part is that this modern, low-slung hotel has the lake as a neighbor, rather than the cluster of neon motels that crowd the casinos several miles down the road.

**THE TAHOE SEASONS RESORT, South Lake Tahoe**
**Saddle Road, at Keller Road**
**(916) 541-6700**
Moderate to Very Expensive

*From Highway 50, turn toward the mountains onto Ski Run Boulevard, then left onto Needle Peak, right on Wildwood, and left on Saddle Road.*

I can't imagine a more rejuvenating place to spend the night after a long day of schussing together than this resort set in the woods within walking distance of Heavenly Ski Resort. Each guest room is a mini-suite with a cozy living room and bedroom separated by a huge whirlpool enclosed in Japanese-style screens. In most rooms, you can indulge in a hot, massaging soak while a gas fire flickers in the hearth and snowflakes dance in the moonlight outside your window. Each room also comes equipped with a microwave and refrigerator for inventive midnight snacks. Ask for one of the newly renovated rooms when making your reservation; they are pleasantly decorated with contemporary furnishings in teals and mauves.

## *Restaurant Kissing*

**TOP OF THE TRAM RESTAURANT, South Lake Tahoe**
**Heavenly Valley Ski Resort, halfway up the California side**
**(702) 586-7000 ext. 6347**
$10.50 per adult round trip on the tram
Moderate (Restaurant)

*To reach the ski resort from Highway 50, turn toward the mountains onto Ski Run Boulevard, then left onto Needle Peak, right on Wildwood, and left on Saddle Road. Catch the tram at the base lodge.*

Skier or sun lover, winter or summer, you can kiss before the view that Mark Twain called "the fairest picture the whole earth affords." Half the fun is riding the large tram as it soars to 2,000 feet above Lake Tahoe, North America's largest alpine lake. Once on top, forgo the cafeteria, which is perfect for heavy-booted skiers, and head to the Top of the Tram Restaurant, which is a bit too posh for skiers anyway. Linen cloths and wood paneling add a touch of elegance to the basic American fare, but the real draw is the wall of windows framing a heavenly view of crystal blue Lake Tahoe embraced by jagged, often snowcapped mountain peaks. If you come for dinner in the summer, be sure to arrive before sunset.

◆    **Romantic Note:** The Top of the Tram Restaurant serves lunch, dinner, and Sunday brunch in summer, lunch only in winter. Tram hours are daily 10 A.M. to 10 P.M. June through September, daily 9 A.M to 4 P.M November through May.

## Outdoor Kissing

**BORGES CARRIAGE AND SLEIGH RIDES,**
**South Lake Tahoe**
**In the meadow across from Caesars**
**(916) 541-2953**
$15 per couple; $30 for two-person cutter sleigh

Dashing through the snow, in a one-horse open sleigh: it's a short jaunt around the meadow, and a nostalgic voyage to romance. The Borges family offers rides in a variety of sleighs, from the six- to 20-passenger rigs pulled by two Belgian draft horses to the two-person, one-horse cutter. Rides skim through a snowy meadow overlooking the sapphire lake. An intriguing history lesson lends a new perspective on glitzy South Lake Tahoe, bringing back a time when wagon trains and the Pony Express stopped here to rest their stock. A rousing carol and a sprightly kiss are all part of the fun.

# Stateline, Nevada

## Restaurant Kissing

**THE SUMMIT RESTAURANT, Stateline, Nevada** ◆◆◆◀
**Highway 50**
**16th and 17th floors of Harrah's Hotel and Casino**
**(702) 588-6606, (800) 334-6741**
Very Expensive

*Call for directions.*

A true love's kiss on a mountain high is only slightly more exquisite than The Summit. A fire blazed in the hearth. Candles flickered in the candelabra on the ebony piano while a tuxedo-clad virtuoso lovingly stroked the ivories. We were shown to our table by the window with unpretentious aplomb. As we gazed into the night, the view of the city lights and the velvet expanse of Lake Tahoe far below made us feel as though we were perched on the point of a star. This lofty setting was once the Star Suite, the secluded aerie of visiting royalty and Hollywood VIPs. Each dining area is intimate, whether you sit by the fire or on the mezzanine with its smoked glass balustrade. The cuisine is as heavenly as the ambience, from the quail with prune sauce and delicate fritters to salads so beautiful they could second as centerpieces to the lamb, venison, or seafood entrees with delicate sauces and perfect vegetables to the sensuous souffle with vanilla cream sauce. The Summit is a touch of heaven.

# Incline Village

## Hotel/Bed and Breakfast Kissing

**HYATT LAKE TAHOE**
**RESORT HOTEL, Incline Village**
**Lakeshore and Country Club Drive**
**(702) 831-1111, (800) 233-1234**
Very Expensive

The first time I entered the Hyatt, a tuxedo-clad pianist blew a melody of kisses through the spacious lobby. Guests lazed in the horseshoe of overstuffed sofas by the blazing fire in the hearth. And I hardly noticed the obligatory casino, set off to the right. This is what this first-class hotel does best: offers something for every taste without imposing on anyone's. Unlike the more developed shores of South Lake Tahoe, this modern high-rise retains its natural forested setting. You'll actually enjoy a moonlit stroll along the curved paths that lead through the woods, past earth-toned cabins, to the lakeshore. Guest rooms are a cross between inn and hotel, with blond pine furnishings, rich floral spreads, plenty of playful throw pillows, and views of the lake or mountains. On the Regency floors, complimentary afternoon wine, liqueurs, and hor d'oeuvres and an expanded Continental breakfast are served in the private common room to stoke romantic hearts.

## Restaurant Kissing

**HUGO'S, Incline Village**                                  💋💋
**111 Country Club Drive, on the lakeshore at the Hyatt**
**(702) 831-1111**
Moderate to Expensive

Windows wrap around two sides of this shoreline restaurant, capturing the shimmering facets of Lake Tahoe like sapphires on a necklace. Above, a simple wood-paneled ceiling stretches to a crowned point. In the center of the room, flames flicker in a free-standing hearth, gladdening the hearts of those not close to a window. Although this dining establishment is owned by the Hyatt, it is removed from the high-rise hotel, nested in the woods on the shoreline. Duck is a specialty here, served with your choice of Oriental, orange, lingonberry, or green pepper sauce. The extensive menu has something for everyone, including chicken, seafood, beef, and veal dishes. Stoke up for a night of romance with the complimentary creative salad and delectable dessert buffet.

## MARIE FRANCE RESTAURANT, Incline Village
### Tahoe Boulevard (Route 28), across from Raley's
### (702) 832-3007
Moderate

Just like lovers, some restaurants shouldn't be judged by their appearance. This unassuming bistro is in a strip mall next to a print shop, but once inside you'll feel you've flown to France. A cheerful pianist playing cabaret tunes at an upright greeted us as we walked into this room of less than a dozen tables. Since the restaurant was full, which it usually is, we settled down in the overstuffed love seat by the blazing fire. On the coffee table lay photo albums of Marie and friends in her restaurant, along with a Paris picture book. This is truly a family-run operation. Marie's husband or daughter may be your waitperson, and, as they banter back and forth in melodic French, Marie is sure to come by and talk of food or her home country in her heavily accented English. The sauces are cooked after you order this country French cuisine, so be prepared for a leisurely dining experience. It's worth the wait for such scrumptious dishes as rabbit in prune sauce or scallops in lobster sauce served in a pastry crust. Ooh la la!

## *Outdoor Kissing*

## DIAMOND PEAK CROSS COUNTRY, Incline Village
### Off Highway 431
### (702) 831-3249
$10 adult day-pass; $11 all-day ski rental

*From Incline Village, take Highway 431 towards Reno. Near the crest of the mountain, park along the street. The entrance to Cross Country Trails will be on your right.*

If a kiss gives you that top-of-the-world feeling, just wait until you kiss at Diamond Peak. High on a mountaintop, groomed cross-country ski trails lead through pristine forest to spectacular, eagle-eye views of crystalline Lake Tahoe and its ring of snowcapped peaks. Even beginners will find rentals, lessons, and one easy trail here; try the rolling intermediate trails if you can laugh together at your snow-softened falls. Along the intermediate Vista View loop, climb up the aptly named "Knock Your Socks Off Rock" and you'll know what kissing on top of the world is all about. Tables are provided at the base of the rock for chilly but heartwarming picnics.

◆    **Romantic Alternative**: Down by the lake, on its western shore, in the Taylor Creek Forest Service Area, off Highway 89, just north of Camp Richardson, about a 15-minute drive from South Lake Tahoe, (916) 573-2600, are several marked cross-country ski trails varying in difficulty. Our favorite is the one that leads past the eagle wintering area to the lakeshore. Follow the lakeshore, then circle back through the rustic but grand historic estates from the 1920s. Along this forested shoreline, you'd never guess that casinos were just a short drive away. Be sure to get the $3 Sno-Park permit in South Lake Tahoe for parking at Taylor Creek.

# Crystal Bay

## Restaurant Kissing

**SOULE DOMAINE RESTAURANT, Crystal Bay**
**993 Cove Street, across from the Tahoe Biltmore**
**(916) 546-7529**
Expensive

*Call for directions*

Curiosity beckoned us to this tiny log cabin set in its own Lilliputian pine grove in a neighborhood of hulking 1950s-style casinos. It was as though the 1927 home had been placed under a bell jar, a precious artifact of old Tahoe. At first I was skeptical, but we ducked inside to discover one of the lake's best and most romantic restaurants. The warmth of the fire in the stone hearth casts a cozy glow on the intimate setting, with its walls of rotund pine logs caulked with rope. Chef and owner Charles Edward Soule's motto is "Every dish is a specialty of the house." The eclectic menu may include prosciutto and artichoke hearts sauteed with garlic, olives, and tomatoes and tossed with angel-hair pasta, or filet mignon sauteed with shiitake mushrooms, Gorgonzola, brandy, and burgundy butter. Even the soups here were scrumptious. If ever a meal will leave you feeling more in love for having shared it together, this one will.

# Tahoe City

## Hotel/Bed and Breakfast Kissing

**COTTAGE INN, Tahoe City**
**1690 West Lake Boulevard**
**(916) 581-4073**
Moderate

*About two miles south of the town center.*

You'll feel like pioneers in this village of rustic, clapboard cabins by the lakeshore. Far from the glitz of the casinos and the sterility of high-rise hotels, the Cottage Inn lives with nature rather than trying to overwhelm it. The cottages, all with private entrances, are simply decorated. Nothing fancy here, but outdoor types will find it refreshing. Some of the two-room suites are warmed by wood stoves, one by a fireplace. You can also warm yourself by the fire in the 1938 Pomin House, where wine and home-baked cookies are served in the evening and a full breakfast in the morning. After a day of hiking, indulge in an evening sauna or stroll to the private beach where you can dig your toes into the cool sand and kiss to the lullaby of Lake Tahoe's quiet, lapping waters.

## SUNNYSIDE RESTAURANT AND LODGE,
**Tahoe City**                                                    ●●◀
**1850 West Lake Boulevard**
**(916) 583-7200, (800) 822-2SKI (California only)**
Inexpensive to Expensive (Lodge)
Moderate (Restaurant)

*About two miles south of the town center.*

A true mountain lodge of wood and gables, Sunnyside takes full advantage of its perch on Lake Tahoe's forested western shore. In the warmer months, put a blush in your cheeks on its expansive, sun-soaked wooden deck. Boaters can pull up to the dock or, if the water is too low, use the restaurant's buoy shuttle. In winter, a blazing fire crackles in the large river rock fireplace in the lounge. A nautical theme flows throughout the lodge. The Chris Craft dining room, paneled in mahogany, is so close to the lake that you'd think it was floating. Guest rooms are sleek and airy, with high ceilings, white pinstriped wall coverings, chests for coffee tables and boat prints decorating the walls. All the rooms are oriented to the sparkling lake view. Some have fireplaces and balconies where you can stand together in the gloaming, kiss, and imagine you're on the prow of your private yacht.

# SQUAW VALLEY

Nestled at the base of jagged peaks, Squaw Valley is one of the High Sierra's most picturesque settings. Although it is some distance from the sapphire sparkle of Lake Tahoe, its soaring mountains rival the Swiss Alps in their rugged beauty. A village of hotels, condominiums, and restaurants is tucked away in the valley, along with stables, golf courses, and other recreational facilities. Although this first-class ski resort first gained renown for hosting the 1960 Winter Olympics, kissing is inspired at any time of year. In the spring, seek out the wildflowers coloring the steep creekside trails. In the summer, float together in your hotel pool, rippling through the reflection of the mountains. In autumn, ride a horse to the midst of the mountains or just enjoy a quiet evening, far from any distractions.

## *Hotel/Bed and Breakfast Kissing*

**SQUAW VALLEY LODGE, Squaw Valley**
**At the base of the Squaw Valley Ski Resort**
**(916) 583-5500, (800) 922-9970**
Moderate to Unbelievably Expensive

I think it was the whirlpool tubs that won me over—three of them, just off the exercise room, with a fireplace in the corner and a view of the snowy peaks outside. Or perhaps it was the spacious, contemporary rooms, from studios to one-bedroom condominiums, with full kitchens that make it possible to warm your lips with a late-night cocoa or cook up a no-hassle, bathrobe breakfast. Then again, the setting, adjacent to some of the best skiing and hiking in the Tahoe area, is a definite plus. This is the place to come to feel good about yourself and each other. You can tone up on Nautilus and Lifecycles in the gym, indulge in a sauna, dive into the outdoor heated pool, or melt in the hands of a masseuse, then celebrate your health together in your room overlooking the mountains.

◆   **Romantic Alternative: THE RESORT AT SQUAW CREEK**, 400 Squaw Creek Road, Squaw Valley, (916) 583-6300, (800) 327-3353, (Expensive to Unbelievably Expensive), is the newest and grandest addition to Squaw Valley's expanding village. The dramatic lobby alone is worth a peek, with its wall of cathedral-high windows framing the mountain face. Outside, the resort's own waterfall tumbles down past its skating rink to three whirlpools. A shopping arcade, spa and health center, restaurants, water slide, and plunge pool—every amenity of a modern resort is here. After all this, the guest rooms seemed a bit standard, with a comfortable but comparatively unimaginative hotel feel.

## Outdoor Kissing

**OLYMPIC ICE PAVILION, Squaw Valley**
**On top of the world (or close to it)**
**(916) 583-6985, (916) 581-5518**
$10 for the cable car, $5 skating, $2 skate rental
$9 for the cable cars, skating, and skate rental after 4 p.m.

*Look for the Cable Car building at the base of Squaw Valley Ski Resort. Take the Cable Car aerial tramway to the top of the mountain.*

Having frequented Tahoe for many years, I thought I had seen the most magnificent views the area could afford, until we rode the Cable Car to the Olympic Ice Pavilion. A kiss on the aerial tramway alone is an adventure in love, as you soar above the eagles, over one pinnacle, then high to the zenith of the mountaintop. An aerie of a building is perched on the edge of the summit, almost like a gateway to heaven, especially in the rosy light of sunset. The outdoor skating rink is nearly cantilevered over the vast expanse of the valley far below. In the distance, an emerald Lake Tahoe winks on the horizon. Skating together here is like gliding on a silvery cloud, and kissing is angelic.

◆    **Romantic Note:** For lunch, **THE TERRACE RESTAURANT**, (916) 583-2555, (Moderate to Expensive), literally on top of a mountain peak, next to the Olympic Ice Pavilion, shares the same extraordinary panorama. Despite this magnificent setting and the pleasant ambience of the restaurant, basic American hamburgers, chili, and sandwiches are served cafeteria-style at very reasonable prices. This may be the only cafeteria in the world that inspires kissing. Nearby, a small bar also peeks out over the peaks and valley.

# BIG SUR

## Hotel/Bed and Breakfast Kissing

**VENTANA, Big Sur**                                    ❤ ❤ ❤
**Highway 1**
**(408) 667-2331**
Expensive to Unbelievably Expensive

*Located on Highway 1 about 28 miles south of Carmel.*

The unspoiled Santa Lucia Mountains seems to tumble directly into the sea. These rocky slopes and jagged outcroppings abut Big Sur's astonishing coastline. Ventana is an inn with a ringside view of all this, and its amenities will satisfy every other need you might have for a sultry weekend away from the world at large. Ventana is a retreat that is far removed from anything vaguely resembling civilization. Its rooms with raised ceilings, roaring fireplaces and sea-struck balconies are designed to direct your interests to romantic interactions. There are two heated pools, Japanese hot baths, a sauna and Jacuzzi. Each of the 62 guest rooms have private patios or balconies that face the towering mountains or the endless ocean below.

A short stroll from the inn, Ventana's restaurant offers another dramatic view of Big Sur and the surrounding mountain majesty. Lunch and dinner are served daily here, but the outside terrace during the summer is by far the most beguiling part. Outside and inside, blazing fireplaces provides solace and warmth. A stay here is a departure from the burdens and pressures of everyday living. The feelings that will fill your souls during your stay may surpass every expectation.

**Romantic Note:** Bathing suits are considered optional attire in the hot tub baths and the sun deck is clothing optional.

## Restaurant Kissing

**NEPENTHE, Big Sur**
**Highway 1**
**(408) 667-2345**
Expensive

*Thirty miles south of San Francisco, take Highway 1 south till you reach Big Sur; there will be signs pointing you toward the restaurant.*

Nepenthe is hardly a secret—you may even call it a tourist attraction of sorts. This famous restaurant, designed by a student of Frank Lloyd Wright, was the honeymoon cottage of Rita Hayworth and Orson Welles. It is also one of the few dining establishments to be found anywhere in Big Sur. The food is casual and good, but not great. What then makes it a kissing location? It is perched on a cliff 800 feet above the Big Sur shoreline. This feature alone is enough to make eating here a rapturous adventure.

Sunset is perhaps the best time to visit Nepenthe for a snack or drink. As the sun begins to settle into the ocean, its light penetrates the drifting clouds with a pale lavender-blue haze. Suddenly, these soft dusk-colors shift into an intense golden amber culminating in a deep red that sets the sky afire. As night makes its definitive entrance, the clouds fade to steel-blue and the sky turns from cobalt to indigo. Awesome is the only applicable word for this scenery. There is incredible outdoor seating perfectly arranged to take advantage of the view. Weather permitting this floor show performs nightly along the Big Sur coast, and Nepenthe has some of the best seats in the house.

**Romantic Suggestion:** The **GLEN OAKS RESTAURANT,** Route 1, (408) 667-2623 (Moderate), doesn't have the view or the star-studded past of Nepenthe, but what it lacks in glamour it makes up for in charisma. Gourmet cuisine, a charming log cabin exterior and intimate candlelit interior are what makes Glen Oaks a ripe kissing location along Big Sur. (There's even morning kissing here: breakfast includes baked trout and fresh muffins.)

# OUTDOOR KISSING

## BIG SUR COASTLINE
*Located on Highway 1 about 150 miles south of San Francisco.*

The drive from Carmel to Big Sur provides unsurpassed scenery in which to lose yourselves in an afternoon together. The road along this rugged, arduous coastline offers some of the most glorious, breathtaking views you may ever see in your life. It is almost guaranteed that once you've passed through Big Sur, its potent impact will be felt in your lives for years to come—it is that visually compelling. Take it slow through here—an experience of this magnitude needs to be approached with patient appreciation and reverent awe. Besides, there is no real destination to head for or to end up at, because there isn't an actual town of Big Sur to be found. According to the signs, though, Big Sur stretches for about six miles along Highway 1 and then continues south for more of the same impeccable scenery.

What makes all this such a heart throb? The road follows a precariously severe landscape, literally snaking its way along the unblemished shoreline. Beneath you, the relentless surf pounds the jagged outcroppings along the water's edge as nature continues to refine her sculpted masterpiece. Isolated beaches and secluded spots in the wilderness nearby provide momentary respite from the road for those who want to stop for private showcase views. Hard though it is to believe, each mile you pass through seems more remarkable and more titillating than the one before. Every moment you share here will be as seductive and as passionate as the first.

**Romantic Suggestion**: Do not confuse **JULIA PFEIFFER BURNS STATE PARK** with Pfeiffer Big Sur State Park; Julia is 11 miles further south then the other, but it offers what feels like 100 miles more privacy and landscape. Pfeiffer Big Sur State Park is exceedingly popular and disappointingly developed. Julia Burns State Park, on the other hand, is 2,000 acres of prime hiking territory in nature's virgin wonderland. Waterfalls, sequestered beaches and spellbinding views are what you can expect along the way. In the same vicinity, **PFEIFFER BEACH**

(just off of Highway 1 on Sycamore Canyon Road) is an exhilarating seascape crowded with massive, eroded outcroppings and haystack rocks that are approachable during low tide. Watching the sunset from this vantage point is a life-altering proposition, it is that beautiful.

# PERSONAL DIARY

This is the section just for the two of you. Here is where you can keep your own record of the special moments you've shared together—where you went, what you discovered, the occasion celebrated, and whatever else you want to remember long after the event has passed. When you're feeling nostalgic, that's the time to read aloud from these personalized pages, to share as an adoring gift with each other, creating a quiet, magic moment at home.

> "I tried to resist his overtures but he plied me
> with symphonies, quartets, chamber music, and
> cantatas.
>
> S.J. Perelman

# ALPHABETICAL LISTING

## A

Acquerello, 106
Act IV Lounge , 107
Adventure Limousine Service, 212
Adventures by the Sea, 182
Agate Cove Inn, 39
Alamere Falls , 22
Alamo Square, 94
Albion, 34-35
Albion River Inn, 34
Alta Mira Restaurant, 2
Amador City, 216-217
Amber House, 209
Amelio's, 108
Angel Island, 134
Angwin, 84-85
Anton and Michel, 202
Apple Lane Inn, 172
Aptos, 169-176
Aquatic Park, 135
Archbishop Mansion, 93
Asilomar Beach, 192
Auberge du Soleil Restaurant and
    Lounge, 73
Aunt Abigail's, 210

## B

B.F. Hastings Museum, 213
Babbling Brook Inn, 167
Bale Grist Mill State Park, 83
Ballads, 216
Barretta Gardens Inn, 223
Bay Bikes, 184
Bay Club, 193

Bay Hill Mansion, 24
Bayview Hotel, 175
Bed and Breakfast Inn, 94
Bella Mia, 157
Bella Vista, 153
Belle du Jour Inn, 60
Bellerose Vineyard, 65
Berkeley, 141-149
Berkeley Rose Garden, 148
Big River Beach State Park, 45
Bistro Ambrosia, 108
Bix, 109
Blackthorne Inn, 18
Blue and Gold Fleet, 137
Blue Fox, 109
Blue Spruce Inn, 170
Boat & Breakfast, 141
Bodega Bay, 24
Borges Carriage and
    Sleigh Rides, 230
Bothe Napa Valley State Park, 83
Brewery Gulch Inn, 39
Buca Giovanni, 120
Buena Vista Winery, 51
Burgess Cellars, 83

## C

Cafe, The, 59
Cafe Belvedere, 190
Cafe Kiewels, 179
Cafe Majestic, 97,98
Cafe Mozart, 110
Cafe Oritalia, 126
Cafe Potpourri, 111

Cafe Sparrow, 175
Caffe Lido Bar & Ristorante, 172
Calistoga, 85-92
Camelia Inn, 61
Campbell, 154-155
Campbell House, 154
Campton Place Dining Room, 111
Campton Place Hotel, 111
Cannery Row, 176
Capitola, 169-176
Caprice Restaurant, 6
Carmel, 193-206
Carmel Beach, 205
Carmel Valley Ranch Resort, 194
Carnelian Room and Bar, 112
Carriage House Inn, 195
Casa Blanca Inn Restaurant, 168
Casa Blanca Motel, 168
Casa Madrona Hotel &
    Restaurant, 1
Casanova, 203
Cazadero, 26
Centrella, 184
Chart House, 4
Chateau Motelena, 87
Chateau Souverain, 58
Chestelson House, 76
Chez Michel, 121
Chez Panisse, 145
Chez Renee, 173
Children's Fairyland
    (Lake Merritt), 149
Children's Playground (Golden
    Gate Park), 136
Chocolate Mousse, 43
Christiana Inn and Restaurant, 227
Christopher's, 8
City Hotel, 222

City Hotel Dining Room, 222
Claremont Hotel and
    Tennis Club, 142
Cliff House, 112
Clubhouse Bar and Grill, 193
Club 36, 113
Cobblestone Inn, 196
Columbia, 222
Columbia State Historic Park, 222
Compass Rose, 113
Conservatory of Flowers (Golden
    Gate Park), 136
Cottage Inn, 235
Country Cottage Inn, 173
Crab Cake Lounge and Bar, 126
Crossroads Inn, 69
Crystal Bay, 234-235
Cutters Bay House, 146
Cypress Inn (Carmel), 199
Cypress Inn (Miramar), 163

**D**

Dancing Coyote Beach Guest
    Cottages, 19
Deer Park Road, 84
Delfino's, 177
Delta King, 213
Diamond Peak Cross Country, 233
Doidge's, 114
Domaine Chandon, 71
Donatello, 115
Driver Mansion Inn, 210
Dunbar House, 220
Dunes, The, 193

**E**

Edward II Bed & Breakfast, 95
Elk, 32-33

Elk Cove Inn, 32
El Paseo, 9
Embassy Suites, 228
Empress of China, 115
Ernie's, 116

## F

Fandango, 190
Filoli Gardens and Estate, 154
Fiorella's, 173
Fisherman's Wharf (Monterey), 182
Fitzgerald Marine Reserve, 161
Five Brooks Stables, 23
Fleur de Lys, 117
Foothill House, 85
Forest Manor, 84
Fort Point, 135
Fort Ross Lodge, 27
Four Seasons Clift Hotel, 95
Fournou's Ovens, 117
Foxes, The, 217
Frank Fat's, 212
French Laundry, 71
French Room, 118
Fresh Cream, 180

## G

Gables, The, 55
Gaige House, 52
Garden Grill Restaurant, 75
Gatehouse Inn, 185
Gaylord's, 118
Gernot's, 191
Geyserville, 58-60
Giramonti, 10
Giuliano's, 203
Glen Ellen, 52-54

Glen Ellen Winery, 54
Glendeven, 36
Glenelly Inn, 53
Golden Gate Bridge, 135
Golden Gate Ferry, 2
Golden Gate National/Recreation Area, 5
Golden Gate Park, 136
Golden Gate Promenade, 135
Gold Quartz Inn, 218
Good Heavens Restaurant, 224
Gosby House, 186
Gramma's Rose Garden Inn, 143
Grape Leaf Inn, 61
Gray Whale Bar and Cafe, 43
Great Balloon Escape, 90
Greenbrae, 12-13
Green Gables Inn, 186
Greenhouse, 174
Greenstone Winery, 216
Gualala, 29-32
Guaymas, 7

## H

Hacienda Winery, 51
Hakone Japanese Garden, 159
Half Moon Bay, 164-167
Half Moon Bay coastline, 166
Hanford House, 219
Happy Landing, 196
Harbor House, 33
Hartley House Inn, 211
Haydon House, 62
Headlands Inn, 40
Healdsburg, 60-65
Healdsburg Inn on the Plaza, 63
Heart's Desire Beach, 20
Heirloom, The, 215

Heritage House (Little River), 36
Heritage House (San Francisco), 96
Hess Vineyards, 88
Highland Inn, 197
Highway 1, 14
Hoffman House, 59
Holly Tree Inn, 18
Hop Kiln Winery, 65
Hope-Merrill House, 58
Horizon's, 3
Hotel Juliana, 96
Hotel La Rose Dining Room, 56
Hotel Pacific, 177
Hotel Triton, 103
Hotel Vintage Court, 97
Hugo's, 232
Hyatt Lake Tahoe Resort Hotel/
  Casino, 231

## I

Il Fornaio, 106
Il Pescatore, 146
Imperial Palace, 116
Incline Village, 231-234
Indian Rock Vineyard, 221
Inn at Depot Hill, 170
Inn at Saratoga, 156
Inn at Spanish Bay, 193
Inn at the Opera, 107
Inn at Union Square, 105
Inn at Valley Ford, 25
Inn by the Lake, 228
International Spa, 91
Inverness, 18-23
Ione, 215

## J

Jabberwock, 189

Jack London State Historic Park, 54
Jack's, 145
Jackson, 219-220
Jacob Horner, 63
Japanese Tea Garden (Golden
  Gate Park), 136
Jenner, 27-28
Jenner by the Sea, 28
Joe LoCoco's, 12
John Ash & Co. Restaurant, 57
Judy's, 114

## K

Kautz Vineyards, 221
Kenwood, 54-55
Kenwood Restaurant, 54
Korbel Champagne Cellars, 65

## L

La Boheme, 204
La Chaumiere, 86
La Fleur, 76
La Folie, 119
La Foret, 155
Lake Merritt, 148
Lake Tahoe, 227-236
La Mere Michelle, 158
La Nouvelle Patisserie, 119
La Pergola, 109
La Playa Hotel, 197
La Seine Bakery, 119
Lafayette, 150-152
Lafayette Park, 101
Lafayette Park Hotel, 150
Lake Meritt, 148
Lark Creek Inn, 11
Larkspur, 11-12
Lascaux, 120

Le Castel, 121
L'Escargot, 122
Ledford House, 35
Lehr's Greenhouse, 121
Le Mouton Noir, 158
Le St. Tropez, 123
Le Virage, 152
Lighthouse Lodge, 187
Lincoln Avenue Spa, 91
Lincoln Green Inn, 199
Little River, 36-38
Little River Restaurant, 35
Lobby, 147
Lodi, 214
Lodi Lake, 214
L'Olivier, 123
Lovers Point Park, 192
Lulu Belle's, 224

**M**
MacCallum House Inn, 44
MacKerricher State Park, 46
MacLean House, 20
Madrona Manor, 62
Magic Flute, 124
Magliulo's, 52
Mai's, 124
Maison Rouge, 72
Majestic Hotel, 97
Mandarin Oriental Hotel, 132
Mangels House, 171
Manka's Restaurant, 21
Mansion at Lakewood, 150
Mansion Hotel, 98
Marie France Restaurant, 233
Marin Headlands, 16
Marina Green, 137
Martine Inn, 188

Masa's, 125
Mason's, 133
Maximillian's, 152
Mc Cormick and Kuleto's, 125
Meadowood, 77
Mendocino, 38-46
Mendocino Cafe, 43
Mendocino Coast Botanical
    Gardens, 45
Mendocino Headlands, 45
Mendocino Hotel
    Dining Room, 44
Mendocino Village Inn, 40
Millefiori Inn, 139
Mill Rose Inn, 164
Mill Valley, 9-10
Miramar, 163-164
Mr. Q's, 8
Monterey, 176-184
Monterey Bay Aquarium, 183
Monterey Hotel, 178
Monterey Plaza Hotel, 177
Montevina Wincry, 212
Moss Beach, 161-162
Mountain Home Inn and
    Restaurant, 9
Mountain Winery, 160
Mount Tamalpais, 15
Muir Beach State Park, 14
Muir Woods, 13-16
Murphys, 220-222
Mustard's Grill, 70

**N**
Napa, 66-69
Napa's Great Balloon Escape, 90
Napa Valley Wine Train, 67
Natural Bridges State Park, 169

Neon Rose, 20
New Orleans Room, 127
Nieman Marcus Rotunda
    Restaurant, 127
Nob Hill Restaurant, 128
North Coast Country Inn, 31

O

Oak Knoll Inn, 66
Oakland, 141-149
Oakville, 73
Oakville Grocery, 73
Ocean View Boulevard (Pacific
    Grove), 192
Old Bath House, 191
Old Milano Hotel, 29
Old Monterey Inn, 178
Old Sacramento, 213
Old Thyme Inn, 165
Old World Inn, 67
Oleander House, 70
Olema, 16-18
Once in a Lifetime Balloon
    Company of Calistoga, 90
Once in a Lifetime Balloon
    Company of Sonoma County, 90
Olympic Ice Pavilion, 238
One-thousand and One Nob Hill,
    128

P

Pacific Grove, 184-193
Pacific Grove Inn, 188
Pacific Grove shoreline, 192
Pacific's Edge, 197
Palace of Fine Arts, 136
Pane E Vino, 129

Paradise Beach Park, 6
Pasta Nostra, 50
Patisserie Boissiere, 204
Pavillion Restaurant, 142
Pelican Inn Restaurant and Pub, 13
Petite Auberge, 99
Petri's, 66
Piano Zinc Supper Club, 129
Piazza D'Angelo, 10
Piazza Lounge, 130
Pier 39, 137
Pillar Point Inn, 162
Pine Inn, 198
Plumed Horse, 159
Plush Room, 130
Point Lobos State Reserve, 205
Point Reyes, 18-23
Point Reyes Lighthouse, 23
Point Reyes National Seashore, 22
Point Reyes Seashore Lodge, 16
Postrio, 131
Prescott Hotel, 100
Presidio, 138
Princeton-by-the-Sea, 162-163

Q

Queen Anne Hotel, 101

R

Rachel's Inn, 37
Rancho Caymus Inn, 75
Reed Manor, 41
Regina's, 102
Regis Hotel, 101
Remillard's, 11
Rent-a-Roadster, 183
Resort at Squaw Creek, 237

Restaurant Metropole, 145
Richardson Bay Audubon Center, 16
Ridge Restaurant, 200
Ristorante Bonta, 122
River's End Restaurant, 27
Robert Stemmler Vineyards, 65
Robinson Jeffers' Tor House, 206
Robles del Rio Lodge, 200
Rochioli Vineyards and Winery, 65
Rodeo Beach at the Marin Headlands, 5
Roth Ranch, 31
Roundstone Farm, 17
Russion Gulch State Park, 46
Russion River Area Wineries, 64-65
Russian River Wine Road, 64
Rutherford, 73-75
Rutherford Hill Winery, 74
Ryan House, 223

S
Sacramento, 209-213
St. Helena, 76-84
St. Orres Inn and Restaurant, 29
Sam's Anchor Cafe, 7
San Antonio House, 200
San Benito House, 165
San Francisco, 93-139
San Jose, 155
San Rafael Avenue, 6
Sans Souci, 204
Santa Cruz, 167-169
Santa Rosa, 55-57
Saratoga, 156-160
Sardine Factory, 181
Sattui Vineyards, 89

Sausalito, 1-5
Schramsburg Vineyards, 89
Scoma's, 3
Scott Courtyard, 86
Seal and Bird Rock, 193
Seal Cove Inn, 161
Sea Rock Inn, 41
Sedona's, 144
Seven Gables Inn, 189
Seventeen Mile Drive, 192
Shabu Shabu, 205
Shadowbrook, 174
Shadows Restaurant, 139
Shattuck Hotel, 144
Shell Beach, 30
Shenandoah Winery, 212
Sherman House, 102
Shore Bird Restaurant, 163
Showley's at Miramonte, 80
Silks, 132
Silver Rose Inn, 87
Silverado Trail, 68
Skates on the Bay, 147
Sobon Winery, 212
Sonoma, 48-52
Sonoma Hotel Restaurant, 49
Sonora, 223-225
Soquel, 169-176
Soule Domaine Restaurant, 234
South Lake Tahoe, 227-230
Spencer House, 103
Spindrift Inn, 179
Spinnaker, 4
Squaw Valley, 236-238
Squaw Valley Lodge, 237
Squire, 132
Stanford Inn by the Sea, 42

Steep Ravine Trail, 15
Stevenot Winery, 221
Stevenswood, 38
Stonepine, 201
Strybing Arboretum, 136
Summit Restaurant, 231
Sundial Lodge, 195
Sunnyside Restaurant & Lodge, 236
Sutter Creek, 217-219

**T**
Tahoe City, 235-236
Tahoe Seasons Resort, 229
Taylor's of Sonoma
    Florist Shop, 48
Telegraph Hill, 138
Ten Inverness Way, 17
Terra Restaurant, 81
Terrace Restaurant, 238
Thunderbird Bookshop &
    Restaurant, 199
Tiburon, 6-8
Tilden Regional Park, 149
Timberhill Country Inn & Tennis
    Ranch, 26
Tomales Point, 22
Tommy Toy's, 133
Top of the Tram Restaurant, 229
Tourelle's, 151
Tra Vigne, 82
Trilogy Restaurant, 82
Trojan Horse Inn, 50

**U**
Umberto Restaurants, 115
Union Street, 94
University of California at
    Berkeley, 143

**V**
Vagabond's House Inn, 202
Valley Ford, 25
Veranda, 175
Vichon Winery, 73
Victor's, 134
Victorian Garden Inn, 49
Victorian Inn on the Park, 104
Villa St. Helena, 78
Vindel's, 180
Vintage Inn, 70
Vintner's Inn, 56

**W**
Walnut Creek, 150-152
Washington Square Inn, 105
Waterfront Plaza Hotel, 144
Whale Watch Inn, 30
Whale Watching, 23
White Swan Inn, 105
Whitegate Inn, 42
Wildcat Beach, 22
Windrose Inn, 219
Wine and Roses, 214
Wine Country Inn, 79
Winterbrook Vineyards, 216
Woodside, 153-154

**Y**
Yountville, 69-72

**Z**
Zinfandel Inn, 80